COPYRIGHT AND INTERNATIONAL NEGOTIATIONS

Copyright and International Negotiations provides a historical study of the development of Chinese copyright law in terms of China's contemporary political economy and the impact that international copyright law has had. The analysis shows how China's copyright system is intertwined with censorship and international copyright law and how this has affected freedom of expression. China still enforces an old censorship regime that clamps down on free expression despite a modern system of copyright rules which should function as an engine of free expression. The book explores the development and architecture of Chinese copyright law in parallel with international copyright law, clarifies China's nuanced patterns of the control of free expression through copyright law, and identifies a breakthrough for neutralising the impact of China's censorship policies through copyright law.

GE CHEN is a Research Associate at the Mercator Institute for China Studies (MERICS), a Berlin-based think-tank. Dr. Chen has held many research and academic posts in China, Germany, and the United Kingdom and provided legal consulting services to both Chinese and German governments in a variety of legal projects under the Sino–EU Dialogue on the Rule of Law.

CAMBRIDGE INTELLECTUAL PROPERTY AND INFORMATION LAW

As its economic potential has rapidly expanded, intellectual property has become a subject of front-rank legal importance. *Cambridge Intellectual Property and Information Law* is a series of monograph studies of major current issues in intellectual property. Each volume contains a mix of international, European, comparative and national law, making this a highly significant series for practitioners, judges and academic researchers in many countries.

Series editors

Lionel Bently *Herchel Smith Professor of Intellectual Property Law, University of Cambridge*

Graeme Dinwoodie *Professor of Intellectual Property and Information Technology Law, University of Oxford*

Advisory editors

William R. Cornish, *Emeritus Herchel Smith Professor of Intellectual Property Law, University of Cambridge*

François Dessemontet, *Professor of Law, University of Lausanne*

Jane C. Ginsburg, *Morton L. Janklow Professor of Literary and Artistic Property Law, Columbia Law School*

Paul Goldstein, *Professor of Law, Stanford University*

The Rt Hon. Sir Robin Jacob, *Hugh Laddie Professor of Intellectual Property, University College, London*

Ansgar Ohly, *Professor of Intellectual Property Law, Ludwig Maximilians Universitat Munchen, Germany*

A list of books in the series can be found at the end of this volume.

COPYRIGHT AND INTERNATIONAL NEGOTIATIONS

An Engine of Free Expression in China?

GE CHEN

Mercator Institute for China Studies, Berlin

CAMBRIDGE
UNIVERSITY PRESS

CAMBRIDGE
UNIVERSITY PRESS

University Printing House, Cambridge CB2 8BS, United Kingdom

One Liberty Plaza, 20th Floor, New York, NY 10006, USA

477 Williamstown Road, Port Melbourne, VIC 3207, Australia

4843/24, 2nd Floor, Ansari Road, Daryaganj, Delhi – 110002, India

79 Anson Road, #06–04/06, Singapore 079906

Cambridge University Press is part of the University of Cambridge.

It furthers the University's mission by disseminating knowledge in the pursuit of education, learning and research at the highest international levels of excellence.

www.cambridge.org
Information on this title: www.cambridge.org/9781107163454
10.1017/9781316681435

First published 2017

A catalogue record for this publication is available from the British Library.

Library of Congress Cataloging-in-Publication Data
Names: Chen, Ge, author.
Title: Copyright and international negotiations : an engine of free expression in China? / Ge Chen.
Description: New York : Cambridge University Press, 2017. | Series: Cambridge intellectual property and information law | Includes bibliographical references and index.
Identifiers: LCCN 2016047638 | ISBN 9781107163454 (Hardback)
Subjects: LCSH: Copyright–China. | Freedom of speech–China. | Foreign trade regulation–China. | China–Foreign economic relations. | BISAC: LAW / Intellectual Property / General.
Classification: LCC KNQ1160.5 .C54 2017 | DDC 346.5104/82–dc23 LC record available at https://lccn.loc.gov/2016047638

ISBN 978-1-107-16345-4 Hardback

It is desirable that we should have a supply of good books; we cannot have such a supply unless men of letters are liberally remunerated; and the least objectionable way of remunerating them is by means of copyright.

– T. B. Macaulay, 5 February 1841

Knowledge is essential for so many human activities and values, including freedom, the exercise of political power, and economic, social and personal development. The Access to Knowledge movement takes concerns with copyright law and other regulations that affect knowledge and places them within an understandable social need and policy platform.

– Knowledge Ecology International

To realise the freedom of press, the current censorship regime must be abolished thoroughly.

– Xinhua Daily, 26 June 1945

CONTENTS

ACKNOWLEDGEMENTS

This book is based on my thesis to obtain a doctorate in law at the University of Göttingen. The laws and materials are updated to the end of 2015.

First of all, I would like to express my sincere gratitude to Professor Peter-Tobias Stoll, my PhD supervisor, who led me into this meaningful research and taught me the Germanic methodology of legal thinking. Had it not been for his continuous support, patience, and company over the years, I would not have been able to carry out this research project to the end. I would also like to say thanks to Professor Andreas Wiebe, a member of the PhD committee, who gave insightful comments and questions on an earlier draft.

I take this opportunity to thank Professor Lionel Bently and Professor William R. Cornish for chairing this significant series in which I could present my research. My thanks go, in particular, to Lionel, a great teacher and friend, for letting me know how to present complex legal thinking in an understandable and precise way.

I am sincerely thankful to the two anonymous reviewers of the manuscript, who provided relevant comments and criticism for its further improvement.

I wish to thank Professor Graeme Dinwoodie for our unforgettable talk on international copyright law and my research. I also wish to acknowledge the enthusiastic help by Dr Rogier Creemers.

I am particularly grateful to the Konrad-Adenauer Foundation for the generous financial support for my PhD project between 2008 and 2012. Its support also came in the form of regular seminar programs, which gave me enlightenment and spiritual pleasure.

I wish to say thanks to the Institute for Sino–German Legal Studies of Nanjing University, the Institute for International Law and European Law of the University of Göttingen, the Programme for Comparative Media Law and Policies (PCMLP) at the Centre for Socio-Legal Studies (CSLS) of the University of Oxford, the Centre for Research in the Arts,

Social Sciences and Humanities (CRASSH), the Centre for Intellectual Property and Information Law (CIPIL), and the Wolfson College of the University of Cambridge. I've benefitted a lot from these institutions where I've worked over the years. Thanks to all those who gave me help in different forms: Professor Björn Ahl, Dr Jennifer Davis, Dr David Erdos, Dr Hagen Kruger, Dr Roslyn Fuller, Dr Iginio Gagliardone, Dr Andrew McKenzie-McHarg, Justice Professor Andreas L. Paulus, Dr Nicole Stremlau, Jia Xu, Dr Hui Xue, and all those whose names I might fail to mention here.

I take this opportunity to express my gratitude to the Cambridge University Press for publishing this book and to Kim Hughes, Gillian Dadd, Rebecca J. Roberts, Helen Francis, Fiona Allison, and Sarah Lambert at the Cambridge University Press for their laudable work and friendly support throughout the production of this book.

I want to thank Anand Shanmugam, Karen Slaght, and Robert Swanson for helping me make it through in the final phase of editing this work.

I am thankful to the Mercator Institute for China Studies for offering me support and a nice workplace.

I wish to give my deepest thanks to my parents for their love and full-hearted support.

Finally, I owe all my thanks to Wenjun, my dearest life partner, for the incredible years of understanding and patience, and to our little daughter for the joy that she's brought to us.

CASES

ICJ Reports

Case concerning the Application of the Convention of 1902 Governing the
Guardianship of Infants (*Netherlands* v. *Sweden*) (1958)
Case concerning the Pulp Mills on the River Uruguay (*Argentina* v. *Uruguay*) (2010)

WTO Panel Reports

US–Section 110(5) Copyright Act, WT/DS160/R (2000)
Canada–Pharmaceutical Products, WT/DS114/R (2000)
China–IPR, WT/DS362/R (2009)

WTO Appellate Body Reports

Japan–Beverages, WT/DS8/AB/R, WT/DS10/AB/R, WT/DS11/AB/R (1996)

CJEU Cases

Case 70/10, *Scarlet Extended SA* v. *Société belge des auteurs, compositeurs et éditeurs
SCRL*, Judgment of the Court (Third Chamber) (24 November 2011)
Case 314/12, *UPC Telekabel Wien GmbH* v. *Constantin Film Verleih GmbH und
Wega Filmproduktionsgesellschaft GmbH*, Judgment of the Court (Fourth Chamber)
(27 March 2014)

Domestic Cases

Canada

CCH Canadian Co. Ltd v. *Law Society of Upper Canada* (2004) 1 SCR 339,
2004 SCC 13

China

Chen v. *Superstar Digital Technology Co. Ltd* [陈兴良诉超星数字数字技术有限公
司], Beijing Haidian District People's Court (2002) Hai Min Chu Zi [海民初字]
No. 5702, 27 June 2002

Germany

UK

US

TREATIES, STATUTES AND LEGAL DOCUMENTS

International Conventions/Treaties

Agreement on Trade-Related Aspects of Intellectual Property Rights (1994)
Anti-Counterfeiting Trade Agreement (2011)
Berne Convention for the Protection of Literary and Artistic Works, Paris Act (1971)
General Agreement on Tariffs and Trade (1947)
Trans-Pacific Partnership (2015)
Universal Copyright Convention (1952/1971)
Vienna Convention on the Law of Treaties (1969)
WIPO Copyright Treaty (1996)
WIPO Performances and Phonograms Treaty (1996)

EU Directives

2001/29/EC of the European Parliament and of the Council of 22 May 2001 on the harmonisation of certain aspects of copyright and related rights in the information society
EC Directive 2006/116/EC on the Term of Protection of Copyright and Certain Related Rights
Directive 2000/31/EC of the European Parliament and of the Council of 8 June 2000 on certain legal aspects of information society services, in particular electronic commerce, in the Internal Market (Directive on electronic commerce), OJ L 178, 17/07/2000

Bilateral Treaties

Implementing Accord between the Department of Energy of the US and the State Scientific and Technological Commission of the PRC on Cooperation in the Field of High Energy Physics (1979)
Memorandum of Understanding on the Enactment and Scope of Copyright Law in the PRC (1989)
The Memorandum of Understanding between the US and the PRC on the Protection of Intellectual Property Rights (1992)

National Legislations

China

Historical Laws Prior to the Founding of the PRC

Statutory Laws of the PRC Promulgated by the National People's Congress

Regulations Issued by the State Council/Its Ministries of the PRC

Judicial Interpretations of the SPC/SPP of the PRC

Germany

France

UK

US

UN Document

WIPO Document

WTO/GATT Documents

Accession Protocol of the People's Republic of China to the WFO, WT/L/432 (10 November 2001)

China's Status as a Contracting Party: Communication from the People's Republic of China, L/6017 (14 July 1986)

DSB Establishes a Panel on China's Protection of IPR and a Compliance Panel to Review US Implementation in "Zeroing" Case, WT/DS362/7 (21 August 2007)

Excerpt from the Minutes of the Council's Meeting, WTO Doc IP/C/M/64 (26–27 October 2010)

Requests for Consultations by the United States, China-Measures Affecting the Protection and Enforcement of Intellectual Property Rights, WT/DS362/1 (10 April 2007)

Submission by the Africa Group, Barbados, Bolivia, Brazil, Dominican Republic, Ecuador, Honduras, India, Indonesia, Jamaica, Pakistan, Paraguay, Philippines, Peru, Sri Lanka, Thailand and Venezuela on TRIPS and Public Health, IP/C/W/296 (19 June 2001)

USTR Documents

1995 National Trade Estimate – People' Republic of China

2011 US–China Joint Commission on Commerce and Trade Outcomes (20–21 November 2011)

21st US–China Joint Commission on Commerce and Trade Fact Sheet (15 December 2010)

24th US–China Joint Commission on Commerce and Trade Fact Sheet (19–20 December 2013)

Fact Sheet: 23rd US–China Joint Commission on Commerce and Trade (19 December 2012)

Fact Sheet for "Special 301" on Intellectual Property (25 May 1989)

Fact Sheet: US–China Joint Commission on Commerce and Trade (29 October 2009)

Out-of-Cycle Review Results (2005)

Special 301 Report Section 306, China [05 January 2003]

Special 301 Report Finds Progress and Need for Significant Improvements: Results of China OCR Released, China Elevated to Priority Watch List (29 April 2005)

Statement by Ambassador Barshefsky (17 June 1996)

US–China Joint Fact Sheet on the 25th US–China Joint Commission on Commerce and Trade (16 December 2014)

US–China Trade Relations: Entering a New Phase of Greater Accountability and Enforcement, Top-to-Bottom Review (February 2006)

WTO Case Challenging Weakness in China's Legal Regime for Protection, Enforcement of Copyrights, Trademarks (April 2007)

European Union Documents

10th China–EU Summit, Beijing, 28 November 2007, Joint Statement, 1607 0/07 (Press 279), Brussels

A Maturing Partnership – Shared Interests and Challenges in EU–China Relations, Commission Policy Paper for Transmission to the Council and the European Parliament, Brussels, 10/09/03, COM (2003)

EU–China 2020 Strategic Agenda for Cooperation, Beijing, 21 November 2013

European Union External Action Service, Joint Statement of the 12th EU–China Summit, 30 November 2009

EU Strategy to Enforce Intellectual Property Rights in Third Countries – Facts and Figures, Brussels, MEMO/04/255, 10 November 2004

EU–China Summit Joint Statement: The Way forward after Forty Years of EU–China Cooperation, 29 June 2015, Brussels

Joint Press Communiqué of the 14th EU–China Summit, Beijing, 14 February 2012, 6474/12, Press 50

Joint Statement of the 8th EU–China Summit, art 15, IP/05/1091, Brussels, 5 September 2005

Memorandum of Understanding on Reinforcing the EU–China IP Dialogue Mechanism, Brussels, 29 June 2015

Miscellaneous

International Intellectual Property Alliance (IIPA), IIPA's 2008 Special 301 Recommendations (2008) app. A 1

Provisions on Several Issues Concerning Dealing with Foreign-related Cases (1995)

ABBREVIATIONS

A2K	access to knowledge
A2R	access to remuneration
ACTA	Anti-Counterfeiting Trade Agreement
AIPLA Q J	*American Intellectual Property Law Association Quarterly Journal*
AJIL	*American Journal of International Law*
Am Econ Rev	*American Economic Review*
Am U L Rev	*American University Law Review*
APP	Administration of Press and Publication
Ariz L Rev	*Arizona Law Review*
ARWU	Academic Ranking of World Universities
Atk.	Atkyns' Chancery Reports (England)
BC	Berne Convention for the Protection of Literary and Artistic Works
BGH	Bundesgerichtshof
CCD Mass.	Circuit Court for the District of Massachusetts
CCIA	Computer & Communications Industry Association
CCMO	copyright collective management organization
CCP	Chinese Communist Party
Chi J Int'l L	*Chicago Journal of International Law*
CJEU	Court of Justice of the European Union
cl.	clause
col.	column
Columbia J Art L	*Columbia Journal of Arts and Law*
Const.	Constitution
Cornell Int'l L J	*Cornell International Law Journal*
CPPCC	Chinese Peoples' Political Consultative Conference
DMCA	Digital Millennium Copyright Act
DS	Dispute Settlement
DSB	Dispute Settlement Body
DSM	Dispute Settlement Mechanism
E Asian Executive Rep	East Asian Executive Report

EC	European Communities
ECETJC	EU–China Economic and Trade Joint Committee
ECIPE	European Centre for International Political Economy
ECJCMHE	Editing Committee of the Journals of the Chinese Modern History of Economy
ER	The English Reports
Eur J Int'l L	*European Journal of International Law*
EU	European Union
EWHC	England & Wales High Court
F 3d	Federal Reporter, 3rd Series
F. Cas.	Federal Cases
Fed. Cir.	Federal Circuit
Fordham Intell Prop Media Ent L J	*Fordham Intellectual Property Media and Entertainment Law Journal*
F. Supp.	Federal Supplement
GAOP	General Administration of Publication
GAOR	General Assembly Official Record
GA Res	General Assembly Resolution
GATT	General Agreement on Tariffs and Trade
GPCL	General Principles of Civil Law
GRUR	*Gewerblicher Rechtsschutz und Urheberrecht*
Harvard J Asiat Stud	*Harvard Journal of Asiatic Studies*
Harvard L Rev	*Harvard Law Review*
ICCPR	International Covenant on Civil and Political Rights
ICJ	International Court of Justice
IDG	International Data Group
IIC	*International Review of Intellectual Property and Competition Law*
IIPA	International Intellectual Property Alliance
ILM	International Legal Materials
ILSA J Int'l Comp L	*International Law Students Association Journal of International and Comparative Law*
Intell Prop Q	*Intellectual Property Quarterly*
IP(R)	intellectual property (rights)
ISP	Internet Service Provider
JBE	*Journal of Business Economics*
JCCT	Joint Commission on Commerce and Trade
J Cop Soc USA	*Journal of the Copyright Society of the USA*
J Intell Prop L	*Journal of Intellectual Property Law*
J Int'l Commercial L Tech	*Journal of International Commercial Law and Technology*
J Legal Stud	*Journal of Legal Studies*

JWT	*Journal of World Trade*
L Contemp Probs	*Law and Contemporary Problems*
LR	Law Reports
MAPIC	Measures for the Administrative Protection of Internet Copyright
MFN	most favoured nation treatment
MICAP	Measures for the Implementation of Copyright Administrative Punishment
Mich St L Rev	*Michigan State Law Review*
MOC	Ministry of Culture
MOU	Memorandum of Understanding Concerning the Protection of Intellectual Property Rights between the Government of the United States and the People's Republic of China
NCB	National Copyright Bureau
NGO(s)	Non-governmental Organisation(s)
Northwestern J Tech IP	*Northwestern Journal of Technology and Intellectual Property*
NPB	National Publication Bureau
NSW	New South Wales
NYT	New York Times
NYU J Int'l L Pol	*New York University Journal of International Law and Politics*
OJ	Official Journal of the European Union
P2P	peer-to-peer
Pub L No.	Public Law number
Pmbl.	preamble
PRC	People's Republic of China
QB	Queen's Bench
RCCM	Regulations of Copyright Collective Management
Rep.	Report(s)
Reuter Asia-Pac Bus Rep	Reuter Asia-Pacific Business Report
Reuter Bus Rep	Reuter Business Report
RICA	Regulations for the Implementation of the Copyright Act
RIDA	*Revue internationale du droit d'auteur*
RIICC	Regulations on Implementing the International Copyright Convention
RMI	rights management information
ROC	Republic of China
RPCS	Regulations on Protection of Computer Software

SARFT	State Administration of Radio Film and Television
SCC	Supreme Court of Canada
SCNPC	Standing Committee of the National People's Congress
SCR	Supreme Court Reports
SDNY	Southern District of New York
SPC	Supreme People's Court of the People's Republic of China
SPP	Supreme People's Procuratorate of the People's Republic of China
Stat.	Statutes
Texas Int'l L J	*Texas International Law Journal*
TIAS	Treaties and International Act Series
TPM	technological protection measure
TPP	Trans-Pacific Partnership
TPSEPA	Trans-Pacific Strategic Economic Partnership Agreement
TRIPS	Agreement on Trade-Related Aspects of Intellectual Property Rights
UCC	Universal Copyright Convention
U C Davis L Rev	*University of California, Davis Law Review*
UCLA L Rev	*University of California, Los Angeles Law Review*
UGC	user-generated contents
UK	United Kingdom
UN	United Nations
UNESCO	United Nations Educational, Scientific, and Cultural Organization
UN GA	United Nations General Assembly
UNHRC	United Nations Human Rights Council
UNTS	United Nations Treaty Series
US	United States of America
USC	United States Code
USPQ	*United States Patent Quarterly*
USSR	Union of Soviet Socialist Republics
UST	United States Treaties
USTR	United States Trade Representative
Vand J Transnat'l L	*Vanderbilt Journal of Transnational Law*
Vand L Rev	*Vanderbilt Law Review*
Wall Str J	Wall Street Journal
WCT	WIPO Copyright Treaty
WIPO	World Intellectual Property Organization
WL	Westlaw Identifier

World Intell Prop Rep	World Intellectual Property Report
WPPT	WIPO Performances and Phonograms Treaty
WT	World Trade
WTO	World Trade Organization
Yale L J	*Yale Law Journal*

~

Introduction

Copyright is said to be designed as an "engine of free expression,"[1] which promotes the production and dissemination of knowledge by giving economic incentives to creators. Copyright protection also spurs further creative production and dissemination of knowledge by allowing access to previously produced and circulated information. In both cases, copyright is seen as an important legal instrument, which aims at regulating a country's economic and social policies. Arguably, such economic and social mandates of copyright may well underpin free speech and facilitate the free flow of information, which are the two most fundamental cornerstones of free expression. These economic and social regulatory objectives, however, may often clash and come into conflict with each other. This conflict used to be termed a "largely ignored paradox,"[2] but is now becoming increasingly palpable in the industrialised world due to the exponential manner in which knowledge is produced and disseminated.

Whereas the development of such regulatory goals in copyright might contain and trigger potential conflicts with free expression in different forms, the outcome in the People's Republic of China (PRC/China) can be particularly interesting. Today, China maintains a copyright system that is playing an important role in facilitating its economic, cultural, and creative industries, such that the software industry has turned into a stunning success. No doubt China also abounds in creative talent that has invigorated its emerging knowledge economies. All this has, however, occurred only recently, because the local infrastructure of cultural industries has been established and social policies have been adjusted after more than three decades of economic reforms – a historical process of unprecedented repercussion between China and the world.

---

[1] *Harper & Row* v. *Nation Enterprises*, 471 US 539, 558 (1985).
[2] M. B. Nimmer, Does Copyright Abridge the First Amendment Guarantees of Free Speech and Press? (1970) 17 UCLA L Rev 1180.

As a matter of fact, China is still wielding an old and rigorous censorship regime that clamps down on free expression, despite a modern system of copyright rules, which should, presumably, function as an engine of free expression. The most notorious example is Article 4 of China's former Copyright Act (the major statutory copyright law in China) prior to its recent amendment in 2010, which denies copyright protection to works that are barred from publication and distribution. In fact, that provision might have had less of a negative impact on copyright protection than on free expression. When a World Trade Organisation (WTO) Panel decided in 2009 against that controversial provision, the dispute manifested the potential conflict between copyright protection and the censorship regime in China. Although China replaced the former provision with a seemingly acceptable clause, the State's will to exercise control of free expression still overshadows copyright protection in China, which is one of the fundamental factors that render China's copyright protection distinct and somewhat isolated from copyright protection in most countries of the world.

This may explain why, in conducting a policy analysis of the intellectual property (IP) law in China years ago, Alford posed a serious question to the Chinese copyright system. He asserted that the real focus of any regulatory policies concerning publication in China was not the protection of individual rights, but the control of the flow of ideas for the purpose of maintaining the political legitimacy of the government.[3] If this argument still holds true, what are its precise legal implications under Chinese copyright law? Considering the manifold recent legal developments, should this point of view be refined in one aspect or another? Are there any other factors in copyright law that may neutralise or counterbalance the Chinese government's efforts, say, to exercise censorship? These are questions this book seeks to answer.

―――――

Indeed, copyright law in China is not only concerned with the economic interests of authors, publishers, readers, and Internet users, but it also assumes a significant role in regulating China's sociopolitical policies, especially in its cultural domains. In fact, besides being an engine of free expression, copyright in China is treated as one of the fundamental

[3] W. P. Alford, *To Steal a Book Is an Elegant Offense: Intellectual Property Law in Chinese Civilization* (Stanford, CA: Stanford University Press, 1995).

means to carry out the government's underlying policy of the control of free expression. It is perhaps for this reason that copyright protection in China remains a perplexing and embarrassing issue. Although authors and publishers who enjoy copyright protection may have a potential conflict of interest with the general public, a more fundamental understanding is that national copyright policies in China tend to be defined by more diverse and complicated contours of historical, social, and political priorities, especially the entrenched censorship regime.

Since the international copyright system came into being in the nineteenth century, China has been perceived (and may still be perceived) as a country where activities of piracy are rampant. Such rampant piracy has been attributed to the traditionally inward-looking Chinese culture, an overall backward (planned) economy, misconception of the whole Chinese society about copyright, loose government control of piracy, and lower legal standards of copyright protection. All these contributing factors underlie the government's mentality of defining copyright protection as part of its national policies, which aim to regulate China's specific economic and social development. Above all, the traditional Chinese society used to view claiming monetary rewards for one's spiritual works as a shameful thing. "Stealing books is an elegant deed," as the saying goes around in China.

More important, the public policy priorities defined by the Chinese government in regulating publication often lie in controlling the production and dissemination of ideas/knowledge. As a corollary, copyright protection, if anything can be termed as such in China, has always been subject to censorship. Such an underlying policy prevailed in the legislative process of copyright laws before and after China's copyright system was established. In fact, the Chinese government has upheld an understanding of copyright based on the vague term of "interest balancing," which the government often defines in the light of the socialist value of placing collective interests above individual interests. Ultimately, this means control of free expression through censorship.

Such a practice has largely impeded the institutionalisation of the proprietary nature of intellectual works produced by individuals and private entities, thwarting free speech to a considerable extent. Moreover, it also renders the commercial distribution of and access to such works difficult and even frustrating, thus hampering the free flow of information. Even today, when China firmly claims to accord copyright protection an unprecedentedly important role in facilitating its process of economic development and globalisation, it remains challenging how

China could interpret and readjust its national copyright system in a coherent way to cater to different needs that arise from "public" and "private" spheres in specific economic and social contexts.

Certainly, these conflicting interests, as they represent a general "paradox" under other jurisdictions, would have to be weighed against one another in terms of the level of China's economic and social development. Therefore, it seems right to start a conversation on Chinese copyright law with the topic on "interest balancing." However, the State's will to suppress free expression remains the sword of Damocles. So far, most scholarship on copyright in China has focused on the issue of interest balancing from the traditional perspective of private law and national law.[4] Unlike the research on copyright laws in other countries, however, any meaningful scholarship concerning Chinese copyright law would only present an incomplete picture if it is oblivious to the crucial role of censorship, for China's copyright system hinges on the control, rather than the encouragement, of free expression from the outset.

————

In fact, there has long been another important element that complicates China's copyright conundrum: the development of China's copyright law can only be better understood from a comparative perspective, ideally in the international context. This is because the fundamental and irreversible factor that catalyses the establishment and development of China's national copyright system is copyright internationalisation. Since the beginning of the twentieth century, international copyright law has exerted considerable influence on the way in which China designs and constructs its copyright system and, in particular, the extent to which China exercises its censorship in the domain of publication. Thus, copyright in China presents a nuanced paradox. The development of Chinese copyright law involves not only the conflict between authorial interests and public interests in general, but also the conflict between China's censorship and international law.

The way international law interacts with Chinese law involves a long diplomatic process. Historically, international negotiations have influenced profoundly the making of China's modern copyright system and the role of censorship in copyright protection. The first process of such

---

[4] See, e.g., G. Tang, *Copyright and the Public Interest in China* (Cheltenham/Northampton: Edward Elgar, 2011).

negotiations occurred toward the end of the Qing Dynasty, when the United States and Japan raised their requests for copyright protection in bilateral commercial negotiations. Around the 1980s, economic and political pressure from both at home and abroad pushed China to develop its own national copyright system in line with international copyright law. After several rounds of international IP negotiations, the PRC accomplished the stunning process of acceding to the most important international copyright treaties, including the Berne Convention for the Protection of Literary and Artistic Works (BC)[5] and the Universal Copyright Convention (UCC).[6] More recently, international trade negotiations brought forth China's accession to the WTO and the Agreement on Trade-Related Aspects of Intellectual Property Rights (TRIPS).[7] In addition, China has become a party to the World Intellectual Property Organisation (WIPO) Copyright Treaty (WCT) and the WIPO Performances and Phonograms Treaty (WPPT).[8] Obviously, China has taken prompt steps toward internationalisation of its copyright law. However, a question remains: does international law neutralise China's censorship regime or vice versa?

In all those historical stages of negotiation, China's partners insisted either on China's accession to or enforcement of international copyright treaties. While China, in the light of China's censorship policies, claimed to be wrestling with balancing private interests against public interests, China's negotiation partners compelled China to look to international copyright law for establishing, improving, and redesigning its national copyright system. As such, China has committed itself to attuning its copyright rules to international copyright law, and is constantly implementing copyright reforms to adapt its own interest-balancing approach to that of the international copyright system. Thus, international copyright law has provided the fundamental legal framework within which China could develop, interpret, and implement its

---

[5] The Berne Convention for the Protection of Literary and Artistic Works, Paris Act, revised 14 July 1971, 1161 UNTS 3.

[6] Universal Copyright Convention, done 6 September 1952, [1955] 3 UST 2731, TIAS No. 3324, 216 UNTS 132 (UCC); UCC revised 24 July 1971, Paris, 25 UST 1341, TIAS No. 7868.

[7] Agreement on Trade-Related Aspects of Intellectual Property Rights, Marrakesh Agreement Establishing the World Trade Organization, Annex 1C, Legal Instruments–Results of the Uruguay Round, vol. 31, 33 ILM 1197 (15 April 1994).

[8] WIPO Copyright Treaty, 20 December 1996, 36 ILM 65. WIPO Performances and Phonograms Treaty, 20 December 1996, 36 ILM 76.

economic and social policies. This legal scenario is sophisticated and warrants an in-depth examination.

————

Based on the aforementioned linkage between Chinese copyright law and international copyright law through international negotiations, this book attempts to explore the development and architecture of Chinese copyright law in parallel with those of international copyright law, clarify China's nuanced patterns of the control of free expression through copyright law, and identify a breakthrough for neutralising the impact of China's censorship through copyright law. In international trade and IP negotiations so far, China has shown its willingness to defer to international copyright law without jeopardising its censorship regime. Such a policy goal, however, presents an uncompromising conflict: copyright is set to be an engine of free expression, whereas censorship strangles it.

Can international negotiations that aim to indoctrinate China with international copyright law breathe an engine of free expression into China? A historical study of the parallel development of Chinese copyright law and international copyright law might reveal how both legal branches are interrelated through negotiations. Such developments are, certainly, accompanied by complicated economic and sociopolitical backgrounds at home. In addition, a comparative study of relevant copyright rules of the PRC and international copyright law would carve out the legal contours concerning how the conflicts between general copyright policies and China's specific policy of controlling free expression might be viewed and mitigated. Through international IP and trade negotiations, the international copyright system has exerted, and might continue to exert, a positive impact on the functionality of China's national copyright law in regulating free expression. Following are the most important findings of this examination.

First, China's will to exercise the control of free expression is recalcitrant, the way China perceives the international copyright system is multidimensional and the strategies that China incorporates into its copyright system are sophisticated. Traditionally, Western countries have dominated the process of making fundamental global economic rules. Global economic rules, however, are invariably the result of contentions and compromises made between nations to reap more important shared interests. Thus, parallel with the negotiations toward China's accession to the BC and the UCC, China infused its will to exercise the control of free speech into its copyright law, as exemplified by Article 4 of its previous Copyright Act, which denies explicitly copyright protection to certain works that fail to pass the threshold of censorship. Further, although China took over a number of international copyright rules, its practice of establishing a copyright system in this stage is characterised by lower standards of copyright protection and reflects the traditional policy of discouraging intellectuals, who are engaged in creating independent works, thus thwarting free speech. This anti-free-speech pattern of copyright law was, certainly, backed up by a planned economy that suppressed the intellectuals' pursuit of financial independence from the State.

Second, international copyright law has been able to infiltrate into China's copyright system and counterbalance certain chilling effects of the practice to dampen free expression. In an incrementally integrated global system that encompasses knowledge as a fundamental engine and new pattern of economic development, a nation's cultural and social policies can be largely assimilated into its trade interests through its IP laws. Upon becoming a Member State of the WTO, China became fully aware of the significance of enforcing international copyright rules when implementing its economic, cultural, and social policies. In that connection, China was not able to dodge its obligations under TRIPS, but was obliged to boost its copyright standards considerably. The subsequent copyright reform reshaped the contours of authorial protection and enhanced their economic status, which contributed to encouraging free speech. Nonetheless, China was able to react and redefine its national IP policies within the purview of international copyright rules to achieve its goal of controlling free expression. For instance, Article 47 of the revised Copyright Act confers authority on administrative departments to enforce copyright protection and define the "public interest." In practice, China has launched regular campaigns that crack down on the piracy of copyrighted materials. These campaigns, however, are targeted practically at the circulation of specific information that fails to rise to the threshold of censorship. By readjusting its copyright law, China shifts the focus of its control of free expression from the production to the circulation of intellectual works and, thus, from control of free speech to control of the free flow of information.

Finally, concerning its future, the Chinese copyright system looks to a trend of modernisation geared to the development of international law. In aligning its national copyright system with international copyright law, China endeavours to balance different kinds of tensions and conflicts of interests, while maintaining its censorship regime. In the ongoing process of IP and trade negotiations, China defines its national copyright strategy as an intellectual framework that defers to international law, but takes priorities in local economic and social development into account. Clearly, under TRIPS, China is obliged to provide for copyright protection on a full scale and remove any barriers that might hinder the functioning of a modern copyright system. As exemplified by the Sino–US copyright dispute, China deleted Article 4 of the earlier Copyright Act. This does not, however, mean that international copyright law could redeem free expression in China once for all. Further, in the era of digital copyright, China is and will be engaged in a spate of negotiations with powerful global players, which will produce diverse new copyright rules. As such, China's digital copyright system, burdened by the task to exercise censorship, grows, collides, and develops with international copyright law. Once they are planted into the Chinese copyright system, these international copyright rules, which render the promotion of free expression irreversible, may present new challenges to, and opportunities for, facilitating free expression in China.

This work is also looking to the future of Chinese copyright law, as China launched its copyright law reforms in 2012, which is going to witness the third, but probably the most significant, revision of its Copyright Act in history. So far several revision drafts have been presented to the public to solicit opinions. Although the formal revision is likely to come in near future, there are still some fundamental issues that give rise to controversies in China. In any event, China proclaims that it will adopt internationalisation as one of its fundamental goals of copyright reform. New dialogues between China and its commercial partners that cover this topic are also under way. Therefore, it is crucial to address Chinese copyright law in a historical lens and, in particular, China's entrenched policy of regulating free expression through copyright law, which represents a cutting-edge issue that underlies the Chinese copyright system and merits attention in the long run.

As such, the title of this book reveals that positioning China in international negotiations would prompt China to reshape its copyright law in terms of international copyright law. Although China adopts sophisticated legal strategies to incorporate censorship into its copyright system, this process of legal integration might become a fundamental engine, which drives China to advance a modern copyright system that contributes to free expression. This book seeks to achieve this end in three dimensions. First, the book explores the historical process of positioning China's national copyright system in international negotiations, which helps channel Chinese copyright law into the international copyright system. Second, this book provides an analysis of positive law, comparing relevant international copyright rules and Chinese copyright rules that might affect free expression. Finally, the book evaluates how the role of Chinese copyright law, in serving the State's will to exercise censorship, has developed and may develop further in parallel with international copyright law. This book will be divided into the following four chapters.

Chapter 1 sets the scene of the whole book by providing an overview of the fundamental problem and methodology. The chapter raises the general question of balancing private interests against public interests in traditional copyright rationales and discusses its relationship with the regulation of free expression. The chapter highlights the specific role of the predominance of the government's interest in conducting censorship in Chinese copyright law. After that, the chapter moves on to the history of legal transplantation in China and focuses on a specific episode of China's international negotiations, which encompasses the imbroglio of copyright issues. This process shows how international negotiations have led China to transplant rules of international copyright law into Chinese law, which compromises China's policy of exercising censorship. Finally, this chapter presents a legal approach in copyright law for the purpose of promoting free expression in the normative dimension.

Chapter 2 reveals how China relies on international legal resources for making its earlier copyright law, which compromises its strategy of controlling free expression. In this dimension, the architecture of Chinese copyright law aims to legitimise the government's interest in controlling free speech by imposing limitations on copyright protection in general or by limiting copyright owners' economic interests. The chapter reviews the history of the economic and social development of the PRC prior to the 1990s, in which China's cultural policies concerning copyright and intellectuals were embedded. In particular, the chapter examines China's accession to the BC and the UCC through a series of international negotiations and how China took steps toward copyright law making. The chapter also explores the international copyright framework with an eye on the legal resources, which are apt to generate a scenario amiable to free expression by facilitating the economic interests of copyright owners. Further, the chapter will probe into the legal framework of China's national copyright system of the 1990s, as China's initial interest-balancing approach aims to suppress such interests to buttress the policy goal of exercising censorship. The chapter ends by evaluating China's inverted legal architecture in a comparative perspective.

Chapter 3 considers China's commitment to the international obligation of enforcing copyright protection, which may further contradict the government's interest in controlling free expression. At this stage, the problem is relocated in controlling the free flow of information by restricting the interests of the general public in accessing intellectual works. This chapter first provides an overview about the historical background concerning the establishment of a new economic system until the beginning of the new century, which hails the advent of an information society. The chapter elaborates on how China underwent harsh rounds of multilateral trade negotiations to accede to the WTO and, thus, to the TRIPS Agreement. The chapter also analyses the new legal framework under TRIPS with regard to its rules that may facilitate public access to copyrighted materials and the free flow of information. The chapter then turns to the 2001 copyright reform and elucidates how China endeavoured to bring a relevant framework under its revised copyright law into harmony with that of international copyright treaties. The chapter ends with an appraisal of China's alternative interest-balancing approach that aims to bring such public interests under control for the purpose of ensuring the censorship regime.

Chapter 4 offers an overall review of China's national copyright system in terms of the government's policy to exercise censorship in the context of copyright internationalisation, which indicates the irreversible tide of aligning copyright with free expression. In this regard, the chapter will explore the new global copyright framework, in which China's international IP and trade negotiations are rooted (within and beyond WIPO and the WTO). The chapter will also enunciate China's copyright reforms and strategies in the new era, considering China's contemporary domestic policies relating to the regulation of free expression. In that connection, the chapter reconsiders China's current copyright framework with respect to the conflicts between the interests protected by copyright and China's censorship policy. Finally, the chapter provides a prospect on China's ongoing reform of its Copyright Act since 2012 in terms of China's peculiar approach of balancing free-expression-oriented interests against its censorship-directed interests.

1

A Tale of Two Engines

As the title may suggest, this study on the interplay between copyright and free expression in China is based on the following analytical framework. First, whereas the instrumentality of copyright can be channelled to the objective of facilitating free expression, Chinese copyright law has a task of controlling free expression through censorship. Second, the genesis of copyright law in China is a result of international negotiations, which mark the beginning of the legal transplantation of international copyright rules into Chinese law and represent a compromise between international copyright law and China's censorship. Finally, international copyright law provides a potential substantive normative framework, which can be employed as the basis for recalibrating and redesigning the role of copyright law in regulating free expression. Thus, copyright and international negotiations may become an integrated engine of free expression.

1.1. Copyright as an Instrument of Regulating Free Expression in China

1.1.1. *Access to Remuneration and Access to Knowledge: The Instrumentality of Copyright*

Copyright is concerned with creative works, creations of the mind, and elements of cultural heritage that are of particular value of knowledge to a society. In contrast to the protection of material goods by property rights, the protection of intangible goods in the form of copyright has been regarded as a legal fiction. Whereas patents directly protect technology know-how, that is, a creative idea, copyright does not protect immaterial knowledge (or an idea) itself.[1] Instead, copyright aims to encourage

---

[1] Agreement on Trade-Related Aspects of Intellectual Property Rights, Art. 9.2, Marrakesh Agreement Establishing the World Trade Organisation, Annex 1C, Legal Instruments–Results of the Uruguay Round, vol. 31, 33 ILM 1197 (15 April 1994) (TRIPS).

copyright owners to produce and disseminate knowledge by giving them the exclusive right to control the availability of the way an idea is expressed, or, availability of a certain form of knowledge goods (books, software, and so on).[2] Most often copyright owners are remunerated for the work they invest in those knowledge goods. In this sense, copyright provides a proprietary system that grants access to remuneration (A2R) to copyright owners in return for permitting their works to be used.

In recent decades, however, copyright as a proprietary system is facing more challenges from nonproprietary strategies and policies deriving from more fundamental sociopolitical values.[3] This is primarily because the digital technology has ushered in a new way of human life now otherwise called the "knowledge economy" or "information society" that has made exchange of knowledge and information easier than ever before. The traditional economic pattern of producing and circulating knowledge goods, which used to be largely limited by state or public funding, has led to strong protection of owner-generated knowledge products. That pattern is now being reshaped and characterised by the "user-generated contents" (UGC) in the digital context.

As every Internet user can upload materials online immediately, these materials could often be copyright-protected contents and may cause tremendous copyright issues.[4] Thus, whereas the market stakeholders readily resort to the traditional regulatory pattern of strong copyright protection for generating huge profits from copyright-protected contents, a different community has long started with its deregulatory efforts by embracing a nonproprietary mode as embedded in a series of intellectual movements and initiatives in different names such as "free and open-source software,"[5] "open access,"[6] or "creative commons (CC)."[7] The ultimate purpose of these initiatives is to counteract the proprietary effects of copyright, improve copyright, or, in some far-fetched circumstances, to subvert copyright.

---

[2] L. Bently and B. Sherman, *Intellectual Property Law*, 3rd edn (Oxford: Oxford University Press, 2009), pp. 1–2 and 31.

[3] Y. Benkler, *The Wealth of Networks: How Social Production Transforms Markets and Freedom* (New Haven and London: Yale University Press, 2006), pp. 2–15.

[4] See, e.g., *Viacom International Inc v. YouTube Inc*, No. 07 Civ 2103, 2010 WL 2532404 (SDNY 2010).

[5] Open Source Initiative: The Open Source Definition, at http://opensource.org/osd.

[6] Max Planck Gesellschaft, Open Access, at http://openaccess.mpg.de.

[7] Creative Commons, Creative Commons Licenses, at http://creativecommons.org/licenses.

Moreover, the rise of the digital technology is also changing the traditional way of realising sociopolitical values such as freedom of expression: it enables peer and cooperative efforts of producing and circulating knowledge products among ordinary citizens in completely new ways. The best example is Wikipedia, the most influential encyclopedia on the Internet nowadays. Although such development may have dramatic economic and social impacts on traditional copyright-protected materials, even totalitarian states cannot isolate themselves from such a centrifugal trend. In short, knowledge is no longer under the monopolistic control of the State.

Consider the Chinese market, which is still dominated by state-owned media. Although Wikipedia is blockaded in China, Baidu, a private web services Chinese company, is expected to take over, at least partially, the role of a channel for free speech and the free dissemination of information by offering the predominant Chinese search engine including Baidu Baike [百度百科], an online Chinese encyclopedia similar to Wikipedia and an influential public forum. Certainly, Baidu is obliged to conduct regular censorship of its UGC in terms of politically and commercially sensitive words.[8] It has also been reported frequently as a rampant copyright infringer with about thousands of articles plagiarised from Wikipedia while claiming copyright over the contents on its website, despite its alleged application of CC license.[9] However, such a private media facility, which relies on the dynamics of copyright, is exerting overwhelming influence on the Chinese information market. Through either copyrighted or copyright-infringing contents, Chinese Internet users have learned to endorse the new mode of producing and receiving information readily, which might produce positive impacts on free expression in the Chinese society.

In fact, the driving force behind advancement of human knowledge is composed of both proprietary and nonproprietary motives that are increasingly coming into conflict with each other in the digital age. Copyright and knowledge are by no means conflicting terms because copyright does not hinder one from gaining knowledge itself. On the

---

[8] S. Wood, 'Baidu's Perfect Paradox: Free Speech and the Right to Censor', *The Conversation*, 9 April 2014, at http://phys.org/news/2014-04-baidu-paradox-free-speech-censor .html.

[9] D. Nystedt, 'Baidu May Be Worst Wikipedia Copyright Violator', IDG News Service, 6 August 2007, at https://web.archive.org/web/20070930182947/www.pcworld.com/art icle/id,135550-c,copyright/article.html.

contrary, copyright can be an instrument that facilitates the advancement of knowledge for humankind. It is often said that copyright was born to serve the learning process,[10] through which one could gain more information and knowledge about the world. Essentially, copyright protects not only "literary and artistic" works, but also works that contain educational, scientific, and technical content. To achieve this goal, however, one has to have lawful access to a copyright-protected work that carries such knowledge, for example, by paying copyright owners and obtaining their permission.

In many digit-oriented circumstances, this process of learning on the condition of obtaining lawful access to copyright-protected works has been referred to as "access to knowledge" (A2K).[11] The substance of A2K does not contradict with that of A2R, as long as copyright law strikes the balance between A2R and the cost for A2K. Apparently, granting A2R to a copyright owner and enabling the general public to have A2K are two sides of the same coin, both of which are fundamental functions of copyright law. If copyright owners are denied proper A2R, or the general public cannot afford to pay the copyright owner for having A2K, copyright law might fail to achieve its goal. Such instrumentality of copyright is where the tension between the "private interest" and the "public interest" in copyright law begins and also the connecting point between copyright and free expression.

1.1.2. Proprietary and Nonproprietary Copyright Rationales: How Is Copyright Related to Free Expression?

The instrumentality of copyright implies that copyright aims ultimately at encouraging the production and circulation of knowledge. This is, in fact, testified by earlier copyright legislation in England and the United States. As such, the US Supreme Court dubs copyright as an engine of free expression.[12] Nimmer, however, points out the inherent tension between copyright and free expression.[13] Indeed, free expression represents a

---

[10] The 1709 Statute of Anne was subtitled "An Act for the Encouragement of Learning." C. Joyce, L. R. Patterson, 'Copyright (and Its Master) in Historical Perspective' (2003) 10 J Intell Prop L 239, at 243. See also the US Const, Art. I, § 8, cl. 8.

[11] A. Kapzynski, 'The Access to Knowledge Mobilization and the New Politics of Intellectual Property' (2008) 117 Yale L J 804.

[12] Harper & Row v. Nation Enterprises, 471 US 539, at 558 (1985).

[13] M. B. Nimmer, 'Does Copyright Abridge the First Amendment Guarantees of Free Speech and Press?' (1970) 17 UCLA L Rev 1180.

universal value, and freedom of expression is recognised as a fundamental right in almost all the countries of the world that have a constitution. Basically, freedom of expression encompasses speech freedom and freedom of information, which aims to enable everyone to transmit ideas and knowledge to others freely. If the ultimate goal of copyright is to facilitate the advancement of knowledge, why would it clash with free expression, which, practically, assumes identical objectives? How can the relationship between copyright and free expression be better perceived? Do copyright theories provide some basic clues?

Traditionally, there have been both proprietary and nonproprietary approaches that justify the role of copyright in facilitating the advancement of knowledge. These approaches are often based on the tension between the private interest in having A2R for producing and disseminating knowledge and the public interest in having A2K contained in such works at certain costs. The most influential rationales include the natural-right theory, the personality theory, the utilitarian theory and the social-planning theory. Although these theories do not constitute an all-inclusive spectrum, they do present some of the most important underlying values of those two interests and have contributed to law making in most countries. More important, although these theories are not perfect, they contain factors that might carve out and build up the relationship between copyright and free expression.

1.1.2.1. The natural-right theory

The most well-known copyright discourse originates in the Lockean theory about human work and the consequent right in the works as a property.[14] Accordingly, any mental or physical work produced as a result of one's own work is regarded as one's property, as the mind is the sole resource of works. As such, one could conceive of the owner's right to a work as naturally bestowed and inalienable. This concept may justify copyright owners' A2R for their copy-based work. Nevertheless, such an understanding of Locke's idea might be incomplete and misleading: Locke did embrace a balancing approach by placing some restrictions on the right to appropriation as he stressed that there should be "enough and as good left for others."[15] Thus, copyright owners would only have a legitimate claim to copy-based remuneration if they are also

---

[14] J. Locke, *Two Treatises of Government*, 2nd edn (Cambridge: Cambridge University Press, 1690, *reprinted* 1967), pp. 305–6.
[15] Ibid., p. 306.

ready to comply with certain principles that limit their act of exercising copyright. Therefore, the Lockean theory would endorse copyright protection only when the wide interest of the general public in having less costly, or at least reasonable A2K, is taken into account. This most fundamental theory of copyright has spawned the idea that A2R must be congruent with A2K.

1.1.2.2.   The personality theory

The natural-right theory seems to justify a copyright owner's monetary interests more than personality interests. In contrast, Kant and Hegel endorsed an owner's right not as a natural gift, but as the result of exercising the right to freedom of expression. They characterised a work without personal character simply as a corporeal product, which differs from a work produced by the author instead of by anyone else, in which case the author should assume an exclusive right.[16] If copyright originates from the protection of authors' act of free expression and, thus, their personality, then authors should assume commercial interests over their own work. This approach seems to emphasise the value of a personal speech embedded in a copy-based work. Nevertheless, not all speeches have a value worth legal protection, and copyright is conferred on an owner not simply because a work is produced by a person. For one thing, it is untenable to assert that a work with low levels of originality also deserves protection simply for the sake of protecting personal dignity.[17]

By contrast, the value of a speech would depend on external standards, that is, its value in being distributed and accepted (the flow of information). It is true that copyright covers both property rights and personality rights.[18] Nonetheless, the functions of these two rights are different. Whereas copyright patronises the production and dissemination of a valuable speech, copyright owners and the audience tend to have more conflicts over the financial gains reaped by the owners. In that sense, copyright has a potential burden on the audience in the process of facilitating information flow. Apparently, such a conflict of interest cannot be reconciled simply by stressing the protection of the personality of a copyright owner. The personality theory, however, shows that a

---

[16] M. Rehbinder, *Urheberrecht: Ein Studienbuch*, 15th edn (München: C. H. Beck, 2008), p. 13.

[17] C. Joyce et al., *Copyright Law*, 5th edn (New York: Lexis Publishing, 2000), p. 65.

[18] The Berne Convention for the Protection of Literary and Artistic Works, Paris Act, Art. 6bis, revised 24 July 1971, 1161 UNTS 30 (BC).

copy-based work is supposed to reach and communicate with an audience. Each intellectual work, if it is worth copyright protection, may constitute a "speech" directed at a large audience and contribute to the "flow of information," though it may require a price to be paid by the audience to the copyright owner.

1.1.2.3. The utilitarian theory

The utilitarian discourse highlights the overall economic interests with a proposition that copyright preserves copyright owners' incentive to create and circulate intellectual works by awarding them with A2R for providing knowledge goods. Notably, economic analysts have differentiated the merit of knowledge goods from their drawback, namely, the nature of being used simultaneously by more than one person without being depleted versus the noncost of reproducing the goods.[19] Above all, this approach renders the idea/expression dichotomy more palpable, as it entertains and justifies the need of the general public to lower the costs for A2K. Although creative expressions may be appropriable, ideas remain a public asset; otherwise, if ideas were protected by copyright, the cost in producing new intellectual works would be raised substantially, and the market would diminish considerably.[20] Despite dwelling on a utilitarian premise of awarding copyright owners with A2R, the approach would disfavour prohibitive prices for intellectual works, which might deter a potential audience from accessing such works.[21] In fact, it is undesirable to grant monopolistic status to copyright owners in defining the costs for knowledge goods.[22] Thus, the utilitarian approach manifests the discrepancy between the process of producing/disseminating a speech and that of information flow in economic dimensions. Whereas copyright owners who are free to utter a speech should be entitled to A2R, the general audience who seek the free flow of information should be able to enjoy A2K at a reasonable cost.

---

[19] W. M. Landes and R. A. Posner, 'An Economic Analysis of Copyright Law' (1989) 18 *J Legal Stud* 325, at 325–7.

[20] Ibid., pp. 347–8.

[21] Cf. S. P. Callandrillo, 'An Economic Analysis of Intellectual Property Rights: Justifications and Problems of Exclusive Rights, Incentives to Generate Information, and the Alternative of a Government-Run Reward System' (1998) 9 *Fordham Intell Prop Media Ent L J* 301, at 304.

[22] E. W. Kitch, 'Elementary and Persistent Errors in the Economic Analysis of Intellectual Property' (2000) 53 *Vand L Rev* 1727, at 1729.

1.1.2.4. The social-planning theory

The social-planning theory focuses on the functions that A2R and A2K might have in promoting sociopolitical development, especially in free expression. This theory has long since emerged and redefined copyright in a way that could help establish a better social order through the production and circulation of knowledge goods.[23] It also aims to counteract the negative impacts of a constantly expanding copyright system by stressing the restrictions on copyright. Early theorists of social planning in major European countries justified the restrictions of copyright by the economic and social conditions in which a work was produced. For instance, in England, Macaulay argued against exorbitant prices of works and extending copyright terms.[24] In France, Renouard posited that the author and his works were the results and products of the times and centuries in which he lived.[25] In Germany, the debate became more radical. According to "Pandects" jurists, rights were independent of any other sociopolitical contingencies.[26] However, von Jhering, who saw such an absolutist right theory as inconsistent with the ideal of the society at large, endorsed the limited social functions of property.[27]

More recently, Netanel has refined the social-planning theory by upholding copyright as a catalyst of the democratic society with its potential of achieving a free and democratic culture. This approach focuses more on how copyright could promote other policy priorities, such as free creative expression and independent communicative activities.[28] According to Netanel, copyright may facilitate free expression through its "production," "structural," and "expressive" functions because copyright can provide incentives, financial freedom from government support, and symbolic meanings of authorship and expression.[29] Such a discourse has wider implications regarding the instrumentality of

---

[23] N. W. Netanel, 'Copyright and a Democratic Civil Society' (1996) 106 *Yale L J* 283, at 306–7.

[24] T. B. Macaulay, 'Copyright: Speech Delivered to the House of Commons on 5 February 1841', *UK Parliamentary Debates*, vol. 56, col. 246–51, 5 February 1841.

[25] A. C. Renouard, *Traité des Droits d'Auteurs dans la Littérature, les Sciences et les Beaux-arts*, 2 vols. (Paris: J. Renouard et cie, 1838), vol. I, p. 436.

[26] Cf. F. C. von Savigny, *System des heutigen römischen Rechts*, 3 vols. (Leipzig: Veit, 1840), vol. I, p. 53.

[27] R. von Jhering, *Der Zweck im Recht*, 3rd ed, 2 vols. (Leipzig: Breitkopf & Härtel, 1893), vol. I, p. 526.

[28] Netanel, 'Copyright and a Democratic Civil Society', 288.

[29] N. W. Netanel, *The Copyright's Paradox* (New York: Oxford University Press, 2008), pp. 84–107.

copyright and free expression. Although stronger copyright reinforces A2R and provides incentives to free speech, the restrictions of copyright result in lower costs for A2K that may, in turn, facilitate the free flow of information.

1.1.3. Regulating Free Expression in Different Dimensions of Copyright

The foregoing discussions envisage an analytical framework of correlation between the instrumentalities of copyright and those of free expression. Indeed, interest balancing is a fundamental issue of copyright. To achieve the goal of advancing knowledge, every one shall be able to express freely by producing and circulating their intellectual works. Copyright law not only protects the impetus of private parties to produce and disseminate knowledge by awarding them with A2R, but also serves to render the costs for the general public to have A2K at reasonable or affordable costs. Thus, copyright law was born with an inherent tension between two fundamental interests that can be defined as the "private interest" and the "public interest," respectively.

The private interest refers to the commercial interests of those private parties such as authors, publishers, performers, and record producers in having A2R for allowing people to enjoy the works that these copyright owners produce or disseminate. The public interest has a far more complicated and elusive nature.[30] In a broad sense, the public interest can be construed as encompassing also the protection of the commercial interests of copyright owners. In the context of this study, however, the public interest in copyright law refers only to the interests of the general public (such as readers or Internet users) in having A2K (learning by obtaining lawful access to copyright-protected works) at reasonable or affordable costs.

The purpose of these discussions is, however, not to establish a precise standard for balancing the private interest against the public interest in copyright law. Rather, interest balancing is treated here as a precondition for considering how copyright is employed as an instrument to regulate free expression. In that connection, it suffices to know that, in balancing different interests, there is a negative correlation between A2R and affordable A2K: copyright owners may hope to increase their

---

[30] *Case concerning the Application of the Convention of 1902 Governing the Guardianship of Infants* (Netherlands v. Sweden), Judgements, Separate Opinion of Judge Sir Hersch Lauterpacht, ICJ Reports 1958, p. 79, at 90 (28 November 1958).

remuneration when prices of their works rise, whereas the likelihood of A2K tends to shrink because higher costs might well deter the general public from accessing the works. On the other hand, if copyright owners make concessions and compromise part of their A2R, there may be a larger chance of materialising affordable A2K. For the purpose of balancing different interests, copyright law takes such inverse interactions between A2R and A2K at reasonable costs into account.

In the light of the aforementioned rationales, however, the instrumentality of copyright can be linked intrinsically to free expression: the tensions between the two fundamental interests are meant not only in *general/proprietary* terms, but also in *specific/nonproprietary* dimensions. In general terms, A2R and A2K at reasonable costs assume economic functions. A2R is based on copyright owners' natural right and, thus, is pivotal for stimulating their impetus to produce and disseminate knowledge (by speech). According to the utilitarian theory, however, the wide public should also be able to afford A2K, so as to facilitate further creativity (by information flow). In specific terms, A2R and A2K can have further sociopolitical implications regarding free expression. For instance, the theory of personality rights justifies A2R by one's freedom of expression (the right to free speech). By contrast, social planning theories treat affordable A2K (the right to seek and receive information) as the general prerequisite for achieving a wide array of specific public interests, such as freedom of information, political discussion, education, cultural enjoyment, and production.

Because the general and specific functions of A2R and A2K are interrelated, copyright can become a dynamic policy instrument in regulating free expression by "balancing the private interest against the public interest," that is, by making use of the inverse interactions between A2R and affordable A2K. In a sense, speech freedom cannot be guaranteed without properly protecting copyright owners' A2R and, thus, their incentive to produce and disseminate knowledge. Likewise, if A2K at reasonable costs is not ensured, that is, the general public cannot even afford to do so due to financial difficulties, then freedom of information, which provides for the right to seek, receive, and impart information, cannot be materialised. Consequently, balancing the private interest against the public interest in general terms is often the precondition of realising the specific function of copyright in regulating free expression. In other words, the State can also achieve its specific regulatory objectives of facilitating or thwarting freedom of expression by designing a specific architecture of copyright law. As such, different states may develop different interest-balancing approaches in copyright law to realise their policy goals.

1.1.4. China's Dualistic Approach of Interest Balancing in Copyright Protection and the Control of Free Expression

The following section probes into such dualistic instrumentality of Chinese copyright law and its role in China's policy of regulating free expression. Certainly, the Chinese copyright system has the general task of striking the balance between A2R and A2K at affordable costs. The way China uses such instrumentality to control free expression has, however, remained an unexplored mystery. As a totalitarian state, China designed its copyright law for the purpose of social regulation in a socialist country from the very beginning. Thus, the Chinese copyright system carries a perverted policy task of enabling the government to maintain social and political control, especially through censorship. To this end, both the private interest and the public interest are subject to the government's control of the production and dissemination of knowledge through censorship. In other words, under the disguise of "balancing the private interest against the public interest," the "weight" of A2R and A2K at reasonable costs can be rendered different by prioritising one of these policy goals and depreciating the other. Consequently, the distorted protection of A2R and A2K will affect free speech and the free flow of information, respectively. By manipulating the instrumentality of copyright law, the government may attain its specific goal of maintaining control of free expression.

Such a dualistic role of China's copyright system in interest balancing is rooted in the supremacy of the government's interest in controlling free speech and the free flow of ideas in ancient China. In fact, the development of copyright law in China was only a recent event: the first copyright statute in China didn't come into being until 1910. Presumably, what was comparable to copyright protection emerged in China as early as in the eleventh century,[31] when the government monopolised the printing and distribution of certain works, forbidding any reprint without its authorisation. In fact, this was due to the fact that the government conducted censorship. Otherwise the conflict between the public interest and the private interest, if there was any, never rendered copyright law a

---

[31] C. Zheng and M. Pendleton, *Copyright Law in China* (NSW, CCH Australia Ltd for CCH International, 1991), p. 17.

necessity. Indeed, Confucianism led most Chinese intellectuals to commit themselves to expounding their life philosophy through their writings, which suppressed the private interest in commercial gains. In a sense, it was the government's initiative to exert social and political control over free production and dissemination of ideas, rather than the copyright owners' incentive to make profits from their work, that gave rise to what could be compared to copyright protection in ancient China. However, it was also the government's censorship that prevented copyright law from coming into being in ancient China.

1.1.4.1.   Censorship: the origin of an embryonic form of copyright protection in ancient China?

If earlier European governments ever tried to control free expression through printed books before copyright law came into being, they did so by granting privilege or patronage to authors and publishers.[32] A similar situation has long since existed in traditional Chinese cultural policies, albeit in a more sophisticated and nuanced way. In fact, the cultural policies in ancient China that underlay the Chinese mentality about publication were much less connected with either A2R or A2K than with the "public interest" as defined by the government in terms of controlling free production and dissemination of printed materials. Indeed, one may ask why there was no copyright legislation at all prior to the end of the Qing Dynasty (1644–1911 AD). This can be attributed primarily to the economic and social development in ancient China, which encouraged the government to maintain ideological orthodoxy by suppressing authors' pursuit of commercial gains through their works and discouraging their impetus to produce and disseminate knowledge.

Feudal China, prior to the Late Qing Dynasty, was an agricultural society that had only a closed natural economy with no national industrial system or market, where almost all dynasties valued agricultural production above handcraft and commercial industries.[33] Thus, the considerable demands for intellectual creation (which justified A2R in earlier Europe) and cultural consumption (a primitive form of A2K), which were necessary for establishing copyright protection in a free market, were almost nonexistent. Further, the ancient Chinese society

---

[32] See, e.g., W. Holdsworth, *A History of English Law*, 2nd edn, 12 vols. (London: Methuen Publishing Ltd, 1939, reprinted 1966), vol. VI, pp. 360–79.

[33] Y. Kuang [匡亚明], *Comments on Confucius* [《孔子评传》] (山东: 齐鲁书社, 1985), p. 387.

never embraced a social pattern based on legal culture (or, more precisely, a culture of "the rule of law"). Rather, Confucianism, which provided the fundamental ethical framework for social conducts, endorsed harmony between the human society and nature and resisted the value of individuality and equality.[34] Accordingly, law was not supposed to provide guidance on telling the right from the wrong, whereas trials that served to assign different interests would disturb a naturally harmonious state.[35] Such an economic and social pattern led to the prevalence of Confucianism and obscurantism. The former suppressed the private interest in commercial gains, whereas the latter required the State to define the public interest in terms of the control of free flow of ideas and knowledge.

1.1.4.1.1. The suppression of the private interest in commercial gains In traditional copyright rationales, the private interest is a most important factor that accounts for the genesis of copyright protection. In ancient China, however, intellectual works were seen as something merely transmitting previous knowledge rather than creating anything at all.[36] Moreover, the traditional Chinese society had a peculiar mentality about the relationship between education and personal development. Whereas the political elites monopolised educational sources, learning was regarded as above anything else. Government officials were selected on the basis of the results of competitive imperial examinations held annually, which tested only one's knowledge of arts and ignored scientific, technological, or commercial knowledge completely.[37] Intellectuals were, thus, encouraged only to learn to become government officials in order to achieve fame and wealth, whereas ordinary illiterate people developed blind worship about knowledge, only because literacy gave the hope of becoming more powerful and richer officials. For those reasons, any direct act of showing financial interests connected with intellectual works would be deemed shameful.

By contrast, there was widespread respect for knowledge itself, and the need to absorb knowledge (a premodern form of A2K) never ceased to grow.

---

[34] D. Bodde and C. Morris, *Law in Imperial China: Exemplified by 190 Qing Dynasty Cases* (Cambridge, MA: Harvard University Press, 1971), p. 178.

[35] E. W. Ploman and L. C. Hamilton, *Copyright: Intellectual Property in the Information Age* (London and Boston: Routledge & Kegan Paul, 1980), p. 142.

[36] *The Analects of Confucius* [《论语》], Book 7, Ch I.

[37] J. Levenson, *Modern China and Its Confucian Past: The Problems of Intellectual Continuity* (Garden City, NY: Anchor Books, 1964), p. 21.

This was partly because many intellectuals had long since attached the pursuit of fame and reputations to their works and respected the intellectual works of others. Although this did not result in the establishment of a "personality right" or freedom of expression in China, it seems to entertain a value of free expression as part of the private interest of authors. Apparently, intellectuals could be discouraged from making a free speech (it was, certainly, never provided as a civil liberty), if they had expected to live on any financial incomes directly from composing intellectual works. It seems, however, that most intellectuals did not care about commercial gains through their works. Instead, authors seemed to care more about the exclusivity of what they said in such works. Although such cultural mentalities suppressed authors' pursuit of commercial gains through their works and hindered their A2R, there was a stronger demand for A2K through intellectual works. As early as the 400–500 BC the famous "Book of Rites" [《礼记》] warned against "taking what others said as what one says oneself [毋剿说,毋雷同]." This can be perceived as the initial criticism of plagiarism, though the wording of plagiarism formally came up about 1,300 years ago in the Tang Dynasty (618–907 AD), when plagiarism became more rampant and was widely denounced.[38]

1.1.4.1.2. The government's control of free expression through censorship and the initial protection of authorial interests Although intellectuals were interested in expressing their ideas through their works and the general public had an interest in an open book market, political obscurantism, which overrode such interests, aimed to bring any production, publication, and printing of works under government control. During the Qin Dynasty (221–206 BC) and the Han Dynasty (206 BC–220 AD), the government was extremely concerned about barring unauthorised reproduction of the classics that might threaten its political rule.[39] It was, however, not until the Tang Dynasty that the government began to regulate publication formally through the "Tang Code" [《唐律疏议》] when the invention of the printing technology facilitated the dissemination of works tremendously.[40] This was because the

---

[38] Y. Yuan [袁逸], 'The History of Plagiarism in China' ['中国古代剽窃史'] (1992) 1 *Copyright* [《著作权》] 48.

[39] D. Bodde, *China's First Unifier: A Study of the Ch'in Dynasty as Seen in the Life of Li Ssu* (Hong Kong: Hong Kong University Press, 1967), p. 39.

[40] T. F. Carter, *The Invention of Printing in China and Its Spread Westward* (New York: Columbia University Press, 1925), p. 17.

development of the printing technology and the publication industry, in the civil society, shook the basis of the dominant ideology of the Chinese empire. Thus, knowledge, which used to represent the mysterious authority monopolised by the political elites, became no longer mysterious through wide dissemination of books. During the Tang Dynasty, Buddhists made a number of copies of their scriptures that preceded the printing technology in the rest of the world.[41] Moreover, the publication of copies of works flourished in the civil society, so that many private printing centres emerged.[42] Finally, even the government itself was engaged in printing books, whereupon the publishing industry and the book market began to thrive.[43]

While the publication industry flourished, the feudal government found it necessary to control acts of free expression, especially those that might jeopardise the political system, by imposing censorship to allow or forbid certain works to be published. From the Song Dynasty (960–1279 AD) to the Qing Dynasty almost every emperor issued an order of forbidding unauthorised printing. At first, the government of the Song Dynasty began to establish different institutions of censorship under the "Song Code" [《宋刑统》].[44] In the Yuan Dynasty (1271–1368 AD) censorship became a regular rule prior to any book printing, whereas the government of the Ming Dynasty (1368–1644 AD) adopted a more stringent policy of government control of publication.[45] In the Qing Dynasty, the government enacted the "Qing Code" [《大清律例》] and imposed even more draconian censorship to control the printing industry and dissemination of books.[46]

In consequence, if there was any government protection of private authorial interests or any expressive acts of producing and circulating one's works, such protection was overshadowed by the government's censorship policies and characterised by cracking down on piracy (rather

---

[41] Ibid., 207.
[42] S. Ye and Z. Yu [叶树声, 余政辉], *A Brief History of Book Printing by Jiangnan Heren in the Ming and Qing Dynasties* [《明清江南和人刻书史略》] (合肥: 安徽大学出版社, 2000), p. 2.
[43] Y. Miu [缪咏禾], *The History of Printing in the Ming Dynasty* [《明代出版史稿》] (南京: 江苏人民出版社, 2000), p. 61.
[44] D. Ye [叶德辉], *Light Comments among the Bookstacks* [《书林清话》] (北京: 中华书局, 1957), p. 145.
[45] K. Wu, 'Ming Printers and Printing' (1942–43) 7(3) *Harvard J Asiat Stud* 230.
[46] S. Zhao [赵胜], 'The Bar of Printing in the Song Dynasty' ['宋代的印刷禁令'] (1982) 4 *Journal of the Hebei Normal University* [《河北师范大学学报》] 39.

than making copyright laws). Certainly, there was no formal legal system of fighting against piracy: the feudal government aimed only at preventing printed materials and ideas from spreading freely and conveniently. In fact, the State cared much less about the private interest of authors/ publishers in reprinting works than about maintaining the political order.[47] By suppressing the private interest in commercial gains, the government could discourage the practice of living on producing and circulating intellectual works.

Nevertheless, while the State tried to bring the private printing industry under its control through government license for publication, authors and publishers had the chance to obtain special license from the State to forbid others to make copies of their works. For this reason, "whoever makes copies will be prosecuted" [翻印必究] became a fashionable warning, which was frequently seen on printed works.[48] According to Chengsi Zheng [郑成思], a leading authority on Chinese copyright law, copyright protection already came into being in the Song Dynasty through such a form of government injunctions of making copies.[49] In any event, an embryonic form of the conflict of interests, which would have engendered copyright law in ancient China, was subject to the government's interest of controlling free expression.

1.1.4.2. The dilemma of subjecting different interests to censorship in the PRC

1.1.4.2.1. The control of free expression in the PRC: from censorship to copyright Since the founding of the PRC, the practice of retaining the government's control of free expression has continued to prevail. Literally, China's cultural policies are laid down in its constitution, Articles 35 and 47 of which explicitly provide for freedom of expression and freedom of scientific and cultural pursuits. Due to the totalitarian structure of the socialist state, however, these rights, especially the right to freedom of expression, are subject to ideological control and lack effective constitutional protection.[50] China has established a notorious

---

[47] F. Yao [姚福生], *The Editing History in China* [《中国编辑史》] (上海: 复旦大学出版社, 1990), p. 292.

[48] M. Li [李明山], *The Chinese pre-Modern Copyright History* [《中国近代版权史》] (开封: 河南大学出版社, 2003), p. 8.

[49] C. Zheng, *Copyright Law* [《版权法》] (北京: 中国人民大学出版社, 1997), pp. 23–5.

[50] G. Chen, 'Piercing the Veil of State Sovereignty: How China's Censorship Regime into Fragmented International Law can Lead to a Butterfly Effect' (2014) 3:1 *Global Constitutionalism* 31, at 37–8.

censorship regime, which boasts of a decentralised institutional frame-work that exercises political control through various public authorities of a Party-state.[51] Censorship works in a multidimensional process that aims to suppress free speech, the free flow of information, and, ultim-ately, the combined force of both that culminates in any protest.[52]

Concerning copyright, Article 13 of the Chinese Constitution pre-scribes citizens' right to lawful income, savings, and private property. This right must, certainly, also be subject to China's censorship system. In this regard, the "public interest" in the context of copyright is defined by a variety of specific laws and regulations, which are, in practice, enforced in a more effective way than the constitution. For instance, the General Principles of Civil Law (GPCL) of the PRC, which is sup-posed to guide the interpretation of Chinese IP laws in general, empha-sises the "actual situation" in China so as to "meet the needs of the developing socialist modernisation."[53] The private interest in A2R through copyright protection, which gives an author the exclusive right to exert control over such works, dwells on the relationship between the intellectual works and the author who creates such works. In Chinese copyright law, however, such private interest must be subject to the "public interest" of the socialist state,[54] which can be defined in terms of the government's priorities.

The recent proliferation of legislations with regard to safeguarding national security testifies the gravity of the public interest in the Chi-nese context. The National Security Act of the PRC [《国家安全法》] enacted in 2015 empowers the Chinese Communist Party (CCP) to guide the work of safeguarding national security with utmost author-ity.[55] In defining the top priorities of national security, for example, the Act refers to fostering the application of IP,[56] while emphasising the maintenance of the dictatorship of the CCP and punishing the dissem-ination of harmful information in the Internet.[57] In doing so, this Act enshrines China's censorship regime in IP protection.[58] Further, the Draft of the Cyber Security Act [《网络安全法草案》] released in 2015 accommodates concrete measures in realising those priorities in

---

[51] Ibid., pp. 39–41.   [52] Ibid., pp. 41–4.
[53] The General Principles of Civil Law of the PRC, 12 April 1986, Art. 1.
[54] The Copyright Act of the PRC, Art. 1, 7 September 1990, revised 27 October 2001 and 26 February 2010.
[55] The National Security Act of the PRC, 1 July 2015, Art. 4.   [56] Ibid., Art. 24.
[57] Ibid., Arts. 15 and 25.   [58] Ibid., Arts. 59–61.

the Internet.[59] Such a legal scenario betrays China's dualistic approach of balancing A2R against affordable A2K in both general and specific terms, that is, in both economic and sociopolitical terms, in order to restrict free speech and the free flow of information by facilitating censorship.

1.1.4.2.2. Censorship and the development of copyright policies in the PRC The traditional approach of subjecting different interests concerning copyright protection to the government's interest in controlling free expression through censorship is largely evident in the development of Chinese copyright law. After the PRC was founded, the government developed a modern copyright policy, which also aimed to strike the balance between A2R and A2K at affordable costs. Nevertheless, the socialist approach of the former Union of Soviet Socialist Republics (USSR/Soviet Union), which emphasised the compliance of creative freedom with the communist ideology through state control, has had a lasting influence on the copyright policies of the PRC. As such, the development of China's national copyright system can be divided grossly into two phases: from 1949 to 1990 (when there was no formal copyright code) and since 1990 (after which there has been a formal code on copyright protection). The development of the copyright policies of the PRC shows that both A2R and affordable A2K are in tension with the government's censorship, as they must be subject to the latter.

In the first phase, the government's copyright policy regarding published works was featured by the focus on satisfying the general demand for scientific and cultural books subject to the ideological predominance of Marxism–Leninism.[60] Before a work was published, the author had to sign a standard contract with a state-owned publishing house that would, in fact, subject the submitted works to government censorship.[61] Moreover, the remuneration to authors was not based on the sale of the books, but on the symbolic rate subject to the disproportionate discount for greater number of reprints (the more copies, the less reward) as provided by administrative

---

[59] The Standing Committee of the National People's Congress (SCNPC) published a draft of the Cyber Security Act of the PRC on 6 July 2015 for soliciting public opinions, at www.npc.gov.cn/npc/xinwen/lfgz/flca/2015-07/06/content_1940614.htm.

[60] A. P. L. Liu, *Communication and National Integration in Communist China* (Berkeley: University of California Press, 1971), p. 150.

[61] C. Zheng, *Chinese Intellectual Property and Technology Transfer Law* (London: Sweet & Maxwell, 1987), p. 97.

regulations.[62] Such a process not only curtailed the authors' economic rights to gain profits from their works, but also imposed a strict limitation on their moral rights to decide whether to publish their works. China's copyright policies at this time were featured by restricting copyright owners' A2R and, therefore, discouraging independent authors from uttering a free speech.

In the second phase, China's copyright policies differ largely from those in the first phase as a result of radical economic reforms since the 1980s and the enactment of its Copyright Act in 1990. Both the need to develop a market economy and the repercussion with classical copyright rationales have brought forth great changes in all other areas of the publishing industry, which leads to copyright owners' increasing monetary income. In this regard, the copyright system of the PRC upholds the private interest in A2R. To reinforce this policy goal, copyright protection is often featured by regular nationwide campaigns of cracking down on piracy. Beneath the rubric, however, government authorities that carry out such campaigns aim to control free circulation of those "pirated" works that may fail or escape censorship. Thus, the public interest in affordable A2K is defined by the government in accordance with its political needs. In other words, the government's interest in controlling the free flow of information (especially any expressive contents that are related to political ideologies) prevails over the public interest in affordable A2K.

Importantly, it must be pointed out that censorship in China is not confined to political content, but may well cover wide content in economic and social contexts, or even recreational domains. Some of the censored materials do not seem to involve political content, but may stimulate an appetite for political discussion.[63] Other content is nonpolitical in nature, but belongs to such a category as may be banned in the name of the public order.[64] Even though there might be a difference in the weight that censorship attaches to such content, both the general instrumentality (A2R and A2K at reasonable costs) and the specific objectives (production and dissemination of information)

---

[62] Ibid., p. 99.

[63] See, e.g., E. Wong, 'China Blocks Web Access to "Under the Dome" Documentary on Pollution', *NYT*, 8 March 2015, at http://cn.nytimes.com/china/20150308/c08dome/dual/.

[64] See, e.g., S. Shakespeare, 'Chinese Ban "Rude" Songs at Prince William's Gala Dinner', *Daily Mail*, 4 March 2015, at www.dailymail.co.uk/news/article-2978504/SEBASTIAN-SHAKESPEARE-Chinese-ban-rude-songs-Prince-William-s-gala-dinner.html.

of copyright law will be affected when censorship works, regardless of the content thus censored.

1.1.4.2.3. Interest balancing in general terms: facilitating censorship indirectly

Copyright protection in China must serve the economic interests of the socialist state. Accordingly, any intellectual creation belongs to the socialist society. Whereas the approach in ancient China takes the idea of a book as a mere transmission of existing knowledge, the socialist doctrine further prescribes that the expression of such ideas forms a communal product that results from the achievements of former generations and cultures.[65] According to the socialist doctrine, IPRs operate in accordance with the market principle that typically arises in a capitalist society.[66] When applied in a socialist legal order, copyright should by no means be absolute or complete, but should be limited and partial. As a result, socialist states can and should impose restrictions on such "capitalist rights" in order to ensure the economic interests of the socialist state at large. This approach is consistent with the traditional Chinese policy of imposing restrictions on authors and publishers to dampen their incentive to produce and disseminate works. In this sense, subjecting copyright protection to such socialist economic doctrines could facilitate the government's interest in conducting censorship indirectly by hindering the instrumentality of copyright.

1.1.4.2.4. Interest balancing in specific terms: facilitating censorship directly

Presumably, restrictions on copyright can also facilitate censorship directly by interfering with the objective of copyright law because copyright protection in China must also serve the sociopolitical interests of the socialist state. A socialist country would grant copyright protection to works only if authors produce intellectual works that are "useful in serving the wellbeing of the society," which is the "value and purpose" of copyright.[67] Generally, any works deemed socially useless for the State would be barred from copyright protection. Specifically, copyright protection in China must be subject to the political doctrine of the socialist

---

[65] G. Boytha and A. Benard, 'Socialist Copyright Law – A Theoretical Approach' (1976) 109 RIDA 63.

[66] K. Marx, *Grundrisse: Foundations of the Critique of Political Economy (Rough Draft) 1857–1858* (Harmondsworth: Penguin, 1973), p. 611.

[67] Q. Huang [黄勤南] (ed.), *The New Textbook of Intellectual Property Law* [《新编知识产权法教程》] (北京: 中国政法大学出版社, 1995), p. 391.

state. To be precise, copyright protection must conform to the fundamental "Four Cardinal Principles" [四项基本原则] that highlight the political rule of the CCP and are laid down as the utmost tenet in the Constitution of the PRC.[68] This rationale was underlying Article 4 of the former Copyright Act, the "censorship provision," a specific legal regime in Chinese copyright law that excludes certain works from the subject matter of copyright protection based on subjective criteria.

To a certain extent, these potential tensions and the need to balance different interests exist behind the legislative goal of Chinese copyright law. In the general/economic dimension, the classical tension between A2R and affordable A2K persists. In the specific/sociopolitical dimension, the government's interest in conducting censorship may come into conflict with both the interest of copyright owners in free speech and the interest of the general public in the free flow of information. According to some Chinese scholars, Chinese copyright law shall serve the education and spiritual enhancement of the people and encourage the cultivation of socialist values and civilisation, where protection of the incentive to create and circulate works conforming to such values is in the interests of the socialist state and society.[69] This approach, however, can be used to justify not only the objective of copyright law in advancing knowledge, but also the "public" interest defined by the Chinese government in conducting censorship in terms of the socialist values.

Certainly, China's censorship regime is antithetical to the specific goal of copyright law in advancing knowledge and facilitating free expression. What is more appealing, however, is that censorship has made it more difficult to materialise the general function of copyright law in providing for A2R and affordable A2K. Such is the dilemma of a dualistic process of interest balancing in Chinese copyright law. While the State endeavours to maintain its censorship regime by bringing the specific instrumentalities of copyright law under control, China is also committed to strengthening copyright protection under international law and striking the general balance between the private interest and the public interest. Can international copyright law, then, breathe an engine of free expression into China? How can it reorient

---

[68] The Const. of the PRC, Pmbl., para. 7.

[69] B. Zhu [朱兵], 'Copyright Legislation Is an Important Content of the Socialist Legal System' ['建立和完善中国特色社会主义文化法律制度'] (2012) 20 *People's Congress of China* [《中国人大》] 8.

Chinese copyright law and, specifically, affect China's regulation of free expression through copyright law?

1.2. International Negotiations: A Historical Model of Prompting China to Compromise Censorship through Development of Copyright Law

The following part will elucidate a historical process with the focus on how international negotiations and international copyright law brought about China's earlier national copyright law prior to the founding of the PRC. Clarifying this historical model is important for understanding why international copyright law is a key factor for exploring and calibrating the role of Chinese copyright law in regulating free expression. In addition, such a historical process also marks the prelude for the development of copyright law of the PRC concomitant with the development of international copyright law in the next chapters. As a focus, what forges the link between international copyright law and Chinese copyright law is international negotiation, which has become the major instrument of catalysing the transformation of international legal rules into Chinese law.

In fact, the role of international negotiations is a catalyst that highlights a compromise between international copyright law and China's censorship regime. The economic and social development of the modern Chinese society has brought forth commercial and cultural exchange with foreign countries. It was through such negotiations that the Qing government was compelled to address the need to balance different interests and enacted China's first copyright statute. In this process, the government's interest in imposing censorship compromised with the need to provide copyright protection of foreign works. Virtually, this is the beginning of the legal transplantation of international copyright law in China. The subsequent development of the national copyright system of the PRC has followed such an approach.

1.2.1. International Law, Legal Transplantation, and International Negotiations

International law, as it is called today, came into being in Europe around the sixteenth century when China was still under the feudal reign of the Ming Dynasty. For a long time in history, China used to ignore the existence of international law and refused to accept the customs, such as the immunity of diplomatic officials.[70] In 1689, however, international law loomed on the horizon, as the Qing government negotiated with Russia on signing the Treaty of Nerchinsk and established the principle of equality between states.[71] In fact, China began to accept modern international law around the middle of the nineteenth century when Western ideas and powers managed to penetrate into the old empire and imposed a humiliating history on China. Indeed, the introduction of international law into China was accompanied by a bitter process of "modernisation": on the one hand, Western priests, government officials, and scholars played an important part in elucidating the principles of international law; on the other hand, Western powers compelled China to accept a series of "unequal treaties" through military invasion.[72] For China, international law used to be a symbol for imperialism that depreciated China's national law.

Today, the situation has changed considerably, and China claims to defer to international law as an important power in the world. In principle, the Vienna Convention on the Law of Treaties provides for the superiority of international law to national law,[73] which has been testified by prevalent international law practice, so that states may not invoke national law "as justification for its failure to perform a treaty."[74] Basically, China endorses this legal principle by prioritising the rules of treaties to which China is a state party where China's national laws come into conflict with such rules.[75] However, this does not mean that international law is directly applicable in China. Nor does it mean that China applies only national law as long as there is no conflict between the two sources. Rather, China would carry out its obligations under

---

[70] T. Wang [王铁崖], 'China and International Law: History and Today' ['中国与国际法—历史与当代'] (1992) Chinese Yearbook of International Law [《中国国际法年刊》] 22.

[71] S. Wang [王绳祖] (ed.), The History of International Relations: From the Middle of the Seventeenth Century to 1945 [《国际关系史(十七世纪中叶-一九四五)》] (北京: 法律出版社, 1986), p. 351.

[72] Z. Xiu [修志君], 'The Dissemination and Influence of Modern International Law in China' ['近代国际法在中国的传播及影响'] (2006) 23:3 Journal of the Normal College of Qingdao University [《青岛大学师范学院学报》] 81.

[73] Vienna Convention on the Law of Treaties, Art. 27, opened for signature 23 May 1969, 1155 UNTS 331.

[74] See the Case Concerning the Pulp Mills on the River Uruguay (Argentina v. Uruguay), Judgements, ICJ Rep. 2010, 14, para. 122 (20 April 2010).

[75] Provisions on Several Issues Concerning Dealing with Foreign-Related Cases [《关于处理涉外案件若干问题的规定》], Art. 1(3), 20 June 1995.

international law by taking corresponding legislative steps under its national law, though such legislative measures may take different forms.

The applicability of international law in China is, however, a complicated issue. China's constitution does not refer to the status of international treaties in the Chinese legal order. In legal practice, the way in which international law is applied can be highly selective. On the one hand, China tends to allow international treaties to be directly applicable, where such treaties relate primarily to civil or business law issues such as an IPR-related case.[76] On the other hand, China is very cautious in applying treaty law involving sensitive issues such as human rights, trade and economies, or criminal affairs.[77] Most often such rules have to be transformed into national law before they are really enforceable. Consequently, courts may decide whether or not to apply international law directly or interpret Chinese law in accordance with relevant treaty law.

Such a change of the status of international law in China is inseparable from the aforementioned, but still ongoing, process of modernisation of Chinese law, which is almost equal to the concept of "legal transplantation."[78] Chinese law, as it is today, does not stem from ancient China, but has been formed largely out of a mixture of Western laws and Chinese customs since the beginning of the twentieth century. From the end of the Qing Dynasty to the Republican period, modern Chinese law took shape in the form of Western (primarily European continental) laws, but carried content featuring the economic, social, and cultural conditions of the Chinese society.[79] Indeed, a number of legal rules in foreign laws were transplanted into Chinese legislation during this period, especially in the domain of civil law. After the founding of the PRC, the previous laws were abolished, but the tradition of a largely continental legislative model has been preserved. Since the 1980s, China has accelerated its pace in absorbing foreign laws, first in the arena of civil and commercial law, and then in the fields of administrative and criminal law.

---

[76] J. Zhao [赵建文], 'The Status of International Treaties in the Chinese Legal System' ['国际条约在中国法律体系中的地位'] (2010) 6 *Chinese Journal of Law* [《法学研究》] 190, pp. 196–7.

[77] Ibid., pp. 198–9.

[78] J. Chen, 'Modernisation, Westernisation, and Globalisation: Legal Transplant in China', in J. C. Oliveira and P. Cardinal (eds.), *One Country, Two Systems, Three Legal Orders – Perspectives of Evolution* (Berlin/Heidelberg: Springer, 2009), p. 91.

[79] Ibid., pp. 94–100.

Today, Westernisation, modernisation, and internationalisation of Chinese law are often treated as categories identical with legal transplantation, as the trend to assimilate foreign laws moves increasingly toward complying with international treaty law and practice. In the past three decades, China has been involved in different international negotiations intensely and played an indispensable part in various negotiations that resulted in international conventions, treaties, or customs, especially with regard to commercial and economic issues. In a sense, international law has become a leading force that facilitated the establishment of a modern legal system in China within a relatively short period of time. As far as copyright law is concerned, however, it is particularly relevant to focus on the initial pattern in which such negotiations brought about the legal transplantation, that is, the origin of China's earlier copyright legislation and the internationalisation of Chinese copyright law. These backgrounds would help understand the underlying force, which, even before the PRC was founded, led China to compromise its entrenched policy of censorship with the need to provide copyright protection and explain how China started to employ copyright as an instrument to regulate free expression.

1.2.2. The Introduction of the BC into China in the Late Qing Dynasty

The earliest and the most influential international copyright treaty, the BC, was signed in 1886. The birth of the BC itself was a difficult process. The idea of a universal law of copyright derived from the nineteenth century. Despite several diplomatic conferences of states, it proved unrealistic to envision a universal substantive code of copyright that could balance the interests of all countries categorically due to the vast discrepancies in their national legislations.[80] Instead, it seemed that only an international instrument based on the principle of territoriality could work. After decades of preparation and conferences full of bitter conflicts, the dust was eventually settled in 1886 when more than ten states attending the Conference signed the BC, and the Berne Union was formed.[81]

---

[80] S. Ricketson and J. C. Ginsburg, *International Copyright and Neighbouring Rights: The Berne Convention and Beyond*, 2nd edn (Oxford: Oxford University Press, 2006), pp. 52–82.

[81] Ibid., p. 82.

At the onset, European countries influenced the process of drafting and signing the BC overwhelmingly, so that relatively high protection standards took the upper hand in the underlying policies of this treaty. After that, the BC gradually extended its influence by establishing a set of minimum protection standards.[82] Accordingly, the goal of the BC was to extend uniform copyright protection standards across borders and ensure mutually equal standards between member countries. The basic assumption of such a widely respected treaty was that the conditions, such as the innovation capacity and publication industry of these countries, were at the same or similar levels. In contrast, where there were far fewer domestic works to be protected, protecting foreign works would simply increase the local costs of publishing such works. This was exactly why the United States did not choose to accede to the BC in 1886 when it was invited to attend the Conference as an observer. At that time, the United States had far fewer domestic works than the United Kingdom (UK) and France so that piracy was rampant in the United States. In fact, the United States did not accede to the BC until 1989.

This might explain why it was difficult for ordinary Chinese to understand what an international convention like the BC would mean for China – a country without copyright traditions. When the BC was being revised for the first time in 1896, China was still at the dawn of earlier political reforms so that many liberal-minded people needed legal protection of their translations of those foreign works. On 4 March 1902, Yuanji Zhang [张元济], the editor in chief of the *Diplomatic Review* [《外交报》], published a Chinese translation of the 1886 version of the BC.[83] On 14 March, a translation of the amendment of the BC was published, and ten days later a translation of the complete revised 1896 version of the BC was published.[84] Because the newspaper was very popular and influential in China, these translations of the BC had a profound impact on the Chinese civil society, and many people began to study the BC. Moreover, Baoxuan Yu [于宝轩] also compiled the translations of the BC and its subsequent amendments into the "Collections of Reserve Essays of the Empire" [《皇朝蓄艾文编》].[85] These versions of translations first introduced the BC into China.

---

[82] Ibid., pp. 85–133.   [83] Li, *The Chinese Modern Copyright History*, p. 70.   [84] Ibid.
[85] Ibid.

1.2.3.   The Earlier Bilateral Commercial Negotiations Concerning Copyright Protection at the End of the Qing Dynasty

However, it was the earlier bilateral commercial negotiations toward the end of the Qing Dynasty that truly helped disseminate the idea of copyright protection as embedded in the BC and materialise the legal transplantation of the copyright rules. The making of the modern Chinese copyright law was, in fact, catalysed by international commercial negotiations at the beginning of the twentieth century as a result of the expansion of Western churches, which "gave rise to the revolution of publication" and new copyright rationales in China that aimed at balancing different interests.[86] To preach their teachings, Western missionaries introduced new printing technology and universal copyright standards into China. Soon they found it necessary to demand copyright protection of their works, but there was no way to bring such needs to serious attention of the Chinese government. After the Boxer Protocol [《辛丑条约》] was signed, many trade-related issues remained unsettled, so that countries such as the United States and Japan kept negotiating with China. Throughout these commercial negotiations the United States and Japan raised the issue of copyright protection, which compelled China to adopt a Western legal framework to cater to the initial foreign trade activities. During this process, however, China succeeded in maintaining the priority of censorship in granting copyright protection to domestic and foreign works.

1.2.3.1.   The economic and social background of the negotiations

The Opium War in 1840 knocked open the Chinese commercial border that the government of the Qing Dynasty had long closed to the world. After that, it became legitimate for Western missionaries to reenter China with the intent to "punish the nation that prosecuted the Christianity" through the "New Crusade."[87] Accordingly, they brought in a large number of books on religion, together with advanced printing technology, so that great changes took place in the publication industry

---

[86] L. Huang [黄林], *Studies on the Publication Industry under the New Politics during the Period of the Late Qing Dynasty* [《晚清新政时期图书出版业研究》] (长沙: 湖南师范大学出版社, 2007), p. 62.

[87] Y. Li [李育民], *The Treaty System in Modern China* [《近代中国的条约制度》] (长沙: 湖南师范大学出版社, 1995), p. 273.

in China. Several trends of such social development paved road to the advent of copyright in China.

First, there was a tremendous growth of publications attributable to Western missionaries. Christianity gained prominent status in such cultural movements as many works were published, and schools and libraries were set up. For one thing, the Mohai Library [墨海书馆], established by a Western priest in Shanghai, published 171 books between 1844 and 1860, most of which were religious.[88] Although these religious books became the spiritual guidance for most Chinese at that time, other books on literature, art, science, and technology also began to be disseminated. The books, as they became more popular on a large scale, could bring in considerable turnover for the Western world. Thereupon, Western priests and missionaries had strong incentive to introduce Western copyright law into China.

Moreover, China's own publication industry was booming. Whereas the private publication industry used to be under the stringent control of the Chinese government, the situation changed considerably during the "Hundred Day's Reform" [百日维新] in 1898, after Japan defeated China in the First Sino–Japanese War. Many leading Chinese intellectuals, who believed that Japan became a powerful country because it had learned thoroughly from the Western politics, advocated translating Western political works into Chinese and launched various political newspapers.[89] While it became possible to pay for high-quality books published by private publishers, a thriving publication industry and a booming domestic market came into being.

Finally, there was a great shift in the layer of authors who relied on their works for a living. Toward the end of the Qing Dynasty, there was a vast demand for works on political, economic, and social studies, many of which had to be translated from foreign works. Accordingly, a group of professional authors arose. At this time, both Western missionaries and Chinese authors became more concerned about the economic interests in their works. Traditionally, the Chinese intellectuals, most of whom were disciples of Confucianism, despised talking about pecuniary matters and never understood why there should be a copyright system.[90] The

[88] Y. Song [宋原放] (ed.), *The History of Publication in China: The pre-Modern Part*, [《中国出版史料·近代部分》], 3 vols. (武汉: 湖北教育出版社, 2004), vol. I, p. 263.

[89] X. Lai [来新夏], *The History of Chinese Publication Industry* [《中国图书事业史》] (上海: 上海人民出版社, 2000), pp. 140–1.

[90] S. Xue [薛松奎], *The Memory of the Empire: A Memorandum of the Late Qing Dynasty by the NYT* [《帝国的回忆:<纽约时报>晚清观察纪》] (北京: 三联书店, 2002), p. 91.

new authors, however, gradually learned that they could make a profit from their works and developed a consciousness of their own private interest. Thus, they began to endorse copyright protection under the influence of foreign laws.

At this moment, piracy became rampant, as publishers saw unprecedented chances for making profits from works written or translated by Western missionaries who, though concerned about their copyright and private interests, disdained the act of seeking copyright protection in a culturally backward country like China.[91] Shortly before international commercial negotiations took place, however, these Western missionaries took the initiative to articulate their concerns about piracy and demanded that the Chinese government grant copyright protection of their works. They introduced Western copyright law into China systematically and disseminated the idea that, once newly published books were protected, authors could have pecuniary gains from their books. Thus, they advocated openly that China adopt copyright law and join the international union to give incentives and do justice to authors and publishers to facilitate social and cultural progress.[92]

Although the United States was not a member of the BC and did not extend copyright protection to foreign works at the end of the nineteenth century, American missionaries, who introduced a Western copyright system into China, helped Chinese intellectuals learn more about how to protect their own economic interests. Young John Allen [林乐知], one of such American missionaries, preached that copyright was a natural gift so that the State was obliged to protect the works "regardless of whatever was written or printed."[93] Such an opinion, which reflected the idea of freedom of expression, challenged the Chinese belief that copyright was granted only because the emperor wanted to patronise the authors.[94] Besides, this missionary held that authors who contributed to the intellectual progress should be rewarded,[95] and that unauthorised copying was an act of stealing and piracy.[96] Further, Young resorted to the public

---

[91] Y. Xiong and W. Zhou [熊月之、周武], *Shanghai: The Chronicle of a Modern Metropolis* [《上海--一座现代化都市的编年史》] (上海: 上海书店, 2007), p. 147.

[92] Y. J. Allen [林乐知] et al. (eds.), *International Communique* [《万国公报》], 60 vols. (上海: 上海书店, 2014), vol. 36, Book 183, pp. 22522–3.

[93] Allen et al. (eds.), *International Communique*, vol. 36, Book 183, 22522.

[94] L. Zhou and M. Li [周林、李明山] (eds.), *Literature of Study on Chinese Copyright History* [《中国版权史研究文献》] (北京: 中国方正出版社, 1999), p. 81.

[95] Allen et al. (eds.), *International Communique*, vol. 36, Book 183, 22523.

[96] Zhou and Li (eds.), *Literature of Study on Chinese Copyright History*, p. 77.

interest element. Traditionally, most intellectuals in China, if they did not
turn into government officials after decades of hard study, would remain
poor for a lifetime because what they produced could not earn them a
decent life due to the default of copyright protection. Unsuccessful
intellectuals often developed resentment toward the government, which
became an element of political instability. Young argued that copyright
protection would enrich intellectuals by selling their works and, thus,
contribute to social stability.[97]

In any event, with more works published by Western missionaries
after the First Sino–Japanese War, there were more cases of copyright
infringement, so that the missionaries had to rely on any available means
to protect their legitimate interests. The missionaries even managed to
ask the municipal supervisory authority in Shanghai to prescribe an
order and have it advertised on the *International Communique* [《万国
公报》], a most influential newspaper in China at that time, to prohibit
an unauthorised act of copying as a criminal deed.[98] However, the effect
of such an order was trivial, and it became inevitable to compel the
Chinese government to ensure the protection of their works through
commercial negotiations. In sum, though they originally came to preach,
Western missionaries helped disseminate Western legal thoughts, in
particular, copyright rationales, and fought against piracy to protect their
own economic interests. This process laid down the foundation for the
upcoming commercial negotiations that spawned the origin of copyright
law in China.

1.2.3.2.   The Sino–US commercial negotiation

Since the United States took cultural influence as the leading diplomatic
policy in the Sino–US relationship, Americans published most of their
works in China without any guarantee of copyright protection. As such,
works written and published by Americans were frequently copied without any authorisation, which caused great economic losses to the Americans in China.[99] Thus, American publishers asked the US government to
negotiate with the Chinese government on copyright protection. The
bilateral commercial negotiations between China and the United States
involving copyright issues, however, did not run smoothly. Obviously,

---

[97] Z. Shao [邵之棠], *Collection of Political Essays of the Empire* [《皇朝经世文统编》] (台
北: 文海出版社, 1980), vol. 6, p. 195.

[98] Allen et al. (eds.), *International Communique*, Book 97, pp. 1897–02.

[99] Song, *The History of Publication in China*, p. 256.

states chose to accede to a copyright treaty based on its willingness and domestic conditions. It seemed unreasonable to expect China to sign a bilateral copyright treaty to protect the economic interests of American authors, while the United States itself did not accede to the BC. Of course, the Chinese did not entertain such a request seriously.

However, as the Chinese government wanted an exchange for compromises on the part of the United States in other matters, China finally agreed with the United States on providing copyright protection. Certainly, the negotiation process did not live up to the principle of equality. The draft negotiation treaty, which was based on the Tianjin Treaty and submitted to the Chinese government in June 1902, provided for copyright protection in accordance with the principle of national treatment.[100] In many circumstances (such as in education), however, China relied on translating those works from the United States, whereas the United States did not need to translate works from China. Besides, as many Chinese had never heard about copyright before, the United States was playing with the words in the draft treaty by rendering the term of copyright protection unclear.[101]

Within a long time thereafter, copyright was a keynote in the Sino–US bilateral commercial negotiations. The representatives of the Qing government dared not to accept any new request from the United States without explicit approval from the central government. Meanwhile, opponents (mainly from the civil society) warned against prohibitive books as a result of protecting foreign works. Even Zhidong Zhang [张之洞], an influential governor and one of the real decision makers behind the scene, agreed to the request for copyright protection only on certain conditions. The term of protection, for example, turned out to be a controversial issue in the bilateral negotiation. On 27 September 1902, a negotiation was held on whether the term of protection should be 5 or 14 years, and ultimately both sides agreed on 10 years.[102]

What the Chinese government was really concerned about, however, was the impact of copyright protection on censorship and the political stability. At this time, many Chinese tried to express their dissatisfaction with and opposition to the Qing Dynasty under the name of foreign

---

[100] Editing Committee of the Journals of the Chinese Modern History of Economy (ECJCMHE) [中国近代经济史资料丛刊编辑委员会] (ed.), *The Commercial Negotiations after the Boxer Protocol* [《辛丑合约订立以后的商约谈判》] (北京: 中华书局, 1994), p. 156.
[101] Ibid., p. 159.   [102] Ibid., p. 160.

works, which caused trouble to the Chinese government. Finally, the
United States agreed with officials of the Qing government who insisted
on adding a clause of public interest (censorship) into the negotiation
treaty banning works that might interfere with public security and
stability in China.[103] It was, thus, provided in the negotiation clause that
"whoever . . . disturbs the public security and stability in China shall not
be exempted under this clause and shall be punished in accordance with
relevant laws and regulations."[104] Such a treaty clause enabled the Chinese government to preserve its specific regime of exercising censorship
while granting copyright protection.

Although copyright protection was not the primary goal of the Sino–
US bilateral commercial negotiations, it had considerable influence on
the publication industry in China. The treaty did not, however, prohibit
the act of piracy effectively. In 1911, an American publisher brought a
case of copyright infringement in Shanghai against the Chinese Commercial Press on the basis of the negotiated treaty clause and required the
Court to prohibit the defendant from selling a book protected by copyright. The Court relied on the treaty and held that the book did not enjoy
copyright protection in China because it was neither translated into
Chinese nor exclusively for use by the Chinese.[105] The Court went on
to explain that prohibiting the sale of American works in several provinces was merely an act of diplomatic courtesy rather than of legal
necessity.[106] Therefore, the negotiated copyright clause did not protect
the interests of the American publishers in China effectively, for it was
difficult for them to find any substantial legal basis for prosecuting piracy
in China. This was why the United States requested renegotiation with
China on copyright clauses later.

1.2.3.3. The Sino–Japan commercial negotiation

Meanwhile, Japan also started to negotiate with the government of the
Qing Dynasty on copyright protection. The importance of copyright in
the Sino–Japan commercial negotiations was not unwarranted. Whereas
Japan and China shared some commonalities in language and culture,
the economic and social development was rather different toward the end

---

[103] Ibid., p. 201.   [104] Ibid., p. 203.

[105] Q. He [何勤华] (ed.), *The Essential Essays of Jurisprudence of the Republic of China: Civil
and Commercial Law*) [《民国法学论文精粹·民商法律篇》], 6 vols. (北京: 法律出版
社, 2004), vol. 3, p. 541.

[106] Ibid.

of the nineteenth century. Japan became a strong power after the Meiji Restoration and won the First Sino–Japanese War. For China, it became fashionable to learn from Japan, and many Japanese books were translated into Chinese. After acceding to the BC in 1899, Japan was aware that, once China started to protect the copyright of foreign works, Japan could reap considerable profits from China. Therefore, Japan decided to raise the request for copyright protection. At this time, the Qing government faced great pressure because many dissidents fled to Japan and launched newspapers to criticise the Qing government.[107] As the Qing government was unable to control these newspapers directly, it was determined to make compromise and exchange copyright protection for the restriction of such expressive activities by the Japanese government.

However, Japan made a more concrete draft for negotiation by specifying that "in order to avoid a loss of economic interest, copyright protection granted by the Chinese government should cover books, maps, sea charts, and all the rest of the works that Japanese citizens prepare for the exclusive use in China."[108] On the one hand, Japan raised very specific request on the subject matter of copyright protection and even went so far as to require the establishment of a bureau for copyright registration.[109] On the other hand, China objected to the broad and vague definition of the subject matter and required Japan to protect Chinese works so as to prevent "false use" [冒用之弊],[110] which corresponded to the intent of the Qing government to control publications by censorship. Despite opposition from the civil society in China, the negotiation process went on intermittently. This was primarily because Japan wanted to reap more economic interests from the protection of Japanese works, whereas China wanted to exchange copyright protection for more compromise on the Japanese side in other aspects of the commercial negotiation.

Finally, on 24 November 1903, China and Japan reached agreement on copyright protection. China agreed to protect Japanese works in the aforementioned way and establish a bureau for copyright registration and protection, on the condition that the Chinese government was entitled to punish anyone, be they Chinese or Japanese, who published

---

[107] T. Bao [包天笑], *The Reminiscence of the Chuanying Mansion* [《钏影楼回忆录》] (台北: 文海出版社, 1980), p. 242.

[108] ECJCMHE (ed.), *The Commercial Negotiations after the Boxer Protocol*, p. 212.

[109] Ibid., pp. 213–14.   [110] Ibid.

works that disturbed the public security in China.[111] This clause was very similar to that signed at the end of the Sino–US commercial negotiation. Thus, both the United States and Japan agreed to the Qing government in paying homage to its censorship in granting copyright protection to Chinese works. To be fair, this was also because similar provisions existed in Western countries. Although the Qing Dynasty was overthrown soon after the negotiation, the effect of this provision on the priority of censorship in copyright law did not come to an end but has continued to exist in China.

1.2.4.   The Influence of the Commercial Negotiations on Copyright Protection at the End of the Qing Dynasty

In any event, the commercial negotiations toward the end of the Qing Dynasty were comparable to an "enlightenment" regarding copyright protection on ordinary Chinese. Whereas most Chinese still had no idea about copyright protection, the negotiations and their consequent debates at home disseminated the concept of copyright protection as a matter of fact. As the Qing government realised the importance of making copyright law, such a process of international commercial negotiations concerning copyright also turned out to be illuminating for the legislators. However, it was controversial whether China should grant copyright protection in the way as required by Western countries. The civil society and the Chinese government held diverse opinions on the requests for copyright protection.

For many ordinary Chinese, foreign powers were insatiable and simply pursuing economic interests. As both the United States and Japan had great pecuniary interests in copyright protection in China, they took their requests for granted because most books in China were published with a warning against unauthorised printing. Although both countries had domestic copyright law, they were fully aware of the importance of protecting domestic culture and the consequence of acceding to the BC. The United States, for example, refused to accede to the BC, as piracy of English books was rampant at home. By contrast, Japan's quick accession to the BC seemed to be a miscalculation as a political strategy for taking back the political power that the Western powers used to have in Japan. Because both countries knew the potential harm of protecting foreign

---

[111] *The Guangxu Treaties* [《光绪条约》] (台北: 文海出版社, 1980), vol. V, Book 68, pp. 2409–10.

works to the local economy, their requests for China to accede to the BC seemed to be unreasonable or even outrageous for many Chinese.

In a feudal country that stood at the turning point toward a modern state, it remained a political inertia for the government to control the free flow of ideas. Copyright protection of foreign works, however, would definitely impinge on the censorship. Thus, the attitudes of the United States and Japan toward copyright protection in China, while the Qing government took both countries for "friendly states," were seen as being more deceptive than real. Their requests for copyright protection were considered a political invasion, which reflected not only their requests for economic interests, but also their strategy of reaping cultural interests through international commercial negotiations. China's opposition to such requests seemed legitimate because it was based on the strategy of protecting national interests. China's acceptance of the copyright clause was only due to its weak diplomatic power toward the end of the Qing Dynasty.

The opinions of government officials, however, often seemed to be ambivalent. For example, Baixi Zhang [张百熙], the minister of education of the Late Qing Dynasty, was strongly opposed to signing such treaties with the United States and Japan. On the one hand, he was very concerned about access to the translated textbooks in China. This was why he advocated strong protection of the interests of translators and publishers to maintain their incentive to produce such textbooks for education's sake.[112] On the other hand, Zhang objected to the protection of foreign works, which might affect the importation of such works and hinder China's acceptance of Western ideas.[113] Because China was obliged to apply the most-favoured-nation (MFN) treatment under other trade treaties, he feared that copyright protection of works from the United States and Japan would mean copyright protection of works from other countries as well.[114]

Other influential politicians like Zhidong Zhang, who did not participate in the commercial negotiations directly but openly expressed his opinions on copyright protection, played a decisive role in the outcomes of the negotiations relating to copyright. Zhang thought it important to recognise the universal principle of copyright protection in Western

[112] S. Wang [王栻], *The Collections of the Works by Fu Yan* [《严复集》], 5 vols. (北京: 中华 书局, 1986), vol. III, p. 577.
[113] Zhou and Li (eds.), *Literature of Study on Chinese Copyright History*, p. 42.
[114] Ibid., p. 41.

countries, but insisted that China negotiate with the United States and Japan over certain restrictions on copyright such as the term of protection and the interest of the Qing government in conducting censorship.[115] At the beginning, he was not really concerned about the private interest of authors in copyright protection, but intended only to exchange copyright protection of foreign works for other conditions such as censorship of foreign publications. Later on, he came to embrace part of the opinions of Baixi Zhang and held it important to protect the cultural progress of the Chinese nation.[116]

Still other officials who participated in the commercial negotiations had their own opinions on copyright protection, though they lacked experience and flexibilities in bilateral trade negotiations. These officials, however, regarded copyright as an extension of the regulatory measures of conducting censorship. Haihuan Lü [吕海寰], for instance, took copyright protection for granted, and held it all right to agree with the United States and Japan on the grounds that there had been a long tradition of forbidding others to reprint in China.[117] Therefore, he worked hard to persuade American and Japanese representatives to agree to the censorship clause in exchange for copyright protection of works from the United States and Japan.

By contrast, Chinese intellectuals were no longer feeling shameful in raising reasonable requests for the protection of their private interests. As life was becoming harder, many intellectuals lived on translating Western works into Chinese. Most of them gave up the Confucian contempt of the act of exchanging intellectual works for money and established stable business relations with publishers. To a certain extent, this enabled many intellectuals to become independent writers. For example, Fu Yan [严复], a famous translator in the Qing Dynasty, required 20 percent of the sale price as the royalties for his translated works.[118] He also fought against piracy by designing printing stamps and signing the first publication contract with publishers in China.[119] Other translators like Shoupeng Chen [陈寿彭] required signing his

[115] Z. Zhang [张之洞], *The Entire Collections of Zhang Wenxianggong* [《张文襄公全集》], 4 vols. (北京: 中国书店, 1990), vol. IV, pp. 239–40.

[116] Ibid., p. 246.

[117] H. Lü [吕海寰], Memorials Submitted by Haihuan Lü [《吕海寰奏稿》] (台北: 文海出版社, 1997), vol. I, pp. 204–17.

[118] Wang, *The Collections of the Works by Fu Yan*, pp. 543–4.

[119] H. Pi [皮后峰], *The Biography of Yan Fu* [《严复大传》] (福州: 福建人民出版社, 2003), p. 323.

name on the translated works.[120] It became essential, then, to provide legal protection for the reasonable interests of both domestic and foreign authors.

1.2.5. The 1910 Copyright Code of the Qing Dynasty: A Product of Compromise

Under domestic and international pressure, the Qing government decided to make its own copyright law. After many debates and coordination, the Ministry of Commerce issued a draft copyright code in 1905,[121] which did not come into effect immediately, as the Qing government had not finished its legislation on censorship. In 1908, the Qing government sent its delegate in Germany to attend the Diplomatic Conference of the BC in Berlin.[122] After that, the draft was revised on the basis of the BC. On 18 December 1910, the first Copyright Code in China came into being. The underlying goal of the Qing government was, certainly, to maintain its control of the Chinese society through censorship. As illustrated earlier, however, it was very difficult to address different interests of publishers, authors, and readers at home. Besides, both the United States and Japan raised their claims for international copyright protection. As a result, this Copyright Code was a product of the compromise between the need to grant copyright protection and the government's policy of conducting censorship.

Indeed, how to balance all these different interests without jeopardising the rule of the Qing government became a real question. According to the Ministry of Civil Affairs, it was essential to grant copyright protection to domestic works to turn China into a strong power in the world.[123] This should be done, however, under the condition of maintaining social security because assembly, association, press, and publication were among the most urgent affairs of government policing.[124] Notwithstanding, the 1910 Copyright Code represented a fundamental change in Chinese legal history, as the State started to recognise the

---

[120] Shanghai Library (ed.), *Letters of the Teachers and Friends of Wang Kangnian* [《汪康年师友书札》], 4 vols. (上海: 上海古籍出版社, 1986), vol. II, p. 2039.

[121] Li, *The Chinese Modern Copyright History*, p. 104.

[122] Q. Wang [王清], 'The Commercial Press and the Chinese Modern Copyright Protection' ['商务印书馆与中国近代版权保护'] (1993) 1 *Publishing Research* [《出版发行研究》] 55.

[123] *Gazette of Politics* [《政治官报》], (台北: 文海出版社, 1965), vol. 38, p. 525.

[124] Ibid.

private interest of authors and publishers and balance such interests against censorship as deemed necessary by the government.

In making the Copyright Code, the government identified two legislative approaches: French copyright law and German copyright law. Those who favoured the French approach dealt with copyright as a classical proprietary right, whereas the German scholarship took copyright for a privilege. Finally, the German scholarship took the upper hand because copyright as a privilege would be granted by the State so that the government could impose more restrictions as it wished. As a result, Japanese copyright law, which was based on the German model, became the model of China's first Copyright Code.[125] This approach, however, seemed to contradict traditional copyright rationales. In the end, the Copyright Code of the Qing Dynasty was divided into five chapters with 55 provisions.

Because the Qing government intended to grant copyright protection simply to better control the free flow of ideas, Articles 3–5 of this Copyright Code provided that, in order to acquire and enjoy copyright protection, one must submit the works to the government for registration. The Copyright Code was far more extensive in laying down the restrictions on copyright. Article 31 excluded certain types of subject matter from protection, such as laws, regulations, charity propaganda, public speeches, and newspaper articles on current events. This Article even specified four circumstances of the public interest (in free A2K): where the term of protection expires, where the author dies and no one is supposed to inherit, where the works have long been circulated, and where the author allows others to reprint freely. Article 39 was most important because it encompassed three circumstances comparable to what is regarded as "fair use" today: first, excerpts for the use of textbooks; second, excerpts for the purpose of citation; and third, imitation of others' graphs for the purpose of making sculptures, or vice versa.

These substantive provisions constituted the initial legal framework for balancing different interests under the 1910 Copyright Code. It incorporated the guiding principle of balance, relatively expansive scope of subject matter, and modern legal doctrines such as fair use. Importantly, the 1910 Copyright Code was not a spontaneous outcome of the economic and social development of the Chinese society toward the end of the Qing Dynasty, but was largely a product of international pressure and legal

---

[125] Li, *The Chinese Modern Copyright History*, p. 110.

transplantation. In this process, the legal framework of copyright protection without jeopardising censorship has become a fundamental chart for subsequent copyright legislation. Although the Qing Dynasty was overthrown almost immediately after the copyright code was promulgated, the influence of the Copyright Code did not stop there, but continued to work during the period of the Republic of China (ROC) (1911–1949) and after the founding of the PRC.

1.2.6. The Aftermath: International Copyright Negotiations and Copyright Legislation of the ROC

1.2.6.1. The international copyright negotiations of the ROC

After the ROC was founded, the government was not prepared to create a whole set of new legal rules for the Chinese society. Thus, disputes relating to copyright were decided on the basis of the 1910 Copyright Code. This was an awkward makeshift because a number of foreign publishers were bringing actions against Chinese publishers for their piracy activities in terms of the 1903 Sino–US bilateral commercial treaty. As a common practice, judges decided in accordance with both Article 11 of that treaty (which granted copyright protection to foreign works that were designed for use in China) and the 1910 Copyright Code (which did not grant copyright protection to foreign works explicitly).[126] Moreover, the US ambassador required in June 1913 that China accede to the BC, which went far beyond the scope of granting copyright protection under the previous bilateral commercial treaties. In 1919, the American Commerce Association warned the China Commerce Press against unauthorised reproduction of its books and submitted the dispute to the US ambassador in Beijing to seek diplomatic solutions.[127] The China Commerce Press submitted its opinions to three ministries of the central government to argue for its standpoint based on Article 11 of the said bilateral treaty[128] and to argue against China's accession to the BC in such a hasty way.[129]

---

[126] Z. Li [李宗辉], 'Legal Transplantation and Traditional Creation in the Hiatus: Comments on the 1910 Copyright Code' ['夹缝中的法律移植与传统创造:《大清著作权律》述评'] (2010) 5 *Journal of the Southwestern University of Politics and Law* [《西南政法大学学报》] 14.

[127] Zhou and Li (eds.), *Literature of Study on Chinese Copyright History*, p. 146.

[128] Ibid., p. 171.   [129] Ibid., p. 148.

On 3 November 1920, France dispatched a diplomat to China who submitted a protocol to the minister of Foreign Affairs of the ROC, urging China to accede to the BC.[130] The circulation of this protocol provoked hot debates all over the country. For example, the Shanghai Books Commerce Association took the initiative to submit its opinion formally to three ministries of the central government, stating its opposition to acceding to the BC based on China's difficult situation of economic and social development and the need to facilitate cultural progress by free translation and reproduction. As a result, the Ministry of Education of the ROC was convinced and replied to the opinion positively and agreed not to accede to the BC.[131] There were, however, different opinions. Duanliu Yang [杨端六], editor in chief of *Oriental Magazine*, advocated China to take an active part in international affairs and suggested that China sign the BC but postpone ratifying it. Yugan Wu [武堉干], a scholar of international trade, held that it was necessary for China to accede to the BC and that China could well make reservations to those provisions that went against China's interests.[132]

1.2.6.2. The copyright legislation of the ROC

The Beiyang Government in Beijing (the central government of the ROC at that time) issued in 1915 another Copyright Code, which was almost identical to the 1910 Copyright Code of the Qing Dynasty. Notably, Articles 25 and 26 of 1915 Copyright Code also required copyright registration with government authorities as a basis for remedy against infringement. In 1928, the Nanjing Government of the Nationalist regime (the subsequent central government of the ROC) enacted a second Copyright Code, which established a complete set of new copyright rules. Compared with the 1915 act, the 1928 Copyright Code had important new features. Above all, it was clarified, not through the Code itself, but through the implementing rules of the Code,[133] that foreign authors could also enjoy the protection of the reproduction right (but not translation right), subject to the principle of mutual reciprocity and on the condition that the works were made for use in China.

Moreover, whereas the previous term of protection started from the date of registration, the 1928 Copyright Code counted the term by beginning with the date of first publication and turned registration into a compulsory formality. This was because the publication law of the

---

[130] Ibid., p.168.   [131] Ibid., p. 170.   [132] Ibid., pp. 159–62.
[133] The Implementing Rules of the 1928 Copyright Code of the ROC, Art. 14.

Nationalist regime issued license for publication only on the condition that the works must be submitted for censorship. This requirement means that without publication the works could never enjoy copyright protection, not to mention a term of protection. Besides, the 1928 Copyright Code strengthened censorship by providing that works such as college textbooks that went against the tenets of the Chinese Nationalist Party or were forbidden by other laws would not be registered.

In sum, the foregoing historical account of the international negotiations between China and the Western countries as well as their influence on the establishment of China's copyright system prior to 1949 shows that international copyright law became an important legal source, which China gradually tried to transplant into Chinese law. However, China was aware that copyright protection could provide incentive to authors and publishers in producing and circulating works freely, which could jeopardise the rule of an authoritarian government. The major reason why China granted copyright protection, however, was that the Western negotiation partners exerted pressure on China in other fields while allowing the Chinese government to subject copyright protection to its censorship. Therefore, copyright was, for China, a bargaining chip for sustaining its censorship and political rule more than it was necessary to protect the private interest. That being said, the initial international negotiations prompted China to make a compromise of its censorship by allowing for the legal transplantation of international copyright law. As the following chapters show, this is a historical legacy that has continued to exist since the founding of the PRC.

1.3. Access Rules as a Legal Instrument in Copyright Law toward Regulation of Free Expression

Whereas international copyright law provides a major legal source for the transplantation of copyright law in China, the following part will explore access rules, a digit-oriented and balance-oriented normative framework of copyright law, which renders copyright protection more akin to free expression. Generally, such a legal instrument aims to fulfil proprietary functions by "restriking the balance" between the private interest in A2R and the public interest in having A2K at reasonable costs. Specifically, however, different countries may rely on this framework to serve the nonproprietary objective of regulating free expression. This general legal framework is important for further discussion.

1.3.1.   International Copyright Law as a Legal Source: The Need to
Restrike the Balance as a Global Issue

As interest balancing in copyright law is a process of distributing the benefits of copyright-protected works, copyrightable works can be regarded as knowledge products that have acquired the nature of "public goods" with such distributive values.[134] Whether and to what extent a country's copyright law strikes the balance well reflects "a country's progress in making knowledge goods accessible to its population," which can be determined in terms of the "affordability" of such goods and the "purchasing power" of the users.[135] No doubt copyright law has played a fundamental role over the past centuries, where authors and publishers gain royalties for allowing readers to access their works at a reasonable price, thus attaining the general policy goal of copyright law in both rewarding copyright owners and enabling the general public to advance knowledge.

In the last few decades, however, there have been increasing efforts toward restriking the balance in copyright laws around the world. Such efforts often involve more specific social needs than general economic concerns. One needs only to take a look at the development in international copyright law, which nowadays is decisive for the development of national copyright law. International copyright law has witnessed the proliferation of its components since the middle of the past century when WIPO and the United Nations Educational, Scientific, and Cultural Organization (UNESCO) took the lead in contracting relevant conventions with different focuses of policy interests. Since the 1990s, two trends, economic globalisation and the widespread use of information technology, have brought forth new challenges and difficulties to international copyright law. In the twenty-first century, the imbalance between different policy goals of these treaties, often intertwined with more complex social interests and larger policy priorities, has led to more institutional segmentation and normative fragmentation of international copyright law.[136] The following section reviews the specific objectives of major international copyright treaties, which have become a primary source for legal transplantation in China.

---

[134] P. L. C. Torremans, 'Is Copyright a Human Right?' (2007) *Mich St L Rev* 271, at 274.

[135] L. B. Shaver, 'Defining and Measuring A2K: A Blueprint for an Index of Access to Knowledge', *I/S: A Journal of Law and Policy for the Information Society* (2008) vol. 4, Issue 2, p. 3, at 20–2, at http://ssrn.com/abstract=1021065.

[136] H. Grosse Ruse-Khan, 'The Role of TRIPS in a Fragmented IP World' (2012) 43(8) IIC 881.

1.3.1.1. The BC and the UCC: the conflicts between developed countries and developing countries

Although WIPO boasts of the most fundamental and sophisticated treaty system of copyright and neighbouring rights, there has been a constant need to restrike the balance even for a mature copyright treaty such as the BC. In fact, the basis for a fixed universal copyright system is virtually shaky because different states with different levels of economic and social development assume different interests and roles in distributing the benefits of copyright-protected works. Thus, although developed countries have taken the lead in designing a global copyright system that aims at strengthening copyright owners' A2R, developing countries have been making efforts to restrike the balance by claiming that the general public should have A2K at lower costs to meet domestic needs.[137]

As early as in the 1950s, a number of developing countries resorted to the UCC initiated by the UNESCO because this convention imposes far looser, if not lower, copyright standards on member states than the BC. The UCC became a competing instrument to the BC, although it was meant only to allow less-developed countries to have a transitional stage of acceding to the BC. In fact, the UCC was important because the United States and the USSR took the lead in acceding to it. After the USSR collapsed and the United States acceded to the BC in 1989, the UCC has lost much of its contemporary significance. In addition, in the 1960s, developing country members of the BC managed to create the "Stockholm Protocol" under that convention to allow more exceptions to copyright protection for developing countries, especially in research and educational matters. The tension between different countries almost resulted in the collapse of the international copyright system.[138] Although the Stockholm Protocol never went into effect, it has become obvious that there is a need to restrike the balance between A2R and A2K at reasonable costs at the international level.

1.3.1.2. The TRIPS agreement: creating a more effective IP enforcement mechanism through trade agreements

The difficulties of creating a universally acceptable and effective copyright treaty become more discernible in the subsequent proliferation of

---

[137] See, e.g., J. H. Reichman, 'Intellectual Property in International Trade: Opportunities and Risks of a GATT Connection' (1989) 22 *Vand J Transnat'l L* 747.

[138] I. A. Olian, 'International Copyright and the Needs of Developing Countries: The Awakening at Stockholm and Paris' (1974) 7 *Cornell Int'l L J* 81.

international organisations and the institutional interactions between them. For instance, the birth of TRIPS in the 1990s is a product of WIPO's "shotgun marriage" to the WTO[139] because a substantive part of the BC is incorporated into TRIPS, and international copyright law is highlighted by the WTO's potential role in dealing with the "trade-linkage" issues.[140] In contrast to the General Agreement on Tariffs and Trade (GATT),[141] which relied on a loose and informal structure of "insider network" of member states,[142] the WTO assumes a formal institutional structure with distinct decision-making facilities and dispute settlement mechanism (DSM), as well as widely respected rule-based capacities.

In fact, it was only the "trade-related aspects" of IP that attracted the attention of major industrialised countries when they discerned the effective enforcement mechanism of the GATT system and the difficulties in enforcing the uniform standards of IP protection. Through such a linkage, developed countries expected to retrieve the remarkable profits for their domestic entertainment industry. Indeed, the WTO system created a comprehensive and powerful mechanism capable of imposing sanctions on countries that fail to comply with universal IP standards. Besides, TRIPS has also created flexible substantive copyright rules, such as the idea/expression dichotomy and the three-step-test, which are related to the balance between A2R and A2K at reasonable costs.

Most important, TRIPS requires members to implement and enforce those substantive rights. What makes TRIPS unique is its self-contained institutional structure that, in practice, makes IP protection more effective than ever. These procedural rules constitute "Bern-plus" copyright standards and give rise to national legislative efforts to pursue "TRIPS-plus" copyright standards such as those in the free trade agreements and bilateral investment treaties. In fact, a number of TRIPS rules, including the fundamental principles and the procedural provisions, are applicable to the substantive copyright-related provisions. In a word, TRIPS calls for more stringent implementation and enforcement of the universal copyright standards: all WTO members need to comply with TRIPS, adapt to

---

[139] A. Taubman, *A Practical Guide to Working with TRIPS* (Oxford: Oxford University Press, 2011), pp. 5 and 31.

[140] J. P. Trachtman, 'The Constitutions of the WTO' (2006) 17 *Eur J Int'l L* 623.

[141] General Agreement on Tariffs and Trade, 61 Stat. A-11, UNTS 55, 194, 30 October 1947.

[142] R. Howser, 'From Politics to Technocracy – and Back Again: The Fate of the Multilateral Trading Regime' (2002) 96 *AJIL* 94.

the radically changing global knowledge economy, as well as readjust their corresponding positions in providing and gaining A2K goods in bilateral and multilateral IP-related negotiations. Therefore, TRIPS can also be perceived as the result of the efforts toward more effective copyright law enforcement.

1.3.1.3. The WIPO Internet treaties: addressing the new technology

Further, international copyright law has to restrike the balance after new information technology has become widely used. WIPO did this by developing the WIPO Internet Treaties, which deal specifically with Internet-related issues. As relatively new WIPO treaties, the WCT and the WPPT are both identified as a special agreement under Article 20 of the BC and provide new legal measures on "digital copyright."[143] Admittedly, it is no easy thing to restrike the balance in face of the challenges posed by the explosive spread of new information technology, which, on certain occasions, has resulted in the "digital divide."[144] At times, authors and producers may be facing an inefficient market where digital technologies have rendered the cost of access to such works extremely low and "free riders" more rampant, so that loss of royalties for copyright owners may often be astronomical.[145] As a result, legislators around the world have created stricter legal measures to make sure that authors could profit from their creative acts at the market. However, such a process, which exists at both international and national levels, seems to be taking place in a one-way direction: ratcheting up the standards of copyright protection.

The WIPO Internet Treaties have consolidated the universal trend of "TRIPS-plus" standards by allowing legal measures that set up electronic fences to copyrighted works.[146] Following WIPO, a number of countries have developed new copyright laws to enhance the standards for copyright protection. There have been, among others, the Digital Millennium Copyright Act (DMCA) in the United States,[147] the Information Society

---

[143] WIPO Copyright Treaty, 20 December 1996, 36 ILM 65 (WCT). WIPO Performances and Phonograms Treaty, 20 December 1996, 36 ILM 76.

[144] UN, Road Map towards the Implementation of the United Nations Millennium Declaration. Report of the Secretary-General, UN GA/56/326 (6 September 2001) 31.

[145] T. Rogers and A. Szamosszegi, *Fair Use in the US Economy: Economic Contribution of Industries Relying on Fair Use* (CCIA: September 2007), p. 6, at www.ccianet.org/wp-content/uploads/library/FairUseStudy-Sep12.pdf.

[146] E.g., WCT, Arts. 11 and 12.

[147] Digital Millennium Copyright Act, Pub L No. 105–304, 112 Stat. 2860, 17 USC (1998).

Directive in the European Union (EU),[148] the HADOPI law in France,[149] and the Digital Economy Act in the UK,[150] all of which have laid down new rules for strengthening copyright protection in the digital environment. Apparently, digital copyright laws around the world are expanding and granting increasingly higher standards of protection to copyright owners, often without taking appropriate regard to the need of the general public for lowering the costs for A2K.

1.3.1.4.   The ACTA and the TPP: a mélange of proprietary and nonproprietary concerns

The difficulties in harmonising the policy goals of different copyright laws have provoked continuing efforts to create multilateral forums that address different regulatory focuses. In October 2011, a coterie of developed countries signed the Anti-Counterfeiting Trade Agreement (ACTA).[151] Due to widespread protests in the civil society, however, the EU voted against the ratification of the ACTA in 2012, which marked a significant stalemate of the ACTA.[152] In October 2015, twelve countries reached the Trans-Pacific Partnership (TPP), a multilateral free trade agreement including an IP chapter that is largely based on the ACTA.[153] In contrast to the bleak prospect of the marathon Doha Development Round of the WTO, the TPP creates a new comprehensive trade regime in the Asia-Pacific area beyond the staggering WTO system. Apparently, both trade agreements aim to establish a new IP framework to reinforce the global IP standards outside the traditional knowledge-related regulatory institutions such as WIPO and the WTO.

More important, by attaching different values to the general goal of balancing A2R against A2K in copyright protection, the ACTA and the TPP present a mélange of both proprietary and nonproprietary concerns. In fact, the development since TRIPS and the WIPO Digital Agenda has

---

[148] 2001/29/EC of the European Parliament and of the Council of 22 May 2001 on the harmonisation of certain aspects of copyright and related rights in the information society, OJ 2001 L 167, p. 10.

[149] The HADOPI law is an abbreviation of the French law on the Dissemination of Works and the Protection of Authors' Rights on the Internet ("Haute Autorité pour la Diffusion des œuvres et la Protection des droits d'auteur sur Internet").

[150] The UK Digital Economy Act 2010 (c 24).

[151] The Anti-Counterfeiting Trade Agreement (ACTA), 3 December 2010. The text is available at www.dfat.gov.au/trade/acta/Final-ACTA-text-following-legal-verification.pdf.

[152] Z. Whittaker, "'Last Rites' for ACTA? Europe Rejects Antipiracy Treaty', 4 July 2012, CNet, at www.cnet.com/news/last-rites-for-acta-europe-rejects-antipiracy-treaty.

[153] The Trans-Pacific Partnership (TPP), at https://ustr.gov/tpp.

highlighted the need to enforce digital copyright rules in terms of a bunch of trade-related and even non-trade-related effects. A prominent example of such effects involves free expression, a nonproprietary value that has not been addressed in the previous international copyright treaties. For one thing, the ACTA, which sets up a new model law for multilateral IP agreement, refers explicitly to the coherence between free expression and IP enforcement.[154] The TPP, which has a wide membership of Pacific countries, contains profound political requirements about free expression in its member countries, though its copyright rules have also aroused wide concerns about Internet censorship. These priorities manifest the future development of global copyright law and may have strong potential in making, construing, interpreting, and applying national copyright law.

1.3.2. The Proprietary and Nonproprietary Significance of Integrating Rebalance Needs into Free-Expression-Oriented Norms

Indeed, copyright law assumes a fundamental feature in the twenty-first century: copyright is undergoing unprecedented, perhaps revolutionary, challenges posed by the progress of digital technologies. Whereas recent development of copyright laws have focused on copyright owners' rights to control unauthorised access to their works, "user rights,"[155] as they are called, or such legal entitlements that are bestowed on the general public to allow for A2K at lower costs are often easily ignored. Arguably, in the digital context the term "copyright law" or "copyright rules" seems to imply that the proprietary structure of copyright law in the past few centuries was designed more to the advantage of copyright owners than to that of the general public, who are "readers" or "users." Clearly, a new framework of A2K-oriented rules, which cover copyright protection not only in the traditional environment but also in the digital environment, should be introduced for restriking the balance. If such new rules are not immediately available, it is necessary to redefine and interpret the existing copyright rules in a more balance-oriented way.

At a time when costs of economic globalisation are heightening and new information technologies are accelerating the pace of producing and disseminating knowledge, a balance-oriented normative framework should reduce asymmetries between A2R and A2K at reasonable costs in the

---

[154] The ACTA, Art. 27.2–4.
[155] J. Litman, 'Readers' Copyright' (2011) 58 *J Cop Soc USA* 325.

existing copyright law and the legal practice. This framework means that, if copyright law allows more flexibility in interpreting the substantive rules, it will be more likely to enable the general public to have A2K at reasonable costs. A2K-oriented or balance-oriented rules are, however, not supposed to eliminate copyright owners' interest in A2R, but to retain their incentive to produce and circulate knowledge goods by ensuring A2R. In the digital environment, in particular, access rules should transform such rebalance needs into the normative framework of copyright law by taking both A2R and A2K at reasonable costs into account.

Furthermore, such a legal framework must be, ultimately, free-expression-oriented and have nonproprietary significance for facilitating free expression by emphasising the role of A2K in economic, social, and political policies around the world. A2R may encourage individual copyright owners to exercise their creativity and freedom of speech. Rendering A2K widely affordable could facilitate the free flow of information, which is the precondition for gearing up education, advancement and dissemination of knowledge, political participation, and so on. These two functions must be interrelated because overbroad restriction of A2R would not only reduce the incentive to create and disseminate knowledge, but also narrow down the potential for expanding A2K. Once such a specific normative framework is defined, copyright law can better fulfil its role of an engine of free expression.

1.3.3.   Access Rules as a Legal Instrument of Regulating Free Expression

As such, "copyright rules," as they are called literally, may not suffice to fully convey the normative significance and structure of restriking the balance. Rather, there have been more attempts to remould copyright law from the angle of "access rights" instead of "copyright."[156] For example, Ginsburg suggests treating the right to control access as "an integral component of copyright law."[157] Certainly, because copyright protects only the expressive forms rather than ideas, access to the idea or A2K as a narrow concept is virtually nonregulatable. Yet, if A2K is construed as the process of paying for access to copyright-protected works, in which knowledge is carried, then A2K is regulatable. Moreover, this is also a process of allowing copyright owners to have A2R. The concept of "access rights" captures the regulatable

---

[156] J. C. Ginsburg, 'News from the US' (1999) 180 *RIDA* 127, 159.
[157] J. C. Ginsburg, 'From Having Copies to Experiencing Works: The Development of an Access Right in US Copyright Law' (2003) 50 *J Cop Soc* USA 113.

part of any conduct or process that enables a person to access copyright-protected works by subjecting it to the exclusive control of copyright owners on the condition of A2R.[158] In contrast, "rights of access" describe the opposite part of "access rights" and refer to a direct form of allowing access to copyright-protected works without any artificial obstacles to such works.[159] In fact, both A2R and A2K can be assimilated into the framework of "access rules," which are understood generally as an architecture that counteracts the negative effects of strong copyright protection and emphasises the importance of A2K.

Accordingly, access rules refer to the substantive norms in copyright law, aim to enable the general public to gain A2K through copyright-protected works at reasonable costs, while taking the interest of copyright owners in A2R for producing and circulating creative works into account. In other words, access rules derive from two approaches that allow the general public to have access to copyright-protected works: either copyright owners control economic and social costs for A2K by A2R, or the public is entitled to A2K without the need to resort to copyright owners. In any event, the policy goal behind access rules lies in restriking the balance between different interests based on the negative correlation between A2R and A2K. Although traditional copyright rules do so only by imposing the "minimum standards," access rules often redefine copyright law in balance-oriented terms by imposing "maximum standards" as "ceilings" on copyright owners' exclusive rights.[160]

Apart from being digit-oriented and balance-oriented, access rules may also represent a free-expression-oriented approach of copyright law by readjusting both proprietary and nonproprietary interests. Indeed, proprietorship is not only an economic term here, but also connotes strong impacts on social relationships, especially with regard to the expressive speech of individuals. According to Netanel, appropriation of others' existing expressions lies "at the heart of free speech," in that one is fully entitled to exploit the culture in which one lives to formulate one's own language.[161] Such an appropriative nature of free expression may, certainly, come into conflict with the proprietary interests of

---

[158] Z. Efroni, *Access-Right: The Future of Digital Copyright Law* (Oxford: Oxford University Press, 2011), pp. 146–7.

[159] Ibid., p. 153.

[160] See e.g., P. B. Hugenholtz and R. L. Okediji, 'Conceiving an International Instrument on Limitations and Exceptions to Copyright' (2008), at www.ivir.nl/publicaties/hugenholtz/finalreport2008.pdf.

[161] Netanel, *The Copyright's Paradox*, pp. 42–4.

copyright owners. Access rules, thus, aim to mitigate such conflicts by prioritising its A2K-oriented policy goal in copyright law, in both traditional and digital contexts.

Therefore, access rules can be designed, interpreted, and applied in different ways to meet different regulatory goals. Where proprietary interests are too strong, more restrictions can be imposed on the rights of copyright owners. Such restrictions would delimit their economic gains or A2R and might even reduce their incentive to create or exercise their freedom of speech, but would enhance A2K on the part of the general public and envision better prospects of freedom of information. In contrast, where such fine-tuning measures underpin proprietary interests considerably more than public interests, the costs for A2K would rise, resulting in inconvenient dissemination of knowledge and often less freedom of information, though A2R and the motive of free speech could be strengthened. Largely decreased A2K would, however, compromise the policy goal of copyright law. As a legal framework representing a balance-oriented approach, access rules manifest the negative correlation between the private interest and the public interest most clearly and may invariably affect free expression, regardless of whether they are driven by a political incentive to realise such policy goals in different types of societies.

1.3.4.   An Acquis *of Fragmented Access Rules in Positive Copyright Law*

Derived from copyright law, access rules aim to sort out "wiggle room" for granting public access to copyright-protected works.[162] In fact, access rules arise from a broad range of norms in positive copyright law and can be divided into different categories. According to Okediji, access rules provide "bulk compensated access," "uncompensated creative access" (unencumbered availability of certain creative work), "negotiated access" (privately negotiated rules between owners and users), and "mandatory compensated access" (conditional use of works under compulsory licenses).[163] Such a categorisation reflects both economic and social policy considerations that can be geared to the general and specific

---

[162] J. H. Reichman, 'From Free Riders to Fair Flowers: Global Competition under the TRIPS Agreement' (1997) 29 *NYU J Int'l L Pol* 11, at 29.

[163] R. L. Okediji, 'Sustainable Access to Copyrighted Digital Information Works in Developing Countries', in K. E. Maskus and J. H. Reichman (eds.), *International Public Goods and Transfer of Technology under a Globalized Intellectual Property Regime* (New York: Cambridge University Press, 2005), p. 142, at 148.

dimensions of the instrumentality of copyright. For one thing, access rules envisage more potential of expanding A2K, which may advance free flow of information and contribute to such policy goals as boosting education. Thus, access rules represent essential norms in copyright law that offer more "wiggle room" toward promoting not only A2K but also free expression on the whole.

Certainly, many rules in international copyright regimes look virtually identical or even overlapping,[164] which presents technical complexities regarding how access rules emanating from different regimes can be brought into harmony with each other. They are, in fact, "multi-sourced equivalent norms" that are "binding upon the same international legal subjects," "similar or identical in their normative contents," and dwell in different institutional contexts.[165] In the global copyright scenario, these rules can be best exemplified by the à la carte incorporation of the substantive provisions of the BC into TRIPS. They are also visible in the incorporation of certain rules of the BC and TRIPS into the WCT. The seemingly fragmented picture of international copyright law, however, will not necessarily result in norms drifting apart. In fact, different sources of international copyright law shape a uniform "acquis,"[166] from which national access rules can be derived to address specific policy issues such as the regulation of free expression.

As such, access rules, which exist in both international and national copyright law, share some basic characteristics and can be crystallised into several subcategories. The most fundamental subcategories of access rules may include, but are not confined to, principles of ascertaining authorship, the rules about subject matter, the ways to exercise copyright (duration of protection and requirement of formalities), the spectra and latitudes of economic rights, "limitation and exception" rules or, alternatively, fair use/dealings, and rules of compulsory license. These access rules comprise the basic toolbox for balancing A2R against affordable A2K. They may, however, also have the potential of carrying out certain economic and social policies, especially promoting free expression.

---

[164] K. Raustiala, 'Density and Conflict in International Intellectual Property Law' (2007) 40 *U C Davis L Rev* 1021.

[165] T. Broude and Y. Shany, 'The International Law and Policy of Multi-Sourced Equivalent Norms', in T. Broude and Y. Shany (eds.), *Multi-Sourced Equivalent Norms in International Law* (Oxford: Hart Publishing, 2011), p. 1, at 5.

[166] *Japan–Taxes on Alcoholic Beverages*, WT/DS8/AB/R, WT/DS10/AB/R, WT/DS11/AB/R, 14 (1 November 1996).

1.3.4.1.   Authorship

Access rules must define authorship because it's important to determine who are entitled to claim protection and allow or deny access to their works that contain a speech of their own. Such rules are also the prerequisites for identifying who enjoys the specific legal protection of an incentive to produce and circulate a certain intellectual work that contains a speech. Obviously, authorship rules affect the regulation of free expression. If the author of a work cannot be identified, the work may become an orphan work and fall into the public domain (in which case everyone has free access to the work and there is no control of A2K in whatever form). Besides, different types of authors (for instance, sole authorship, coauthorship, or deemed authorship) may enjoy different contents and scopes of copyright, so that the extent to which an author may control others' access to her/his work varies. Because authors will be given different economic and social status in different social systems, there may be different ways of attributing authorship in different countries.

The needs for both copyright protection and A2K at reasonable costs, however, disregard nation borders. In the cross-border sphere, the question of authorship, which determines who will be considered authors or copyright owners in a foreign country, is subject to different applicable laws. Nevertheless, whether a country intends to extend copyright protection to foreign works is decided in accordance with the universal principles of formal and material reciprocity. The former principle, known as the "national treatment," requires that a country protect foreign works in the same way as its domestic works, whereas works originating in that country will be accorded the same level of protection as the domestic works originating in the foreign country. In contrast, the latter principle accords substantially equivalent protection to foreign works, as is conferred on the works in that original foreign country. These principles for determining authorship will have impacts on the outcome of regulating the speech and information flow in cross-border contexts.

1.3.4.2.   Subject matter

The rules about the subject matter of copyright determine whether certain intellectual achievements, which carry a speech themselves, contain elements that deserve copyright protection and, thus, whether and to what extent copyright owners may have A2R and the public may have A2K. In that connection, such access rules have a direct impact on regulating free expression. For instance, the rules about subject matter are important for China's cultural policies because, by imposing censorship, China aims to prohibit certain subject matter from being circulated. In general, however, there are three essential criteria for determining copyrightable subject matter.

First, the idea/expression dichotomy determines the scope of human intelligence to be protected by copyright. Accordingly, the copyrightable matter is the "ordered expression of thought," whereas the idea encapsulated in the knowledge goods cannot be protected.[167] This doctrine, which arises from the proposition that the cost incurred by dissemination of ideas is higher than that incurred by developing ideas,[168] draws the line between the subject matter eligible for copyright protection and the matter that should be left in the public domain.[169] The clear border between an idea and its expression, however, is often rather vague and difficult to define, which might lead authors to conduct self-censorship so as not to call an infringing act into question.

Consequently, not all forms of expression can be protected. Rather, a minimum degree of originality is required.[170] Originality determines the level of human intelligence or endeavours that could amount to "work of the mind."[171] Together with the idea/expression dichotomy, it restricts the profitability of knowledge goods.[172] In addition, authors will cause any of their ideas/speeches to be fixed in certain tangible medium, such as books or software, but it remains widely divided under national legislation whether the requirement of fixation constitutes a necessary precondition for copyright protection.[173] Even though it may not be the decisive criterion for determining the subject matter of copyright protection, fixation underscores the commercial feature of copyright-protected works, that is, knowledge or ideas should generally be fixed in a certain tangible form as A2K goods.

---

[167] J. A. L. Sterling, *World Copyright Law*, 3rd edn (London: Sweet & Maxwell, 2008), pp. 248–9.

[168] Landes and Posner, 'An Economic Analysis of Copyright Law', 349–50.

[169] J. E. Cohen et al., *Copyright in a Global Information Economy* (New York: Aspen Publishers, 2006), p. 72.

[170] Ricketson and Ginsburg, *International Copyright and Neighbouring Rights*, pp. 402 and 404.

[171] S. Strömholm, 'Copyright – Comparison of Laws', in E. Ulmer and G. Schricker (eds.), *Copyright: International Encyclopedia of Comparative Law* (Tübingen: Mohr Siebeck, 2007) vol. 14, § 3–13, p. 7.

[172] Ibid., p. 8.   [173] Ibid., p. 5.

1.3.4.3.   Exercising the rights

Duration of protection and formalities determine to what extent copyright owners may exercise their exclusive rights in temporal and procedural dimensions. These access rules may affect A2R and the costs for A2K and, thus, the regulation of free expression, in either positive or negative ways.

1.3.4.3.1. Duration of protection   Copyright protection granted to a work is not permanent. For a long time in history, the need to shorten the duration of copyright protection on the ground of the public interest was beyond doubt.[174] Recently, however, duration of protection has been extended under a number of major copyright laws.[175] This would certainly affect the chance of A2K in a negative way. Arguably, such expansive legislations have met with strong opposition on the grounds of having affordable A2K.[176] Indeed, unreasonably long terms of copyright protection may readily deter the general public from accessing copyright-protected works and, thus, their freedom to seek and receive information. In fact, works created long ago may not be worth protecting anymore due to the accelerated pace of knowledge production. Moreover, authors are not tempted to create works simply because of longer terms of protection. Rather, it is often the publishers that are more likely to benefit from a prolonged period of copyright protection.

1.3.4.3.2. Formalities   Another category of access rules that may concern the interest-balancing process and free expression in copyright law is the formalities of acquiring and exercising copyright. A2K can be rendered more convenient to the public when it is easy for those who produce and circulate knowledge goods to acquire copyright and be entitled as copyright owners. In most cases, copyright law provides automatic protection to authors, and no formalities are required,[177] which enables the general public to identify the existence of copyright and copyright owners without any difficulty. Further, free-expression-

---

[174] Sterling, *World Copyright Law*, p. 777.

[175] See, e.g., EC Directive 2006/116/EC on the Term of Protection of Copyright and Certain Related Rights, Art. 1.1 and 1.3, OJ L372, 27 December 2006, pp. 12–18.

[176] S. von Lewinski, 'EC Proposal for a Council Directive Harmonizing the Term of Protection of Copyright and Certain Related Rights' (1992) 23 IIC 785.

[177] Cf. C. Masouyé, *Guide to the Berne Convention for the Protection of Literary and Artistic Works* (Geneva: WIPO, 1978), p. 33.

oriented access rules also include the collective management by "collecting societies," which undertake to negotiate with copyright owners on behalf of the general public.[178] As a mechanism of licensing, administering, and enforcing copyright uniformly, the collective administration can benefit copyright owners by ensuring their A2R and an incentive to produce/disseminate free speech.

1.3.4.4. Economic rights

Admittedly, copyright is divided into economic rights and moral rights. Economic rights give copyright owners the chance to benefit from different uses of works, such as reproduction, adaptation, distribution, translation, and communication. They are often couched in tandem with moral rights that are exclusively associated with the author's personality. Economic rights differ from moral rights, in that they do not pertain exclusively to the copyright owner, but they can also be acquired, assigned, transferred, disposed of, or even inherited on remunerative terms. Thus, copyrightable works can be commercialised and become knowledge goods in a real sense. Because moral rights do not directly affect the access opportunities of the general public, they will not be dealt with here. Rather, it is the nature and content of economic rights that invariably set forth the latitudes of access for the general public. Although a number of copyright scholarships have attempted to describe traditional "copyright" as "access rights," economic rights are important access rules. By providing for convenient A2R, economic rights establish a decent social status for copyright owners who can find significant economic support for an independent living – a fundamental prerequisite for exercising freedom of expression.

1.3.4.5. Limitation and exception rules

An important function of access rules is to render the costs for A2K more reasonable by imposing restrictions on copyright owners' economic rights. Thus, those rules that explain the purposes, reasons, measures, and consequences of restricting copyright protection will be of particular interest. International conventions generally allow free use of works such as public speeches, lectures, use of short excerpts by quotation or illustration for teaching, use for private study and research.[179] By contrast, national rules that serve to restrict copyright

---

[178] G. Davies, 'The Public Interest in Collective Administration of Rights' (March 1989) *Copyright* 81.

[179] BC, Arts. 2*bis* (1) and (2), 9(2), 10*bis* (1), (2) and (3).

are widely disparate in contents and scope. Usually, in civil law countries, they are referred to as "limitations or exceptions," whereas in common law jurisdictions such rules have been specifically dubbed "fair use" or "fair dealing." By reducing economic obstacles for A2K, these rules help facilitate knowledge transfer and free flow of information.

In principle, "limitations and exceptions" or "fair use" are rules in copyright law that allow for copyright-protected works to be accessed without any explicit authorisation by copyright owners. Traditionally, reproduction of works for any use that does not prejudice authorial interests is permitted,[180] whereas compensation shall be made only in case of "serious loss of profit for the copyright owner."[181] The fundamental purpose of such access rules is to prevent creators of works from holding any monopoly over their works so that others may learn from them and create new works on that basis. Different countries, however, tend to design such rules in different ways.

A salient example of such rules is the fair use doctrine founded in the United States. It virtually stems from the old English law[182] and has evolved into a unique statutory provision under the US copyright law that outlines four integral factors for ascertaining a "fair use" of works.[183] Whereas the fair use doctrine has become a general defence to infringement claims,[184] its legal prerequisites exemplify how limitation and exception rules affect A2K in more precise and visible parameters: (1) fair use shall be "transformative" and serve the purpose of advancing works protected by copyright;[185] (2) the nature of works in being socially useful may trump alternative features of works to justify fair use;[186] (3) the substantiality of works being used defines the boundaries of fair use;[187] and (4) the effect of fair use shall not significantly harm the original and potential commercial profitability of works.[188]

As such, US courts have often resorted to the fair use doctrine to provide the protection of free speech as enshrined in the First Amendment of the

---

[180] See, e.g., BC, Art. 9(2).   [181] Masouyé, *Guide to the Berne Convention*, p. 56.

[182] *Gyles* v. *Wilcox, Barrow, and Nutt* (1740) 3 Atk. 143; 26 ER 489, Court of Chancery (England).

[183] Copyright Act, 17 USC § 107 (1976). See also *Folsom* v. *Marsh*, 9 F. Cas. 342, No. 4, 901 (CCD Mass. 1841).

[184] *Campbell* v. *Acuff-Rose Music Inc.*, 510 US 578 (1994).

[185] P. N. Leval, 'Toward a Fair Use Standard' (1990) 103 (5) *Harv L Rev* 1105.

[186] *Time Inc.* v. *Bernard Geis Associates*, 293 F. Supp. 130 (SDNY 1968).

[187] *Harper & Row* v. *Nation Enterprises*.

[188] *Video Pipeline Inc.* v. *Buena Vista Home Entertainment Inc.*, 342 F 3d 191 (3d Cir. 2003).

US Constitution. There are, however, two distinct approaches to interpreting the fair use doctrine on a case-by-case basis. On the one hand, the Supreme Court has maintained a property-centred view by requiring copyright owners' consent and evidence of potential harm to markets.[189] On the other hand, other US courts have embraced a civil-rights-based approach by emphasising the status and significance of free expression.[190] Such a bifurcated scenario seems to cast shadow on the predictability of the role of fair use in defending the value of free expression.

As the development of digital technology poses genuine challenges to copyright protection, it becomes more difficult to preserve the balance between different interests in the digital environment. Internet users are able to reproduce works in exponential volumes and deal with them at random, which cannot be defined as "normal exploitation" anymore and may largely prejudice the interests of copyright owners.[191] While copyright owners require higher protection standards, Internet users also hope to legitimise their act of taking full advantage of modern technology under the aegis of achieving A2K. Therefore, access rules must address such unprecedented challenges by taking different needs into account, especially through limitation and exception rules.

1.3.4.6. Compulsory license

Further, a category of access rules is designed especially for mandatory use of copyright-protected works. In case, reasonable efforts have been made in vain to acquire permission from copyright owners to use their works, the government may grant a compulsory license subject to certain forms of remuneration to the copyright owners. Under such circumstances, the State is intervening and playing its role as arbitrator in dealing with the supply of works, if it is impossible for the general public to negotiate with copyright owners under reasonable terms. Copyright-protected works are, however, generally not such urgent products as patent-protected medicines, in which case the compulsory use can be easily understood. Rather, such needs are often warranted in countries where knowledge products are undeveloped and financial resources are limited. Otherwise access rules would go disproportionately against the private interest of copyright owners. This is why, in judicial practice,

---

[189] *Harper & Row v. Nation Enterprises*, para. III A.
[190] See, e.g., *SunTrust Bank v. Houghton Mifflin*, 60 USPQ 2d 1225, 1260 (11th Cir. 2001). See also *Mattel Inc. v. Walking Mountain Productions*, 353 F 3d 792 (9th Cir. 2003) 803.
[191] WCT, Art. 10(2).

national courts may allow restriction of copyright owners' exclusive right
to prevent others from accessing their works, but leave them with the
right to claim equitable remuneration for accessing the works.[192] Therefore, a compulsory license may help facilitate A2K by lowering the
threshold for obtaining permission from copyright owners.

1.4. Conclusion

This chapter raises the question about the balance between the private
interest and the public interest and its implication for free expression in
Chinese copyright law. Indeed, copyright not only protects the private
interest in A2R, but also facilitates the public interest in affordable A2K.
This is, however, merely the general function of copyright law. Different
countries will confer specific functions on copyright law in different legal,
economic, and social terms. Arguably, A2R reflects an instrument of
promoting the incentive to exercise free speech, whereas affordable
A2K represents a parameter of facilitating the free flow of information.
In traditional Chinese cultural policies, however, the government's interest in controlling the production and dissemination of ideas through
censorship was rendered superior to both A2R and A2K. Such an
intransigent policy has had a profound influence on China's approach
toward copyright protection until the present. It may often sound con-
fusing that the government's interest in maintaining social control,
which reflects a mixture of Confucianism and the socialist ideology, is
also referred to as the "public interest." Such regulatory goals, however,
will invariably come into conflict with the regulatory objectives of copyright law.

A historical study of the censorship regime in ancient China reveals
that there were some sporadic efforts of copyright protection concomitant with the government's censorship in as early as the Song Dynasty.
However, owing to the particular economic and social background of
the ancient Chinese society, such efforts did not lead to any copyright
law making. The earlier development left trace on the mentalities of the
Chinese society about copyright protection and the development of
the publishing industries. The accounts of the general understanding
of copyright at the end of the Qing Dynasty may help interpret such
development from a microhistorical perspective.

---

[192] *Tonband*, 17 BGHZ 266, 278 (1955).

Typically, many Chinese government officials at that time were unaware of the dichotomy between the ideas that a work carried and the expressive form of such ideas. They upheld copyright protection simply because this seemed to legitimise the government's efforts of forbidding certain books from being circulated. Whereas the government forbade free print of works in terms of the needs of censorship, the ordinary publishers intended to do so primarily because they were more concerned about their economic interests (even if the authors did not always want to acknowledge this). Thus, in a more objective lens, the ordinary Chinese were taking advantage of the government's censorship regime to claim copyright protection. Indeed, considering traditional Chinese intellectuals' interest in and dedication to spreading their life philosophy through intellectual works, it would be hard to imagine that nongovernment Chinese authors/publishers were also (or more) interested in forbidding others from "copying" their ideas, that is, conducting censorship. On the contrary, some authors (whose works are politically sensitive) may be even happy to have their works pirated. In a sense, the historical development has formed the path-dependency of the mentalities about copyright protection in China today.

As far as the development of copyright law in China is concerned, the public international law approach counts more substantially. The path-dependency of contemporary Chinese copyright law originates from the development of China's earlier copyright law starting in the Late Qing Dynasty. Although the emergence of China's national copyright law could not be entirely attributed to foreign factors, international copyright law did affect the making of the modern Chinese copyright system decisively through commercial negotiations. Certainly, the public interest as defined by the Chinese government encompasses the control of free exchange of ideas, which differed from the public interest as understood by ordinary Chinese intellectuals and their Western counterparts. Nonetheless, the government could not ignore the emerging market of copyright-protected works driven by the private interest. Thus, while the Qing government endeavoured to maintain its censorship, the legislators started to wield the balance between different interests in copyright law making. Such a trend continued to prevail in the copyright legislation of the ROC. In sum, Chinese copyright law came as a result of both international pressure and the domestic needs of economic and social development. It is, thus, fair to say that Chinese copyright law was rooted in international copyright law and reflected a balance of different interests subject to the outcome of government censorship.

Finally, to better understand how international copyright law influences Chinese copyright law with regard to the regulation of free expression, it is necessary to introduce a legal methodology of assessing the weight of the protection of different interests, that is, the negative correlation between A2R and A2K at reasonable costs in copyright law. Indeed, the dynamic interplay between A2R and A2K reflects a picture of the corresponding change in the policy goal of regulating free expression. Although international copyright law forms the primary legal source for Chinese copyright law, access rules, which assume an important role in the global context, constitute such a normative framework for restriking the balance in copyright law. Accordingly, the better copyright owners are remunerated, the more control they will have in providing A2K through their copyright-protected works, which represents a picture of strong protection of free speech. Alternatively, the lower the costs of A2K are, the easier it will be for the general public to seek and receive information, while the incentive to exercise free speech may not necessarily dwindle. As such, access rules emanate from the substantive rules of copyright law, but may contribute to the objective of regulating free expression. By readjusting and redesigning access rules, different societies can reorient their copyright laws to serve different regulatory goals.

2

Little Gain Makes Work Hard

The international IP negotiations that led to China's accession to the BC and the UCC also prompted China to transpose fundamental international copyright rules into the legislative framework of Chinese copyright law. However, the way China perceives the international copyright system is ambivalent because China's will to exercise control of free expression remains recalcitrant. On the one hand, international copyright law poses challenges to the predominant status of China's entrenched censorship regime in copyright law making, which China cannot ignore. Generally, Chinese intellectuals see a chance of exercising speech freedom through the establishment of a modern copyright system backed up by the economic reforms. On the other hand, while Chinese copyright law encapsulates the modality of access rules under the BC and the UCC, the first Copyright Act of the PRC claims to address "interest balancing." Indeed, such interest balancing takes place in an anti-A2R manner, which aims to attain China's policy goal of exerting control on speech freedom. Thus, the strategies that China incorporates into the architecture of its copyright system are sophisticated, as China designs its copyright law in a way that seemingly entertains the goal of rendering A2K affordable for the general public, but with an aim to control the economic gains of copyright owners and dampen their incentive to produce and disseminate ideas freely.

2.1. The Birth of Copyright Law in the PRC: Compromising China's Censorship-Oriented Copyright Legislation in the Context of International IP Negotiations

2.1.1. Copyright Protection in the PRC Pending the End of the 1980s: Unfettering Intellectual Creation?

2.1.1.1. The censorship-oriented copyright legislation

The founding of the PRC in 1949 ushered in a new phase for copyright legislation in China, as the Communist regime declared the entire corpus of law of the Nationalist regime (1927–1949) void and invalid. The subsequent development must be understood against the economic and social contingencies before the turn of the 1950s. The first decade of the Nationalist regime of the ROC (1927–1937) was a relative peaceful period that witnessed rapid industrial and commercial development. In the eyes of leading authorities, China might have continued its development toward a modern economy and perhaps a modern society, if Japan had not invaded China and the Second Sino–Japanese War (1937–1945) had not broken out.[1] That war had irreversible consequences for China, not only because of the discontinuance of the previous economic development, but also because it gave the CCP a precious chance to survive the impending military confrontation with the Nationalist regime and develop its own military force, which enabled the CCP to defeat the Nationalists in the ensuing Chinese Civil War (1946–1949).

In principle, the Nationalist regime embraced a capitalist economy and recognised private ownership. By contrast, the Communist regime introduced the socialist economic system from the USSR. In the 1950s, the Communist regime nationalised industrial and commercial sectors and collectivised agricultural sectors and handcraft sectors around the country, hallowing a planned economy as China's fundamental economic system.[2] Accordingly, any private ownership was largely abrogated, derogated, and despised. In this instance, the laws enacted during the Nationalist regime were "reactionary" and did not fit in with the new national economic system of public ownership. While the ideals of Marxism–Leninism were quite far from those of the Confucianism, the laws of the former Soviet Union became a wonderful model for the Communist regime. Indeed, like Confucianism, Marxism–Leninism as interpreted by the CCP values the "unity of ideas" and rules out free expression.

In the earlier days of the Communist regime, Mao's ideology permeated and prevailed in all areas relating to public policy. For example, regarding the creation of literary and artistic works, Mao advocated serving the public interest of the socialist society by making use of such works as a "revolutionary machine" and "weapon." In other words, the CCP used to treat works carrying revolutionary thoughts as a "free speech" that must be facilitated and disseminated among the public and, in fact, adopted a

---

[1] J. K. Fairbank and M. Goldman, *China: A New History*, 2nd enlarged edn (Cambridge, MA: Belknap Press of Harvard University Press, 2006).

[2] Cf. R. Coase and N. Wang, *How China Became Capitalist* (Basingstoke: Palgrave Macmillan, 2012), p. 10.

censorship policy that banned "counterrevolutionary" works from circulation. This also explains why copyright law and even those related international agreements that were in force under the Nationalist regime were abolished after 1949. Meanwhile, there was no substitute for the legal void left by such a political movement, as there was no copyright law under the rule of the CCP in the so-called liberated zone prior to 1949.[3]

After the founding of the PRC, however, the CCP promised to establish a new legal system, including IP law, which is a process that has continued to the present. The General Administration of Publication (GAOP) of the central government [中央人民政府出版总署], soon after it was set up in 1949, promulgated the Resolutions Concerning the Improvement and Development of Publication [《关于改进和发展出版工作的决议》]. As the first formal document concerning copyright protection in the PRC, the resolutions were adopted in 1950 at the First Conference of National Publications and delineated broad guidelines on the relationship between authors and publishers. Moreover, the document laid down the fundamental policy of granting authors a fixed sum of basic remuneration for their creative works on the basis of the number of copies printed. In addition, authors were granted the right to prohibit alteration of their works, which was subject to the approval of the socialist state – a model taken over from the former USSR. Subsequently, the GAOP enacted the Regulations on Editorial Organisations and State Owned Publishing Houses [《关于国营出版社编辑机构及工作制度的规定》] in 1952, which allowed the publisher to sign a contract with the authors when publishing their works. Such contracts, however, could not be made on the basis of the principle of private autonomy, but the contents must be predetermined according to the State's plan.

Before the Cultural Revolution (1966–1976) commenced, the legislative work of copyright protection did grow slowly, though not systematically, in the form of several administrative regulations. In 1954, the GAOP even attempted to call for copyright legislation, which would have covered a definition of copyright and treatment of foreign works, through a political document that was issued only to an international bookstore and never went into the public.[4] Shortly before the GAOP was repealed due to the organisational reforms of the State Council in 1954, it

---

[3] M. Sidel, 'The Legal Protection of Copyright and the Rights of Authors in the PRC, 1949–1984: Prelude to the Chinese Copyright Law' (1986) 9 *Columbia J Art L* 479.

[4] M. Li et al. [李明山 等], *The Contemporary Chinese History of Copyright* [《中国当代版权史》] (北京: 知识产权出版社, 2007), p. 12.

submitted a draft to the Ministry of Culture (MOC), which, importantly, became the basis of the Interim Regulations Concerning the Protection of Copyright of Published Works [《保障出版物著作权暂行规定》].[5] The MOC then promulgated these draft regulations in 1957 and subsequently issued an illustration, which provided that "all works published within the PRC are granted copyright protection, regardless of the nationality of the author" and that "copyright protection also extends to works of Chinese nationals that are published outside the PRC."

Unfortunately, this process of evolving copyright legislation was interrupted by the Anti-Rightist Movement in 1957 and the Great Leap Forward Movement in 1958, both of which overshadowed the legitimacy of giving pecuniary and material incentives to those who were engaged in intellectual creations.[6] Even in 1958, the MOC was still trying to "balance" the private interest against the "public interest" (as upheld by the socialist state) through a draft of the Interim Regulations Concerning the Remuneration for Books of Arts and Social Sciences [《关于文学和社会科学稿酬的暂行规定草案》]. The underlying policy goal, however, was to treat copyright as an instrument to maintain the socialist order of the State rather than to protect the private interest of copyright owners.

In 1963, for instance, the State Council promulgated two sets of administrative regulations: Regulations on Encouraging Inventions [《发明奖励条例》] and Regulations on Encouraging Improvements in Technology [《技术改进奖励条例》]. Both regulations contained provisions that discouraged copyright owners from obtaining remuneration for their works. Thus, while an embryonic legislative framework was being shaped to establish the remuneration system for authors, the underlying considerations were mainly political rather than economic. As a result, the MOC had to revoke the system of remunerating authors through a circular in 1961 in response to the nationwide ethos of embracing the public interest in nationalism and collectivism and despising the thoughts and acts of defending private monetary interest.[7] Authors were no longer able to secure copyright protection, as the State used private works freely and allowed the act of reproduction without

---

[5] Ibid., p. 34.

[6] R. MacFarquhar, *The Origins of the Cultural Revolution: Contradictions among the People, 1956–1957* (New York: Columbia University Press, 1974), vol. 1, p. 240.

[7] B. Gale, 'The Concept of Intellectual Property in the People's Republic of China: Inventors and Inventions' (1978) 74(2) *China Quarterly* 350 at 351.

soliciting the permission of authors, paying any remuneration to them, or even acknowledging their authorship.

The Cultural Revolution was a complete disaster that invalidated all the legislative efforts made in the first years of the PRC toward copyright protection. Moreover, the political movement focused on the class struggle and encouraged ordinary Chinese people to despise the intellectuals who dedicated themselves to creative works and wished to be recognised as authors. A famous analogy was that because steelworkers never carved their names onto a steel ingot they produced in carrying out their duty, there was no need for intellectual workers to put their names on the works they produced.[8] Thus, the Cultural Revolution further facilitated the combination of certain controversial principles in the traditional Confucian teaching and those in the socialist doctrine, that is, that a work produced by intellectuals came merely from previous knowledge and should be treated as a common property, which belongs to all members of the socialist country. Consequently, there was no copyright legislative measure during this period of time. In fact, copyright protection was almost demolished completely owing to the violent impingement of the prevalent political ideologies and movements. Many creative literary and artistic works were swept away or banned from publication and dissemination simply because they were treated as a symbol of "bourgeois liberalism."

The negative influence of the Cultural Revolution on copyright protection (as well as on the legal system) went far beyond those ten years: China did not have any formal copyright act until 1990. According to some scholars, this was due to the CCP's underlying policy of censorship and the weakening influence of intellectuals who might otherwise threaten the rule of the CCP by disseminating their dissenting ideologies.[9] This might be the most fundamental reason why the CCP was reluctant to accord creative intellectuals legal entitlements to their works through formal legislation, lest they might become an elite group that would go out of control. This may also explain why, on the other hand, legislation in other IP areas, such as patent and trademark, which had less to do with politics and ideologies, was growing more steadily at the same time.[10]

---

[8] C. Wang and X. Zhang (eds.), *Introduction to Chinese Law* (Hong Kong: Sweet & Maxwell Asia, 1997), p. 443.

[9] T. Hsia and Y. Haun, 'Law of the PRC on Industrial and Intellectual Property' (1983) 38 *L Contemp Probs* 479.

[10] M. Sidel, 'Copyright, Trademarks and Patent Laws in the People's Republic of China' (1986) 21(2) *Texas Int'l L J* 270.

Thus, even though the aforementioned two Regulations in 1963 extended the rewarding system to works of natural science, the traditional ideology about the futility of copyright protection seemed to remain intact. This led the Chinese government to articulate openly that all fruits of intellectual creation were the common heritage of humankind.[11] Certainly, such kinds of mentalities about copyright became an obstacle in attracting foreign investment and technology. In this regard, China's economic growth in an opening environment gradually made it necessary to bring the distorted IP policies back to a normal track. Indeed, at this time, it was desirable to establish a modern patent system to attract foreign technology and further international exchange. As a result, it became inevitable for the PRC to readjust its fundamental economic policies and the agenda of copyright protection in terms of international standards.

2.1.1.2. Copyright as a policy of controlling Chinese intellectuals

In fact, the copyright legislation in the earlier years of the PRC well reflected the continuance of the policies of the Communist regime with regard to intellectuals. The military victory of the CCP in the Chinese Civil War was based largely on an organised campaign of the peasants in the countryside. Whereas most Chinese intellectuals were living in the cities under the rule of the Nationalist regime, the CCP maintained a good control of the revolutionary enthusiasm of a smaller number of intellectuals in the liberated zone. On the one hand, Mao required the intellectuals to organise and educate the ordinary (in most cases illiterate) people through literature and arts to encourage them to fight against the enemies.[12] On the other hand, Mao admonished other party members not to tolerate those intellectuals who were disloyal to the CCP.[13] To implement his ideology, Mao carried out the notorious Yan'an Rectification Movement [延安整风运动] against the intellectuals in as early as

---

[11] M. D. Pendleton, 'Intellectual Property Regimes of Selected Asia-Pacific Jurisdictions', in K. C. D. M. Wild and M. R. Islam (eds.), *International Transactions: Trade and Investment, Law and Finance* (Sydney: The Law Book Co. Ltd, 1993), p. 361.

[12] Z. Mao [毛泽东], 'The Talk at the Meeting on Literature and Arts in Yan'an' ['在延安文艺座谈会的讲话'], in Z. Mao, *Selected Works of MAO Zedong* [《毛泽东选集》], 5 vols. (北京: 人民出版社, 1991), vol. III, p. 847.

[13] Z. Mao, 'Taking in a Number of Intellectuals' ['大量吸收知识分子'], in Z. Mao, *Selected Works of MAO Zedong*, vol. II, p. 618.

1942. Accordingly, to ensure the victory of the revolution, the CCP must control, inculcate, and reform the intellectuals, while those who do not obey the disciplines of the CCP must be purged out of the CCP.

Thus, there was a natural tension between the CCP and the intellectuals from the very beginning.[14] As the CCP aimed to subject the intellectuals to the service of the revolutionary goals, there was no reason to grant any proprietary protection of the intellectual works on the intellectuals, for any independent creative activities and accumulation of wealth, according to Mao, might enervate their revolutionary enthusiasm.[15] Besides, Mao also adhered to the traditional Chinese view about intellectual works, that is, literary and artistic works were no creation themselves, but something made on the basis of the daily life of the people. These views also corresponded to the Marxist theory, which denies granting private property to individual intellectual works.

Considering these profound philosophical conflicts, the copyright policies of the CCP, at least in the first decade of the PRC, might be regarded even as generous for the intellectuals who were allowed to receive some meagre pay for their works in accordance with the standards laid down by the State. As mentioned earlier, the MOC even prepared an interim draft act on copyright protection, which almost came into force. Starting in the earlier 1950s, however, the communist state managed to control intellectuals and their creative activities through two organisations: the China Federation of Literary and Art Circles [中国文学艺术界联合会] and China Writers Association [中国作家协会]. In fact, through these two organisations, Mao and his party could decide the fate of a work by judging its political value. As a result, copyright owners received either admirable remuneration or merciless punishment.

In the late 1950s, however, Mao launched again a series of stern political movements that were directed at the intellectuals on a large scale, as he saw his rule being threatened increasingly by the intellectuals through their free expression of critical views about the government and the society. During that time, one of the best-known remarks about intellectuals was: "The more knowledgeable one is, the more reactionary one is [知识越多越反动]." As a result, many innocent intellectuals were prosecuted ruthlessly and died a miserable death. During the subsequent two decades, the Chinese intellectuals suffered unprecedented tragedy in

---

[14] Coase and Wang, *How China Became Capitalist*, pp. 8–11.
[15] Z. Mao, 'The Analysis of the Classes in the Chinese Society' ['中国社会各阶级的分析'], in Z. Mao, *Selected Works of MAO Zedong*, vol. I, p. 3.

the Chinese intellectual history and were labelled widely as the "Stinking Ninth Category [臭老九]." They were condemned for disdaining the physical labour and derogating from practice and politics, largely because they received remuneration for putting a few lines on paper simply. For many members of the CCP, such practice militated against the cornerstone of the socialist economic system and might encourage a corrupt and decadent lifestyle of the intellectuals.

Certainly, the MOC, which was in charge of the policies of authorial remuneration, could not withstand the scathing criticism on the uselessness and harmfulness of remunerating individual authors: the standards laid down by the MOC for remuneration fluctuated widely from several thousand Yuan to none.[16] In consequence, most writers who used to rely on the remuneration for a living found it increasingly difficult to carry on an independent life without such income. For instance, Shaotang Liu [刘绍棠], a famous Chinese writer who used to live only on such remunerative income before the Anti-Rightist Movement, earned 18 thousand Yuan (an astronomical sum at that time) for publishing four novels.[17] After 1957, however, it became impossible for him to publish anything because he was labelled bourgeois Rightist. As far as the fates of ordinary writers were concerned, the State managed to assign different jobs to these intellectuals: they became teachers, journalists, editors of publishing houses, or members of different associations.[18] In a word, through the political movements the authors lost their personal and financial independence and became authors who were financially dependent on different "working units [单位]."

Therefore, A2R was rendered extremely difficult, if not entirely impossible, for most Chinese authors prior to the beginning of the 1980s. Although the government did not issue any formal regulations banning authorial remuneration, the previous remuneration system stopped running. Authors, as they were so called, were deprived of any entitlement to remuneration for their works, even if such works were printed and distributed in hundreds of thousands of volumes,[19] or made into films that brought back considerable incomes for the working units to which

---

[16] Li et al., *Contemporary Chinese History of Copyright*, pp. 50–77.
[17] S. Liu [刘绍棠], *Unbearable to Recall the Past* [《往事不堪回首》], at www.oklink.net/99/1208/sywc/102.htm.
[18] Li et al., *Contemporary Chinese History of Copyright*, p. 80.
[19] Y. Song [宋原放] et al. (eds.), *The History of Publication in China: The Modern Part* [《中国出版史料·现代部分》], 3 vols. (济南: 山东教育出版社, 2001), vol. II, p. 281.

the authors belonged.[20] In fact, the deprivation of A2R was not the most miserable fate of an author. A number of famous Chinese writers such as Lei Fu [傅雷], Shuli Zhao [赵树理], and Libo Zhou [周立波] were forbidden to create any works because they were accused of writing politically incorrect pieces.[21] In many cases, they were even deprived of their moral rights (to publish or revise their works or sign their names on the works).

2.1.1.3. The impacts of the policy of reform and opening up on copyright and intellectuals

The historical event after the end of the Cultural Revolution was that Xiaoping Deng [邓小平] rose to power in 1978. As a pragmatic leader, Deng overturned Mao's economic policies completely, but retained strict control of political power, albeit in a seemingly more lenient way. Claiming that China was still a country situated "at the rudimentary stage of socialism" [社会主义初级阶段], Deng and his colleagues decided to adopt the economic policy of Reform and Opening up to the outside world. At this juncture, Deng advocated the ideology of "emancipating the mind" and "seeking truth from facts." This meant that the State would no longer care so much about the tutelage of a socialist economy but recognise private ownership again, including the ownership of IP. Soon, the remunerative system regarding authorial creation was reinstated, while the government adopted other policies to improve the status of intellectuals such as restoring college entrance examinations and resuming the system of higher education. All of these measures seemed to encourage the production and dissemination of knowledge in the Chinese society.

To be fair, Deng's policy of economic reforms was rooted in the imperative of rescuing the monopolistic rule of the CCP. Toward the end of the 1970s, the leadership of the CCP found it impossible to carry on Mao's ideology of class struggle and attributing all the resources to the public ownership. As one of the CCP's favourite political jargons formulated, the fundamental principle of the work around the country was "one central task (economic construction) and two basic points (adherence to the Reform and Opening up on the one hand and to the Four Cardinal Principles on the other) [一个中心,两个基本点]." After the

---

[20] J. Cui [崔建农], *The Red Past Events: Chinese Films in 1966–1976* [《红色往事 1966–1976 年的中国电影》] (北京: 台海出版社, 2001), p. 223.
[21] Li et al., *Contemporary Chinese History of Copyright*, pp. 91–2.

Tiananmen Movement in 1989, Deng regretted that economic development (the first basic point) rather than political control (the second basic
point) took the upper hand. As Deng accentuated later, the Party must
"attach equal importance to both hands (tasks)" [两手都要硬] so that
the CCP could maintain a tenacious grip on the power in the long run. At
the onset of the economic reforms, however, the focus was to stay aloof
from Mao's practices and leave as much leeway for economic development as possible. Therefore, there was a relative peaceful period before
the end of the 1980s, which one might refer to as a political vacuum.

For copyright protection, this political vacuum meant, above all, a
compromise on the public ownership in the socialist economy. One no
longer needed to take traditional political ideologies into account as
seriously as before, but would be content to find a convenient pretext
for giving a green light to copyright protection. It was even not necessary to fabricate a well-founded IP theory that accommodates copyright
protection in the socialist state: most proponents of reestablishing a
copyright system tried to persuade decision makers of the need to
overlook the ideological fences by justifying the specific and immediate
advantages that copyright might bring about for China's economic
modernisation, such as cultural propaganda and foreign trade.[22] On
the surface, this required an abrupt demarcation between the public
ownership and the private ownership of intellectual works. Beneath
the ruse, this meant ignoring or postponing the debate on the potential
conflict between copyright as a private right that might facilitate free
expression and censorship as a policy instrument of controlling free
expression.

In a sense, the economic reforms were driven by the incentive
of harmonising the Chinese society that was standing at the brink of
disintegration after the Cultural Revolution. However, the reestablish-
ment of a copyright system in China did not emanate from a free market
economy, but from the underlying monopolistic power of the CCP in
distributing economic and social resources. It is also true that the basic
policy of controlling free expression and especially the Chinese intellectuals remained intact per se in any historical period of the Communist
regime. The abrupt boom of copyright development, however, did take
place in a period when the control of speech freedom was said to be
less tight than before the reforms and even than after the Tiananmen

---

[22] See, e.g., P. Feng, *Intellectual Property in China* (Hong Kong: Sweet & Maxwell Asia,
1997), pp. 4–5.

Movement in 1989.[23] For many Chinese intellectuals who had suffered sufficient ordeals in the Leftist movements that swept over the country in the past decades, the recognition of copyright meant far more than recognition of their economic income. Although no one dared to put it explicitly, recognising the legitimacy of copyright was almost equivalent to endorsing their right to express their ideas freely. Driven by the conventional Chinese intellectuals' sense of social and political responsibilities, these intellectuals, who awoke with keen awareness of the domestic needs for knowledge, became an important force in shaping the national copyright system.

For example, to pacify and unite the intellectuals after the Cultural Revolution, the CCP allowed a number of famous writers and scholars to attend the Chinese Peoples' Political Consultative Conference (CPPCC), which appealed mostly to non-CCP members of the Chinese society who were concerned about the economic and social development of the country. Although the role of the CPPCC was often compared to a vase that lent more legitimacy to the CCP's "democratic dictatorship," many intellectuals still embraced it as a forum where one might express some different views and make themselves heard by the decision makers. In May 1984, Youlan Feng [冯友兰], an influential scholar and philosopher, presented a speech to the CPPCC in which he criticised the government for not respecting the publication of intellectual works and advocated enactment of relevant laws on the protection of publication.[24] According to him, the incentives of authors would be dampened, as long as it always took a long time for their works to be approved for publication while state-owned publishing houses did not respect their economic rights at all.

Another typical example of such intellectuals was Jin Ba [巴金], a famous professional writer in modern China, who relied almost completely on authorial remuneration and royalties for a living. As a traditional Chinese intellectual, he used to be ashamed of receiving monetary income for "saying a few words" that he wanted to say, before he became accustomed to doing so with his "labour."[25] According to Ba, however,

[23] Q. He [何清涟], 'The Status Quo and Prospects of China under Authoritarian Rule' ['威权统治下的中国现状与前景'], *Modern China Studies* [《当代中国研究》] 2 (2004) 5.

[24] Y. Feng [冯友兰], 'The Written Speech at the Second Conference of the Sixth Session of the National CPPCC' ['全国政协六届二次会议的书面发言'], in Y. Feng, *The Collected Works of Sansong Tang* [《三松堂全集》], 15 vols. (郑州: 河南人民出版社, 1994), vol. XIII, pp. 983-6.

[25] J. Ba [巴金], 'On Copyright' ['谈版权'], in J. Ba, *The Book of Telling the Truth* [《说真话的书》] (成都: 四川人民出版社, 1995), p. 823.

the most creative part about creative works was not the monetary reward but the dissemination of progressive ideas among the readers. Thus, he would rather give up his remuneration or give away his royalties than create a work for monetary purposes. Moreover, Ba valued copyright protection but regarded a published work as a social product that no longer belonged to the author because it would take effect among readers. Ba's view on copyright represented that of many authors/intellectuals in China at that time: it went beyond authorial remuneration and took copyright as a breakthrough for free expression.

There were still other intellectuals who started to be more concerned about authorial remuneration and economic incentives. Ming Ying [应明], a pioneering software designer, set up a software company earlier in the 1980s and developed the first software products in China. However, these products failed to yield economic profits because there was no copyright protection. As a result, one copy would suffice to ensure numerous pirated copies in the market. While he reported the case to the Chinese government in vain, he gave up his job and became an expert on copyright law: Ying himself took part in the process of drafting the Regulations for the Protection of Computer Software (RPCS) [《计算机软件保护条例》] that was enacted in 1991.[26] This was a good example that shows the futility of creative intellectual work without strong copyright protection. In a sense, such economic incentives on the part of many Chinese intellectuals rendered it easier for the government to accept copyright protection as an exigent instrument to promote economic development.

2.1.2.   Calling for a Compromise: The Initial International Negotiations of the PRC after the Reform and Opening Up and the Establishment of a National Copyright Framework

During this time, international negotiations exerted increasing pressure on China and became a catalyst that was driving the establishment of a legislative framework of copyright protection in the PRC after the end of the 1970s. This pressure rendered it necessary for China to consider making a compromise of its censorship-oriented legislative framework that relies on dampening the authorial interest in A2R.

---

[26] H. Wu [吴海民], *Toward the Berne Convention: The Memorandum of Chinese Copyright* [《走向伯尔尼—中国版权备忘录》], at www.oklink.net/a/0008/0822/zouxiang/index .html.

2.1.2.1.   The initial international IP negotiations till the 1989 Memorandum of Understanding

For the proponents of resuming copyright protection in China, any external pressure would provide a more convenient reason for neglecting the ideological barriers at home. At this time, China also faced international pressure for quickening its steps toward new copyright legislation, which was well palpable in the initial international IP negotiation process. Of particular importance were the negotiations with WIPO and the United States. As a matter of fact, WIPO was the first international organisation that attempted to negotiate with the PRC on IP law making. At the end of the Cultural Revolution, Dr Árpád Bogsch, Director of WIPO, contacted certain departments of China's central government to urge China to improve its IP system and join the Berne Union.[27] Due to the domestic political and social environment in China at that time, however, these efforts did not produce any positive results.

Shortly after the United States reinstated its diplomatic relationship with the PRC, two bilateral talks were held in Beijing and Washington, which resulted in the signing of two treaties in 1979: the Sino–US Agreement on High Energy Physics and the Sino–US Agreement on Trade Relations. In both negotiations the United States insisted on adding a clause on IP protection (including copyright protection) into Articles 6 of both agreements. While the Chinese delegation resorted to the diplomatic pretext that there was no copyright law in China, the United States threatened not to sign the agreement without IP protection clause.[28] Because the Chinese delegation did not want to break down the consensus that had been reached after hardworking negotiations, the principle of copyright protection was written into Article 6 of the Sino–US Agreement on High Energy Physics.[29] In addition, Article VI of the Sino–US Agreement on Trade Relations recognises the importance of copyright and ensures the effective protection of copyright.[30]

---

[27] Li et al., *Contemporary Chinese History of Copyright*, p. 195.

[28] L. Zhou [周林], 'Several Clues to the Study of Chinese Copyright History' ['中国版权史研究的几条线索'], in L. Zhou and M. Li [周林、李明山] (eds.), *Literature of Study on Chinese Copyright History* [《中国版权史研究文献》] (北京: 中国方正出版社, 1999), p. 10.

[29] Implementing Accord between the Department of Energy of the US and the State Scientific and Technological Commission of the PRC on Cooperation in the Field of High Energy Physics, 18 ILM 345 (1979).

[30] The US and the PRC: Agreement on Trade Relations, 18 ILM 1041 (1979).

Soon after these two Sino–US IP negotiations and bilateral treaties, the PRC became a member of WIPO on 3 March 1980. Indeed, throughout the first decade of China's Reform and Opening up, the United States was playing a principal role in pushing China to take steps toward copyright legislation and reforms. As such, these initial IP-related trade negotiations led to China's assumption of the obligation to provide copyright protection under international law. Since then the United States continued to exert political and economic pressure on China to bring forth a modern copyright system. Behind such a political veil stood unhappy US industries claiming that their IPRs had been violated rampantly in the PRC and that they had, thus, suffered great economic losses. These industries were lobbying the US Trade Representative (USTR) to press China to comply with its obligation to protect IP through bilateral or multilateral trade negotiations, such as the Uruguay Round of the GATT.[31]

In 1984, the US Congress gave the USTR authority to impose trade sanctions on countries that failed to protect IPR effectively, whereas Section 301 under the 1988 Omnibus Trade and Competitiveness Act became a major weapon in the IP-related negotiations.[32] Accordingly, the Office of the USTR shall issue an annual Special 301 Report and identify countries that fail to provide "adequate and effective protection of IPRs" or "fair and equitable markets access" as "priority foreign countries."[33] In practice, the Special 301 Report may also contain a "priority watch list" and a "watch list" of such countries as determined by the USTR.[34] Thus, while the Special 301 clause aims at protecting US IPR abroad and facilitating market access of US IPR products, the USTR would place such foreign countries on one of the aforementioned lists and impose different trade sanctions on these countries. Since 1989, the USTR has been placing China steadily on one of those lists.[35]

During this period, the tension over copyright/IP protection between the United States and the PRC was being escalated to the political level. At the moment of the Tiananmen Movement in 1989, the USTR placed

---

[31] General Agreement on Tariffs and Trade, 61 Stat. A-11, UNTS 55, 194, 30 October 1947.

[32] The Omnibus Trade and Competitiveness Act, sec. 1303(b), Pub L No. 100–418, 102 Stat. 1179 (1988) (codified as amended at 19 USC § 2411).

[33] 19 USC § 2242.

[34] See, e.g., WTO Panel Report, *United States-Sections 301–310 of the Trade Act of 1974*, WT/DS152/R, 22 December 1999.

[35] IIPA, Chart of Countries' Special 301 Placement (1989 to 2014) and IIPA 2015 Special 301 Recommendations, at www.iipa.com/pdf/2015SPEC301HISTORICALCHART.pdf.

China on the "priority watch list,"[36] threatening to impose trade sanctions if China did not extend copyright protection to software. It might be fair to remark that the United States aimed to draft and reach a new IP agreement on the protection of computer software with China by taking advantage of the political pressure on China at that time. From 18 to 19 May 1989, the delegations of both countries held talks in Washington and concluded a memorandum on IP protection without signing it: the Memorandum of Understanding on the Enactment and Scope of Copyright Law in the PRC (1989 MOU),[37] the first MOU between the PRC and the United States regarding copyright protection.

In the 1989 MOU, China promised to submit a Copyright Act based on the international copyright treaties to the National People's Congress, which would extend copyright protection to computer software and to foreign works. Besides, China would draft a set of implementation rules relating to the copyright act on the basis of international standards. In addition, China would also facilitate the process of acceding to the international copyright treaties and promoting the consciousness of copyright protection. In return, the United States promised not to list the PRC as a "priority foreign country" under the Special 301. At this point, it became obvious that, no matter how harsh the negotiations were and how clear the treaty obligations were, China was unable to provide substantial protection for foreign investors without a comprehensive national copyright system. This was why it was urgent for China to design and establish a national copyright framework through a formal Copyright Act.

2.1.2.2. The copyright legislation after the reform and opening up

As noted by Professor Ping Jiang [江平], a most renowned civil law expert, the road to copyright law was "as tortuous as the fate of Chinese intellectuals."[38] Despite the policy of Reform and Opening up, the Chinese government was still trying to control free expression in China. However, serious efforts toward setting up a new copyright system were

---

[36] USTR, Fact Sheet for "Special 301" on Intellectual Property, 25 May 1989, at https://ustr.gov/sites/default/files/1989%20Special%20301%20Report.pdf.

[37] The Memorandum of Understanding between the People's Republic of China and the United States, signed on 19 May 1989, reprinted in 'PRC Agrees to Push for Copyright Law that Will Protect Computer Software', *World Intell Prop Rep*, July 1989, 151.

[38] P. Jiang and R. Shen [江平、沈仁干], *Lectures on the Copyright Law of the PRC* [《中华人民共和国著作权法讲析》] (北京: 中国国际广播出版社, 1991), p. 18.

also under way. In April 1979, the Publication Bureau of the MOC [文化部出版局] delivered a report that suggested China's accession to international copyright treaties and drafting a copyright act.[39] Yaobang Hu [胡耀邦], one of the highest-ranked party leaders who was in charge of "propaganda" in China at that time, approved the report immediately and ordered a team to be organised to draft a copyright act. The approval of this report could be seen as a seed that sparked off the contemporary Chinese copyright law. Since then, the making of the Chinese copyright system has been influenced deeply by Western copyright laws, and IPR has been protected as a private right.

After signing the bilateral treaties with the United States, China reinstated a number of copyright regulations, which were in force in the earlier decades of the PRC but revoked during the Cultural Revolution. Moreover, China resumed the remuneration system. For example, the 1952 Interim Regulations on the Remuneration for Manuscripts of Literary and Artistic Works were revised and reenacted as the Interim Regulations on Remuneration for Book Manuscripts [《关于书籍稿酬的暂行规定》] in 1980. In 1982, the Publication Bureau of the MOC brought major revisions to these Regulations, which were promulgated as the Provisional Regulations on Remuneration for Book Manuscripts [《书籍稿酬试行规定》] in 1984. In 1985, the MOC also issued the Provisional Regulations on the Copyright Protection of Books and Periodicals [《图书、期刊版权保护试行条例》], the Implementation Rules of the Provisional Regulations on the Copyright Protection of Books and Periodicals [《图书、期刊版权保护试行条例实施细则》], and Provisional Measures for the Remuneration for Manuscripts of Works of Fine Arts [《美术出版物稿酬试行办法》]. These regulations and measures have shaped the fundamental framework of subsequent copyright rules, such as the subject matter, scope of rights, term of protection, and even the applicability of protection to foreign works.

In 1982, the Ministry of Broadcasting and Television issued the Interim Regulations on the Administration of Audio-video Products [《录音录像制品管理暂行规定》]. They were the first legal source in the PRC on related rights, which emphasised effective protection of the rights of authors, performers, and recorders. Article 6 of the Interim Regulations, for instance, recognises "the legitimate interests of authors and performers" who "shall enjoy the right of publishing the audio-video

---

[39] The Publication Bureau, The Report on Copyright Issues Involved in the Sino–US Trade Agreement [《关于中美贸易协定中涉及版权问题的请示报告》], 21 April 1979.

materials." Furthermore, the Ministry of Radio, Film and Television issued its Provisional Regulations on Copyright Protection for Audio-Visual Publications [《录音录像出版物版权保护暂行条例》] in 1986. Finally, the GPCL promulgated in 1986 marks the milestone of copyright legislation in the PRC. The GPCL defines copyright protection in this way:

> Citizens and legal persons shall enjoy rights of authorship and be entitled to sign their names as authors, issue and publish their works and obtain remuneration in accordance with the law.[40]

Thus, the GPCL granted protection of both economic rights and moral rights in principle, even though courts, at this time, could rely on no more detailed clarification about copyright than the CCP's policy and a common sense of fairness. After the GPCL came into force on 1 January 1987, copyright owners could claim A2R in a full sense and are entitled to bring an infringement action against any potential infringers.

2.1.2.3. Drafting the 1990 Copyright Act: control of free expression versus a legislative framework of the national copyright system

Although drafting a Copyright Act was an unprecedented process at this time, China still treated copyright as an instrument that contributed to the overall national policy of economic modernisation and social stability. This means that political stability is superior to economic growth and that copyright protection must be subject to stringent censorship. This may explain why the law granted copyright protection only to foreign works that are first published by Chinese publishers and not in a foreign country.[41] Moreover, although the translation rights of the right holder are protected,[42] the law also set limits on the authors' right to receive remuneration by providing that "where foreign works are translated into Chinese, authors of the original works shall not be paid."[43] In fact, the publication of foreign works or translated works is subject to the approval by relevant government departments or a state-owned publishing house. In a sense, the selective protection of certain rights represents

---

[40] The General Principle of Civil Law of the PRC, Art. 94, 12 April 1986 (GPCL).
[41] Provisional Regulations on the Copyright Protection of Books and Periodicals of the PRC, Art. 21, 1 January 1985 (PRCPBP).
[42] Ibid., Art. 5(5).
[43] Provisional Regulations on the Remuneration for Book Manuscripts of the PRC, Art. 3, 19 October 1984.

a selective anti-A2R approach that recognises only the production of works that might survive the censorship.

Thus, copyright law in China aims to place the government's interest in controlling dissemination of foreign ideas above the private economic interest of individuals, which can be justified by the explicit statement that the ultimate aim of copyright protection was to "foster and develop the socialist publication career and facilitate the construction of socialist spiritual and material civilisation."[44] For this reason, the MOC may even decide to nationalise certain copyrightable works for the purpose of the national interest and to extend the term of ownership.[45] In addition, certain state-owned units may, under certain circumstances, enjoy the privilege of using works protected by copyright under the title of free use or a compulsory license without being treated as copyright infringement.[46] Such a tension between the private interest and the "public interest" (in this case the government's censorship) provoked the debate on how to draft the first Copyright Act of the PRC. According to those who emphasised the importance of the protection of A2R and copyright internationalisation, such a lower threshold of protection would impede the process of technology transfer from abroad. In addition, these proponents maintained that domestic software producers needed stricter means of protection. Accordingly, China should comply with the international minimum standards of copyright protection.

In contrast, the opponents, who were more concerned with the "national interest" and "social stability," held that copyright law in China should undertake the responsibility and functions of the press law, at least temporarily, as the latter had not been drafted yet. Since it is one of the functions of the press law to regulate matters relating to censorship, these opponents insisted that socialist copyright law should serve the economic foundation and the superstructure of socialism so that works whose publication and dissemination were forbidden by laws cannot enjoy copyright protection.[47] Moreover, they advocated that foreign works that were useful for ordinary Chinese should not be protected or should only be accorded lower levels of copyright protection.[48] Still

---

[44] PRCPBP, Art. 1.   [45] Ibid., Art. 14.   [46] Ibid., Arts. 15(5), (6) and (7), 17(1) and (2).
[47] X. Xiao [肖峋], 'Solving Controversial Problems in Copyright Legislation from the Perspective of the Practice in China' ['从我国的实际出发解决版权(著作权)立法中有争议的问题'], in China Copyright Study Association (ed.), *Selected Essays on Copyright Studies* [《版权研究文选》] (上海: 商务印书馆, 1995), p. 25.
[48] Ibid.

others contended that the legislation rather than the enforcement should be improved in substance so that China could win over more time to adapt its own copyright system to the international standards.[49] In short, the first Copyright Act must be compatible with the economic and social development of China as a country at the "rudimentary stage of socialism," for otherwise it could not be enforced in reality. The best explanation that might cover up the policy considerations of thwarting free speech and conducting censorship, therefore, was to facilitate the public interest in lowering the costs for A2K. To meet those needs, copyright legislation in China could only progress gradually.

In this regard, it is fair to remark that the first Copyright Act of the PRC in 1990 was a mixture of paradox and conflicts of interests, which did not produce the effect of copyright protection as China had claimed beforehand. Apparently, China was ambivalent in setting its policy goal of copyright legislation between prioritising the government's interest in strengthening social control and meeting international copyright standards. In fact, as early as in 1985, the State Council decided to establish the copyright system in the light of the international copyright conventions, to provide copyright protection to foreign works.[50] The drafting committee included both domestic and international legal scholars and used the BC as a blueprint in the drafting process. At the end of 1986 when the BC celebrated its centenary, China even submitted a document entitled "Ten Major Points of Copyright Law" to Dr Bogsch for comments.[51] Nevertheless, because China's copyright policies involved such different economic interests and political views, the drafting history of the first Copyright Act was doomed to be highly complicated with more than twenty drafts having been presented.

The complexity of the tension between copyright protection and control of free expression is also perceivable in the capricious development of the relevant government institutions in charge of copyright administration and publication. In July 1985, the Publication Bureau of the MOC, a successor of the previous GAOP of the central government, turned into the National Publication Bureau (NPB) [国家出版局], which

[49] C. Zheng [郑成思], 'Information Industry Property and Copyright Law' ['信息产权与版权法'], in China Copyright Study Association (ed.), *Selected Essays on Copyright Studies*, p. 89.
[50] Li et al., *Contemporary Chinese History of Copyright*, p. 253.
[51] Zheng and Pendleton, *Copyright Law in China* (NSW, CCH Australia Ltd for CCH International, 1991), p. 66.

was also named the National Copyright Bureau (NCB) [国家版权局]. In China, it is a typical and convenient approach of empowering a government department with a second administrative function by giving it two names [一个机构,两块牌子]. In 1987, however, the State Council replaced the NPB with the Administration of Press and Publication (APP) [新闻出版署] while retaining its second name as NCB. The new name might be attributable to the need of tightening the control of news reporting in the middle of the 1980s when student activism was reaching its peak in China.

Finally, in September 1990, the National People's Congress approved the Copyright Act, which went into effect on 1 June 1991. On that day, the State Council promulgated the Regulations for the Implementation of the Copyright Act (RICA) [《中华人民共和国著作权法实施条例》], which contains more specific provisions that help interpret the Copyright Act. On 4 June 1991, the RPCS were also adopted to provide specific rules with respect to software protection. To address the concern that China did not have a copyright registration system for software protection, the Ministry of Machinery and Electronics Industry issued the Measures for the Registration in Computer Software [《计算机软件著作权登记办法》] on 6 April 1992. By this time, the initial legislative work toward establishing the national copyright system of the PRC had been completed.

2.1.3. Setting the Standards: The International Negotiations of the PRC toward Acceding to the BC and the UCC

While China was starting to make a compromise between its censorship-oriented copyright framework and the pressure emanating from international negotiations, there is a question of what should be the criteria for China to look to when improving its copyright legislation. The subsequent international negotiations soon made it clear that, by acceding to the BC and the UCC, China was to embark on its long march toward copyright internationalisation and align its copyright lawmaking with the framework of international copyright law.

2.1.3.1. The negotiations with WIPO toward accession to the BC

In fact, there were many debates during the process of drafting the 1990 Copyright Act. The most controversial one, however, was not about domestic issues, but about international issues. When the draft of the

Copyright Act was published in 1987 to solicit opinions from the civil society, a prevalent view was that if the Copyright Act were enacted like that and China acceded to the international copyright treaties on that basis, it would become extremely difficult for China to import foreign works.[52] This would affect China's scientific and technological development negatively. Accordingly, China should neither accede to the international copyright treaties nor enact a Copyright Act.

As early as in 1985, however, the Chinese government held a conference on whether China should accede to the international copyright system, and the conclusion was "yes."[53] In December 1988, the State Council held a conference on the feasibility of issuing a copyright act, which gave an affirmative answer to the question and put an end to the debate.[54] It remained a challenge, however, how to balance compliance with international treaties against adapting the law to the domestic situations in China. Virtually, Articles 2 and 3 of the 1990 Copyright Act adopt the approach of the national treatment including the principle of territoriality and the principle of reciprocity, which paved the road for China's accession to the international copyright treaties.

Indeed, the first decade of China's Reform and Opening up witnessed China's increasing exchange with the international community in political, economic, and cultural fields. In particular, cultural exchange is a process of importing foreign culture and exporting Chinese culture. Toward the end of the 1980s, international copyright protection was no longer confined to cultural and technological areas, but extended to economic and trade areas. Nonetheless, as China was not a member of any international copyright treaty, problems often came up in the process of trading knowledge goods such as books, films, or software.

On the one hand, piracy of both Chinese and foreign works was extremely rampant at home, as the leadership emphasised China's status as a developing country that was unable to pay high royalties to foreign countries. On the other hand, China often purchased software at an astonishingly prohibitive price in comparison with the normal price. The reason was that foreign copyright owners believed that the sale of

---

[52] M. Song [宋木文], 'Speech (in Hangzhou) at the Seminar of the Leadership of Copyright Administration around the Country' ['在杭州全国版权局局长研讨班上的讲话'], in M. Song (ed.), *Collections of Essays on Publication by Song Muwen* [《宋木文出版文集》] (北京: 中国书籍出版社, 1996), p. 681.

[53] 'Big Events of the Publication in the PRC 1987' ['中华人民共和国出版五十年大事记 1987年'], in Song et al. (eds.), *The History of Publication in China*, vol. II, p. 495.

[54] Ibid.

one copy to Chinese customers meant more than one copy because there was no effective copyright protection in China.[55] Meanwhile, Chinese films were also being pirated rampantly where the foreign government would take no measures to protect Chinese works as China was not a member of the international copyright system. Thus, it became a necessity for China to accede to the international copyright treaties.

By that time, only a few countries, such as China and North Korea, remained aloof from the system of international copyright treaties. It was hard to imagine that such a culturally rich country as China should continue to stay outside this system, although accession to the treaties might cause some economic problems for China. Finally, Yaobang Hu, then the General Secretary of the CCP, agreed to solve this problem in a prompt way. On 30 January 1985, Gao Liu [刘杲] and Rengan Shen [沈仁干], the leaders of the NCB, took part in a conference held by WIPO and the UNESCO and articulated China's willingness to consider acceding to the international copyright treaties after China produced its first Copyright Act.[56] On 24 June 1985, Yaobang Hu held a meeting of the Secretariat of the Central Committee of the CCP. At this meeting, it was decided that China should accede to the international copyright treaties.[57] Nevertheless, because China had not promulgated its Copyright Act yet, it was not entitled to accede to any copyright treaty in practice. For this reason, China began to speed up its steps to draft the first Copyright Act on the basis of the BC.

In September 1986, Gao Liu came to Geneva again to participate in the centenary Conference of the BC, while Dr Bogsch, Director of WIPO, in his address at the conference, expressed his wish that China should join the Berne Union as soon as possible.[58] Apparently, this was because any international union without such a large country as China, which boasts one-fourth of the world's population, would be incomplete. More important, international copyright protection was being extended to new areas, such as computer software, audio/video products, or databases. Therefore, the international copyright system needed to be redesigned, which meant a reshuffling of state interests. As long as the international copyright system was dominated by developed countries, it would be

---

[55] Li et al., *Contemporary Chinese History of Copyright*, p. 252.
[56] C. Liu [刘春田], *Twenty Years of China's Copyright 1978–1998* [《中国知识产权二十年 (1978–1998)》] (北京: 专利文献出版社, 1998), p. 54.
[57] Li et al., *Contemporary Chinese History of Copyright*, p. 253.
[58] Wu, *Toward the Berne Convention*.

difficult to enforce treaties such as the BC eventually. The membership of developing countries in the Berne Union could be strengthened considerably if China joined in. These might be the underlying reasons why Dr Bogsch hoped that China could accede to the BC and exert its influence as a large developing country.

In September 1991, when the 1990 Copyright Act was already in force, Gao Liu brought a Chinese copyright delegation to Geneva to negotiate with WIPO on China's accession to the BC.[59] For the first time in history, China started a formal and substantial negotiation with an international copyright organisation. While WIPO was holding its annual General Assembly, Dr Bogsch met with the Chinese delegation three times and took part in the negotiation with China on its accession to the BC.[60] Later on, Dr Bogsch confirmed the details that WIPO and China had agreed on in written form. Accordingly, although there might be certain conflicts between the 1990 Copyright Act and the BC, it was possible to find a compromise on the condition that both the international standards reflected by the BC and the situation in China should be taken into account and that China's accession to the BC would fit into the social, economic, and cultural situations of China and meet the interests of foreign copyright owners.

At the same time, the Chinese delegation also went to Paris to hold negotiations with UNESCO on acceding to the UCC. UNESCO expressed the same standpoint as WIPO, that is, that China could accede to the UCC on the basis of its 1990 Copyright Act, and gave China a transitional period to prepare for the accession.[61] At this time, it became clear that China would adapt its national copyright system to the international copyright system. The question was simply when it was going to do so.

2.1.3.2. The Sino–US IP negotiation leading to the 1992 Memorandum of Understanding

As mentioned earlier, the 1989 MOU, though not signed, played an important role in pushing China on the way to enact its Copyright Act. On 17 January 1992, however, China signed the Memorandum of Understanding Concerning the Protection of Intellectual Property Rights between the Government of the US and the PRC (1992 MOU), in which

---

[59] Li et al., *Contemporary Chinese History of Copyright*, p. 252.
[60] Wu, *Toward the Berne Convention*.
[61] Li et al., *Contemporary Chinese History of Copyright*, p. 255.

China undertook to improve its copyright law in accordance with international standards.[62] Although signing the 1992 MOU was not the most attractive event in the earlier 1990s, the MOU, as a result of several years of negotiations, turned out to be not only an important step for the Sino–US economic relation, but also a milestone for China to head for its accession to the BC and copyright internationalisation.

Above all, the 1992 MOU granted a broad scope of copyright protection. Considering the special situation in China, however, there were more concerns about effective implementation and enforcement. Presumably, the 1992 MOU was to exert profound economic influence on China. China would then have to forfeit its free access to all those copyright-protected materials that most Chinese had enjoyed previously without being bound to such international obligations as those under the 1992 MOU. After China signed such a bilateral IP agreement with the United States, China should be responsible for banning free access to such knowledge goods unless royalties were paid. In contrast, the 1992 MOU meant for the United States that works of US copyright owners would enjoy full protection. This was why it took several years of intermittent but continuous bilateral IP negotiations between China and the United States to reach the final agreement.

Indeed, as the most important foreign works protected by copyright in China came from the United States, it was the United States that first raised and continued to stress the request on China for copyright protection. After the Tiananmen Movement in 1989, the United States started a unilateral process of requesting IP protection in its negotiations with the PRC. On 16 December 1989, the United States delivered an ultimatum to China, stating that China must revise its IP law in accordance with the US's request within one month or face the sanction of an astronomical sum of punitive customs.[63] Starting in 1989, the USTR placed China on the watch list of the Special 301 Report. On 26 April 1991, however, the United States, for the first time in history, listed China as a "priority foreign country" because of serious infringement on the IPR of US citizens in China.[64]

---

[62] The Memorandum of Understanding between the United States and the People's Republic of China on the Protection of Intellectual Property Rights, *signed* on 17 January 1992, TIAS No. 12036, 34 ILM 676 (1995).

[63] Wu, *Toward the Berne Convention*.

[64] See, e.g., J. A. Massey, 'The Emperor Is Far Away: China's Enforcement of Intellectual Property Rights Protection 1986–2006' (2006) 7 *Chi J Int'l L* 231, at 235.

On 26 May 1991, the USTR decided to investigate IP protection in China, which would last for six months.[65] Once it was confirmed that China's policies had seriously harmed US economic interests, the United States would launch trade retaliation against China. On 11 June 1991, the USTR sent a negotiation delegation to Beijing to negotiate with China on IP issues beyond the Sino–US Agreement on Trade Relations signed in 1980.[66] The USTR alleged that the United States suffered an estimated loss of 400 million US dollars due to piracy of books, video products, and software in China.[67] Besides, the USTR maintained that the 1990 Copyright Act provided an insufficient threshold of copyright protection far below the international standards and required China to revise its copyright law and accede to the BC prior to 1 February 1992.[68]

By contrast, China argued that the United States failed to provide convincing evidence of its loss and that the decision to revise the copyright law was a matter of China's sovereignty, which was not to be intervened by any other state. Moreover, China emphasised that there was already an IP framework in China, but because China was still a developing country, it could not impose an IP system equivalent to that in most developed countries. Finally, China also clarified that it would accede to the BC, but when it would do so was subject to a schedule decided by China itself. As there was a great gap between the standpoints of China and the United States, the negotiations broke down.[69]

Subsequently, China and the United States attempted to reinstate the negotiations. In August, October, and November of 1991, China and the United States held three talks in Washington and Beijing, which, however, yielded no fruit.[70] On 26 November 1991, the investigation process of the USTR concerning IP issues in China ended, with no agreement being reached between China and the United States.[71] For the first time in history, the United States was prepared to invoke the Special 301 Section to retaliate against another country: the United States declared that it would charge 100% tariff duty on 106 products exported from China to the United States that were worth 1.5 billion US dollars.[72] In return, China declared on 21 December 1991 that it would revoke all of its promises on copyright and patent protection and that China would

---

[65] Wu, *Toward the Berne Convention.*   [66] Ibid.   [67] Ibid.   [68] Ibid.
[69] W. Yang and Q. Fu [杨文玉、傅强国], 'On the US 301 Section' ['试论美国三零一条款'], in C. Zheng [郑成思] (ed.), *Studies on Intellectual Property* [《知识产权研究》] (北京: 方正出版社, 1996), vol. I, p. 56.
[70] Wu, *Toward the Berne Convention.*   [71] Ibid.   [72] Ibid.

take countermeasures if the United States were to take its retaliatory measures.[73] After that, China released its plan of countermeasures that would charge punitive tariffs on US products that were worth 1.2 billion US dollars, including Boeing aircrafts, which would be a serious blow to the US economy.[74]

On 10 January 1992, the final negotiation took place, which meant that any failure would kick off the Sino–US trade war and bring a disaster to both countries. At this time, the negotiations of the Uruguay Round of GATT achieved the preliminary result in a draft of the TRIPS Agreement, which provided an important basis for furthering the Sino–US IP negotiations. For China, a failure of the negotiations would mean the end of the MFN treatment, and it would become more difficult for China to retrieve its status as a Contracting State of the GATT. At this time, the Chinese delegation felt it necessary to concede that China must undertake international standards and communicate with the international community according to international law. Eventually, China and the United States signed the MOU on 17 January 1992.[75] The most relevant provision under the 1992 MOU for Chinese copyright law is Article 3. Accordingly, China agreed that the Chinese Government would take steps to accede to the BC, that the BC will be integrated into the framework of the GPCL and prevail in case of any inconsistency with China's domestic law, that China would protect computer software and foreign works in terms of the BC.

Thus, China was bound to accede to the BC, as China was also negotiating with WIPO on its accession, apart from the Sino–US IP negotiation. Nevertheless, the 1992 MOU was also directed at overhauling the existing copyright law in China. For example, Article 3(7) of the 1992 MOU requires China to grant copyright protection to foreign works, regardless of their contents or country of origin. By contrast, the 1990 Copyright Act imposes restrictions on copyright protection of foreign works in terms of those conditions. Article 3(6) of the 1992 MOU, however, clarified the prevailing status of international copyright law in China. These principles mean that China would have to revise its domestic copyright law where there is a conflict. In any event, China reached agreement with its most important copyright trade partner through hard negotiations, which consolidated the foundation for

---

[73] Ibid.   [74] Ibid.
[75] The Memorandum of Understanding on the Protection of Intellectual Property of 17 January 1992, 34 ILM 676 (1995).

China's upcoming process of copyright internationalisation. In accordance with the 1992 MOU, China was about to accede to the BC in October 1992, a date earlier than that negotiated with WIPO.

2.1.3.3.   China's accession to the BC and the UCC

Shortly after the 1992 MOU was signed, Deng pointed out that China should comply with the international copyright standards when he was visiting Shenzhen.[76] On 27 May 1992, Peng Li [李鹏], the premier at that time, submitted a protocol for China's accession to the BC and the UCC to the SCNPC.[77] Entrusted by the State Council, Muwen Song [宋木文], chief of the NCB, delivered a report on the protocol in June, elucidating the necessity of China's accession to the BC and emphasised that China could accede to the BC on the basis of its existing copyright law.[78]

On 1 July 1992, the 26th session of the seventh SCNPC approved the protocol with an absolute majority, stating that the PRC enjoyed the rights provided by Articles II and III of the Appendix to the BC (Berne Appendix).[79] This meant that China could apply a compulsory license in copyright law for the purpose of education and research – an important example of China's standpoint as a developing country for protecting the public interest. Thus, where foreign copyright owners unreasonably decline the publication of their works in China, the NCB may, at the request of domestic publishers, and after completing the legal formalities as provided under the BC, issue a compulsory license that allows translation or reproduction of such works protected by foreign copyright law.

On 10 July 1992, the representative of the PRC at the UN in Geneva submitted China's protocol for accession to the BC to Dr Bogsch, who told the Chinese representative that this was "a great historical event of global significance."[80] On 15 July, Dr Bogsch notified the Foreign Minister of the PRC that the BC was going to take effect on 15 October 1992, and confirmed that China, as a developing country, enjoyed the rights

---

[76] Li et al., *Contemporary Chinese History of Copyright*, p. 258.   [77] Ibid.

[78] G. Liu [刘杲], 'Crossing the History: The Stories before and after China's Accession to the International Copyright Treaties' ['历史的跨越—我国加入版权公约的前前后后'下] Part II (1999) 4 *China Publishing Journal* [《中国出版》] 52.

[79] The Decision of the SCNPC on China's Accession to the Berne Convention on the Protection of Literary and Artistic Works [全国人民代表大会常务委员会关于我国加入《伯尔尼保护文学和艺术作品公约》的决定], *Gazette of the State Council* [《国务院公报》], Issue 21, (1992).

[80] Wu, *Toward the Berne Convention*.

under Articles II and III of the Berne Appendix.[81] On the same day, WIPO declared that China had acceded to the BC as a developing country. On 30 July 1992, the representative of the PRC at the UNESCO in Paris submitted China's protocol for acceding to the UCC to the Director of UNESCO, and on 9 September 1992, UNESCO notified China that the UCC would come into effect in China on 30 October 1992.[82]

2.1.3.4.   The steps toward implementing international copyright treaties

In a sense, China's attitudes toward copyright internationalisation, under the pressure of international negotiations and the treaty obligations, were serious. Therefore, on 25 September 1992, the State Council issued the Regulations on Implementing the International Copyright Convention (RIICC) [《实施国际著作权条约的规定》] to ensure the international community and foreign investors that foreign works would be protected under Chinese copyright law.[83] In addition, these regulations serve to fill the gap between the existing copyright law in China and the international copyright treaties. It is provided explicitly that these Regulations aim to protect "legitimate rights and interests of owners of copyright in foreign works."[84] Thus, these regulations reinforced the national copyright system, which was composed of several regimes, including the 1990 Copyright Act, the RICA, and the RPCS.

Besides, as a member of the BC and the UCC, China issued a number of administrative regulations and judicial interpretations to implement its obligation to protect copyright. The Supreme People's Court of the PRC (SPC) issued the Notice on Several Issues in Implementing the Copyright Act of the PRC (1993) [《关于深入贯彻执行<中华人民共和国著作权法>几个问题的通知》] and the Interpretation on Several Issues of Applying the SCNPC's Decision on Sanctioning the Crimes of Infringing Copyright (1995) [《关于适用<全国人民代表大会常务委员会关于惩治侵犯著作权的犯罪的决定>若干问题的解释》]. The NCB issued the Notice on Prohibiting the Use of Illegally Made Copies of Computer Software (1995) [《关于不得使用非法复制的计算机软件的通知》], Notice on Registration of the Contract Concerning Copyright Authorisation in Publishing and Reproducing Overseas Electronic

---

[81] Li et al., *Contemporary Chinese History of Copyright*, p. 259.   [82] Ibid.

[83] Regulations on the Implementation of the International Copyright Treaties of the PRC, Art. 2, 25 September 1992 (RIICC).

[84] Ibid., Art. 1.

Publications and Computer Software (1996) [《关于对出版和复制境外电子出版物和计算机软件进行著作权授权合同登记和认证的通知》], Measures on Registration of the Contract Concerning the Pledge of Copyright (1996) [《著作权质权登记办法》], and Measures for the Implementation of Copyright Administrative Punishment (1997) [《著作权行政处罚实施办法》] (MICAP). These regulations were important components of the Chinese national copyright system, in its initial stage, when the overall task was to deal with the inconsistency between Chinese copyright law and international copyright treaties.

2.2. The BC and the UCC as Traditional International Legal Sources for Deriving a Framework of Free-Speech-Oriented National Access Rules

Before the middle of the 1990s when TRIPS came into being, the BC was the most significant multilateral instrument. In practice, the national treatment, minimum standards, and automatic protection are distinct features of public international copyright law. Besides, the legal framework of the BC also includes a provision concerning censorship, as well as the Berne Appendix. National legislators may interpret these international standards when redesigning their national copyright system. Some of these rules could help determine the borderline of access rules in national laws. Most important, they may also be free-speech-oriented. For China, the BC is the fundamental source for designing access rules that cater to the specific needs of regulating free speech.

The development of the UCC under the auspices of the UNESCO was not meant to engender any confrontation between countries that acceded to the UCC and those member countries of the Berne Union.[85] Rather, it aimed at giving developing countries a chance to participate in designing different copyright rules in terms of different levels of economic and social development, so as to reach higher levels of copyright protection as enshrined in the BC. What posed a genuine menace to the BC, however, was that the UCC offered a system of nebulous, if not lower, level of protection to authors to attract more members. There was, provokingly, almost no minimum standard for copyright, as the UCC allowed contracting countries to provide for "the adequate and effective protection of

---

[85] See Universal Copyright Convention, Art. VII, done 6 September 1952, [1955] 3 UST 2731, TIAS No. 3324, 216 UNTS 132 (UCC 1952); UCC revised 24 July 1971, Paris, 25 UST 1341, TIAS No. 7868 (UCC 1971).

the rights of authors and other copyright proprietors in literary, scientific and artistic works."[86] By tentatively creating a somewhat different copyright system, the UCC grants more national autonomy to member states in designing their copyright laws and, thus, more wiggle room in regulating free expression.

2.2.1.   The National Treatment: Free Expression in Cross-Border Context

The principle of national treatment mandates a rule of nondiscriminatory treatment of domestic and foreign authors alike in an international economic relationship and has been hallowed as the cornerstone of the international copyright system.[87] It provides a "common sense," which may allow judicial organs to decide on similar issues in accordance with familiar domestic copyright rules. Presumably, the national treatment justifies equal treatment of existing property in the case of works (and, thus, the A2R) instead of equal treatment of personality. Behind the veil of the national treatment, however, the BC ensures more stringent control of the circulation of foreign works, as countries may choose to impose certain standards of censorship, allowing or denying A2K through certain foreign works. In fact, it is the applicable law determined by the national treatment that virtually determines other access rules. Thus, the overall effect of national treatment on free speech exists and is subject to those laws, where states may derogate lawfully from the national treatment to meet the needs of interest balancing at home, for example, in the form of specific limitations or general exception rules under the BC.

2.2.2.   The Minimum Standards: Materialising the Protection of Speech

The minimum standards lay down the lowest threshold for copyright protection, that is, for the protection of the private interest of copyright owners. By doing so, they may safeguard the private interest of copyright owners in A2R and materialise the protection of free speech.

2.2.2.1.   Subject matter: forms of speech

By defining elements of works that deserve copyright protection, the subject matter nails down the form and scope of intellectual achievements

---

[86] Ibid., Art. I.
[87] J. C. Ginsburg, 'Berne without Borders: Geographic Indiscretion and Digital Communications' (2002) 2 *Intell Prop Q* 114–5.

(a form of speech) accessible by the public. Under Article 2 of the BC, the subject matter is defined in a "general plus enumeration" style, which enlists those literary and artistic works amounting to "intellectual creation" eligible for protection.[88] Such an inexhaustible list, which ranges from original works to derivative works (for instance, translations), assumes a mandatory nature and shall be implemented in the domestic legislation of member states.[89] In contrast, the UCC does not regulate the subject matter specifically with a detailed list. Rather, the UCC provides a general formulation in a loose style with a few examples under the category of "literary, scientific and artistic works."[90] By avoiding a rigid doctrine that determines the subject matter categorically, the UCC offers a flexible set of standards. As a result, member states enjoy considerable leeway for copyright law making and may exercise legislative discretion on what kind of works shall assume such economic and social importance as to deserve protection at home.

2.2.2.2.   Specific limitations of the economic rights: A2R in the focus

2.2.2.2.1.   The reproduction right: a fundamental instrument of ensuring A2R   The reproduction right is a fundamental instrument granted to copyright owners for attaining their private interest in A2R, while it affects the public interest in having affordable A2K and the right of the general public to reproduce works for private and public purposes. Being the most entrenched copyright, the reproduction right allows members of the Berne Union to define the content and scope of this right. Besides, Article 9(2) of the BC encompasses unspecified flexibilities under the "three-step test," which is the precursor to the same rule under TRIPS and the WCT. By prescribing the exclusive right of authorising the reproduction of works "in any manner or form," Article 9 of the BC represents a normative rather than technical understanding subject to its fundamental objective.[91] Thus, member countries can invoke the flexibilities in Article 9(2) of the BC to provide statutory exceptions to

---

[88] Berne Convention for the Protection of Literary and Artistic Works, Paris Act, Art. 2(1) and (5), revised on 24 July 1971, 1161 UNTS 30 (BC).

[89] Ibid., Art. 2(6).   [90] UCC, Art. I.

[91] E.g., P. B. Hugenholtz, 'Adapting Copyright to the Information Superhighway', in P. B. Hugenholtz (ed.), *The Future of Copyright in a Digital Environment* (The Hague: Kluwer Law International, 1996), pp. 81–102.

certain copying acts, tailoring the protection of the reproduction right to their domestic balancing needs.

2.2.2.2.2.   The transformative rights: a derivative means of achieving A2R   Some rights are a derivative means of copyright because they allow the transformation of a work into another. The transformative use of copyright is of particular significance for copyright owners to achieve A2R. For one thing, translated works and compiled works often play an irreplaceable role in educational and research activities, a significant form of producing a speech and spurring information flow. Thus, the BC allows for sufficient legislative flexibilities in transformative use of works such as the translation right;[92] the general right of making adaptation, arrangements and other alterations;[93] and the specific right of making adaptations of works into cinematographic works.[94] By contrast, the substantive rights under the UCC are not prescribed as systematically as those under the BC. In fact, the only right provided explicitly for copyright owners is the translation right,[95] which is subject to a compulsory license.[96] This exclusive translation right highlights the role of the UCC in abetting economically and socially inferior countries in expanding their opportunities of A2K by lowering the costs for foreign works.

2.2.2.2.3.   The rights pertaining to physical copies: multiplying A2R through circulation   In a complete sense, copyright should define not only A2R through production of knowledge but also A2R through circulation of knowledge goods. Thus, copyright should preordain the rights pertaining to physical copies, such as the right to access, distribute, import, and resell copies of the works. Admittedly, these rights are of great importance for copyright owners to multiply A2R because they go beyond the activity of reproduction and extend to dissemination of copyright-protected materials to an indefinite number of the general public. Therefore, national legislators rely heavily on these rights to regulate speech by exploiting them in conjunction with the reproduction right. The BC merely provides a "patchy" regime of physical rights such as an initial right of seizure of infringing copies or reproductions imported from other countries, which may be important for countries that impose censorship on imported materials.[97] The BC also allows

---

[92] BC, Art. 8.   [93] Ibid., Art. 12.   [94] Ibid., Art. 14(2).   [95] UCC, Art. V(1).
[96] Ibid., Art. V(2).   [97] BC, Art. 16(1).

member countries to determine the procedure and methods of seizure.[98] Nonetheless, the BC fails to establish a universal threshold for a general seizure of any imported copies made without the author's consent.

2.2.2.2.4. The related rights: expanding A2R through new technologies With revolutionary technological development, the production and dissemination of a speech became increasingly easier in the twentieth century because works can be disseminated everywhere in the world by means of performance or transmission. Because the BC came into being much earlier than the advent of the Internet, it fails to provide a uniform provision that incorporates all acts of communication of works to the public. Nonetheless, the BC defines different ways of communicating the works to the public by allowing acts of performance and transmission of works.[99] Admittedly, both performance and transmission belong to the category of "neighbouring rights," which highlights the distinction between the "author's right" and "copyright." In both cases, national legislators enjoy flexibilities in defining such ambiguous terms as "public," "performance," or "cinematographic work." Further, Union members are allowed to apply compulsory licensing to broadcasting and retransmission rights, subject to providing remuneration.[100] These neighbouring rights may profoundly expand copyright owners' A2R and affect their response to the requests of the general public for affordable A2K in the context of telecommunications.

2.2.2.3. General limitation and exception rules

Apparently, limitation and exception rules are important legal measures that allow member countries to restrict the private interest in A2R in favour of the public interest in having A2K at reasonable costs. By such fine-tuning of proprietary interests, States aim to attain different regulatory objectives relating to nonproprietary interests. Generally, the BC provides for both compensated and uncompensated limitation and exception rules, which is significant for determining A2R. Compensated limitations, such as the specific compulsory licenses,[101] allow particular use of copyright-protected works subject to the payment of reasonable compensation to right holders. On the contrary, uncompensated limitations would have to be examined on a case-by-case basis, depending on whether their specific purposes are justifiable by the three-step test.

---

[98] Ibid., Art. 16(3).   [99] See, e.g., Ibid., Arts. 11(1) and 11*bis* (1).
[100] Ibid., Art. 11*bis* (2).   [101] Ibid., Arts. 11*bis* (2), 13, and the Appendix.

2.2.3.   Automatic Protection: Relieving the Formalities of Granting A2R

Basically, the need to comply with formalities would affect the outcome of balancing the private interest in A2R against the public interest in A2K at reasonable costs. In this regard, the former practice of complicated domestic rules of formalities, which used to exist in many Latin American countries, has been disposed of in the international protection of copyright. The rule of formalities under Article III of the UCC marks a distinct deviation from the principle of automatic protection under Article 5(2) of the BC (no formalities for copyright protection). For most countries today, this issue has become largely irrelevant concerning the regulation of free expression. It remains, however, a problem for countries that require censorship as a precondition for copyright protection.

2.2.4.   The Provision on Censorship

By allowing member countries "to permit, to control, or to prohibit" the dissemination of certain works, Article 17 of the BC represents a compromise of copyright to censorship. It would be hard today to imagine that an international copyright treaty allows censorship in such an explicit way. This may be attributed to the prevailing status of the principle of sovereignty in international law in the nineteenth century when the BC was created. The provision, however, remained uncontroversial at the diplomatic conferences in Rome (1928) and Brussels (1948). A generally accepted view interpreted Article 17 as governing matters of "public order," which should allow the State to maintain social and political order.[102] This differs from the general "public interest" that lies in, say, lowering the costs for A2K through copyright-protected works. Considering that it was placed in a copyright treaty, the provision was meant to be applicable only in very limited circumstances.

At the 1967 Stockholm Conference, however, the UK proposed to delete the wording "to permit," which resulted in a hot debate.[103] The proposal aimed to avoid any misunderstanding that member countries

---

[102] S. Ricketson and J. C. Ginsburg, *International Copyright and Neighbouring Rights: The Berne Convention and Beyond*, 2nd edn (Oxford: Oxford University Press, 2006), p. 841.

[103] WIPO, *Records of the Intellectual Property Conference of Stockholm*, June 11 to July 14, 1967, 2nd vol., Document S/171, p. 704 (WIPO, Geneva 1971).

could, for one thing, impose a compulsory license without an author's permission.[104] The proposal did not succeed because of the opposition by South Africa so that Article 17 has been retained today as it was.[105] Nevertheless, it has been officially documented that, according to most Members, Article 17 should not be understood as allowing member countries to permit any dissemination of works "without the consent of the author."[106] Therefore, although the legitimacy of censorship remains a controversial issue among the states, it seems that Article 17 should be construed in the way that the "public order" as defined by the government shall not prejudice against the private interest of copyright owners. This can be decoded in three aspects: first, the existence of copyright over works must be upheld; second, the measures taken by the State to restrict copyright must be legally provided; and third, such restrictive measures are confined to the dissemination (instead of the production) of works to the public.

2.2.5.   The Berne Appendix

Subject to the procedural rules, the system of compulsory licensing was, for the first time in history, incorporated into the UCC to facilitate the circulation of works in favour of developing countries. Later, the whole system of securing a compulsory license was modified and assimilated into the Berne Appendix to the BC. The Berne Appendix is an important source for expanding opportunities of A2K at reasonable costs and, thus, for regulating nonproprietary objectives in relevant countries. It derived as a special instrument that caters to the specific needs of developing countries to circumvent unnecessarily high levels of copyright protection and gain convenient access to educational materials. The Berne Appendix allows a developing country member to provide for the issuance of "non-exclusive and non-transferable" compulsory licenses for translation and reproduction.[107] Although a compulsory license is largely confined to public interests including "teaching, scholarship or research,"[108] the Berne Appendix could be regarded as a model law for a compulsory license the aim of enhancing affordable A2K.

---

[104] See Ibid., pp. 907 and 1174.   [105] Ibid., pp. 929 and 806.   [106] Ibid., p. 1174.
[107] BC, Appendix, Special Provisions Regarding Developing Countries, Arts. II and III (Berne Appendix).
[108] Ibid., Art. II (5).

2.3. Controlling Free Speech: The Anti-A2R Structure of Access Rules under the 1990 Copyright Act of the PRC

2.3.1. The Institutional Nature of the 1990 Copyright Act: A2R Overshadowed by Censorship

In comparison with the GPCL, the 1990 Copyright Act makes dramatic improvements in protecting copyright owners' private interest in A2R. There are six chapters and fifty-six articles that lay down systematically the fundamental principles of copyright protection. Many provisions were further clarified in the implementing regulations and the RPCS, which form an integral part of the Chinese national copyright system and help interpret and implement the Copyright Act. As the backbone of China's national copyright system, however, the 1990 Copyright Act suffers from institutional drawbacks and provides limited A2R for copyright owners. In practice, copyright protection in China is subject to the censorship system, which aims to control the free production and dissemination of ideologies and speeches.

In 1985, the NCB was merged into the NPB, the most notorious state organ that exercised the authority of government censorship of the press. The State Administration of Radio Film and Television (SARFT), another state organ set up in 1982, combined similar functions in censorship and copyright administration in audiovisual products. Under the leadership of such state organs, cultural entities and their editors must fulfil "editors' responsibility" and conduct "self-censorship" in terms of publication-related laws and regulations.[109] Such practice enables the government to suppress production and dissemination of free speeches in the name of copyright administration, which would often reduce copyright owners' A2R without differentiating between "illegal" and "legal" contents. As a result, it would also be more difficult for the general public to gain A2K.

According to Article 4 of the Copyright Act, to qualify for copyright protection, a work must meet the requirement of "legality," which means that the content of the work must conform to the State's definition of social and public order. For example, the 1990 Copyright Act takes the government's mainstream ideologies into account and prohibits such works from being published and disseminated that might go against the "Four Cardinal Principles" set forth in the Chinese

---

[109] E.g., Regulations on the Administration of Publication of the PRC, Art. 25, 25 December 2001 (RAP).

Constitution. Moreover, nonpolitical or commercial speeches, such as recreational products, are also subject to the government's censorship. Where the NPB/NCB or the SARFT regards a work as having the potential of jeopardising the mainstream social or cultural values, it could exert stringent control not only by direct censorship, but also by indirect sanctions, such as denying the issuance of a standard book/film number.[110]

Therefore, copyright law is channelled to China's censorship regime systematically. Alone the NPB/NCB and the SARFT have created a wide range of censorship regulations in the name of regulating the cultural development in China,[111] covering the markets of books,[112] newspapers,[113] periodicals,[114] audiovisual products,[115] and the Internet.[116] As the State controls most media entities in the PRC, it would be easier for the Chinese government to legitimise its control of free speech by imposing institutional limitations on the A2R of copyright owners. The government could censor individual works either in the name of administering the price of cultural goods for the purpose of allowing the general public to have affordable A2K, or even in the name of rewarding copyright owners for works with specific content.[117]

Thus, the institutional structure of the 1990 Copyright Act appears to be anti-A2R. The availability of remuneration to authors, a most important and fundamental factor for copyright protection, is overshadowed by what the Chinese government defines as the "public interest." On the surface, the government claims to promote wide A2K through a reasonable and affordable system of remuneration to copyright owners. As a matter of fact, this promise merely covers up the government's interest in controlling the production and dissemination of free speeches through

---

[110] Alford, *To Steal a Book Is an Elegant Offence*, p. 70.
[111] Human Rights Watch, *Freedom of Expression and the Internet in China: A Human Rights Watch Backgrounder* (2001), at www.hrw.org.
[112] Regulations on the Administration of Book Publishing of the PRC, 21 February 2008.
[113] Regulations on the Administration of Newspaper Publication of the PRC, 21 October 2005.
[114] Regulations on the Administration of Periodical Publication of the PRC, 20 September 2005.
[115] Regulations on the Administration of Publication of Audio and Video Products of the PRC, 17 June 2004.
[116] Interim Provisions on the Administration of Internet Publication of the PRC, 27 June 2002.
[117] Cf. Committee to Protect Journalists, *Falling Short: As the 2008 Olympics Approach, China Falters on Press Freedom*, A Special Report of the Committee to Protect Journalists (August 2007), p. 27.

censorship. Indeed, although the NCB issued the Notice on Properly Raising the Remuneration for Book Manuscripts [《关于适当提高书籍稿酬的通知》] in June 1990, it was widely held that such a remuneration system imposed overdue limitations on the economic rights of authors because the market price of works as allowed by the regulation could never exceed that of the national standards per se.[118]

Certainly, the first Copyright Act of the PRC played a positive role in copyright protection, as it sets up a framework of copyright law that is based on the legal principles of the prevalent international copyright treaties. Since the 1990s, the 1990 Copyright Act has served as the legal basis of protecting the legitimate rights and interests of copyright owners and encouraged intellectuals to create more works to facilitate the cultural development of the PRC. In addition, improvements have been made in copyright-related areas including administration, judicial practice, theoretical research, international exchange as well as the consciousness of the public in copyright protection.[119] Specifically, however, access rules provide a normative lens to see to what extent the 1990 Copyright Act facilitates the control of free speech by making use of the negative correlation between A2R and A2K. Considering the need to balance different economic and social interests, access rules under the 1990 Copyright Act can be divided into several layers.

2.3.2.   General Access Rules

The general access rules are based on universal standards for copyright protection and can justify the protection of the private interest and the public interest in any type of society. Under the 1990 Copyright Act, however, access rules are constructed in an anti-A2R way to allow for better control of free speech.

2.3.2.1.   The national treatment: controlling cross-border speeches

Generally, IP protection is subject to the principle of territoriality. International copyright treaties, however, require contracting countries to

---

[118] G. Liu [柳谷书], 'Several Questions of Worldwide Interest in the Chinese Copyright Law' ['举世关心的著作权法中的几个问题'] (1991) 4 *China Patent & Trademark* [《中国专利与商标》] 19.

[119] M. Song [宋木文], 'On the Revisions of Chinese Copyright Law' ['关于我国著作权法的修改'] (2001) 6 *Copyright* [《著作权》] 30.

provide copyright protection according to universal standards. Since China did not accede to the BC or the UCC when the 1990 Copyright Act was enacted, the national treatment was not fully assimilated into the statutory law. Accordingly, certain published foreign works could enjoy copyright protection in China, whereas unpublished foreign works would not be protected.[120] Indeed, before the 1990 Copyright Act was enacted, there had been no case law of copyright infringement of foreign works in the PRC. After 1990, Article 2 provided the prima facie legal basis for certain foreign copyright owners to demand A2R and copyright protection of their published works. Even such a claim of copyright infringement is, however, subject to the condition that government authorities allow relevant foreign works to be imported after reviewing the content of the works. Above all, importers and subordinate departments of the NCB and the SARFT at provincial level must review foreign printed materials and films before they can be imported into the Chinese market.[121] Otherwise they cannot be circulated in the PRC at all.

In fact, prior to the 1990s, even the importation and circulation of published foreign works or even translated works were extremely limited in the Chinese market, not to mention unpublished foreign works. Consequently, foreign copyright owners who intended to have their published works circulated in China would have to pass the government censorship, or refrain from exporting their works into China, or witness their works being pirated in China without any recourse to legal remedies (depending on the content, however, the Chinese government may launch campaigns to eliminate such piracy activities).[122] Authors of unpublished works would, at best, only be able to see their works circulated in China through copyright-infringing activities. Thus, Article 2 of the 1990 Copyright Act is a flawed version of the national treatment and does not guarantee free speech of foreign copyright owners.

2.3.2.2. Authorship rules: pigeonholing authors

The 1990 Copyright Act provides a rough definition of authorship as those who create, translate, rewrite, adapt, transform, edit, or annotate certain works. Precisely, authorship can be granted not only to authors themselves, but also to other persons or entities.[123] In this regard, nine categories of works/authorship rules are enumerated to confirm different types of authorship such as "employment works" and "works of

---

[120] The Copyright Act of the PRC, Art. 2(1)–(3), 7 September 1990 (1990 Copyright Act).
[121] RAP, Art. 45.   [122] See Chap. 3, 3.3.4.3.   [123] The 1990 Copyright Act, Art. 9.

employees created in the course of carrying out their duties."[124] Virtually, the authorship rules put authors into different "pigeonholes" in which there might be certain other rules that exert pressure on authors who try to deliver free speech.

Admittedly, Chinese copyright owners may enjoy copyright protection regardless of whether their works are published or not. By defining different forms of authorship, however, the foregoing rules lay down different boundaries of granting A2R to copyright owners, some of which tend to restrict A2R of copyright owners. For instance, concerning works that are created in the course of employment, the law provides that the legal entity to which an author belongs enjoys priority in exploiting such works.[125] Prior to the 1990s, China had primarily a planned economy with very few privately owned enterprises/entities, and the concept of property, including IP, was overwhelmingly state-oriented or collective-oriented. This provision reflects such a situation at that time, but may encumber A2R and creative freedom of authors, especially in educational entities.

For instance, in the 2002 *Gao* case,[126] the plaintiff had been a teacher of a public primary school (the defendant) for more than 10 years and prepared 48 volumes of teaching plans for the school. When the plaintiff required the defendant to return these plans, however, the defendant claimed that they were lost or sold to others. The plaintiff then brought an action of copyright infringement against the defendant. The court of the first instance held that the plaintiff was not the owner of the teaching plans due to his employment by the defendant and turned down his claim. The court of the second instance maintained that verdict. It was not until in the third instance that the court overruled the former decision on the grounds that the work was original (though not innovative) and that the plaintiff was the author of a copyright-protected work.

2.3.2.3.   The scope of copyright: ambiguous A2R rules

Interestingly, the 1990 Copyright Act divides economic rights into the right of exploitation and the right of obtaining remuneration.[127] Concerning the rights of exploitation, the 1990 Copyright Act simply refers to

---

[124] Ibid., Arts. 11–19.   [125] Ibid., Art. 16.
[126] *Gao v. Nanan District Four Kilometer Primary School* [高丽娅诉南岸区四公里小学], Chongqing First Intermediate People's Court, (2005) Yu Yi Zhong Min Chu Zi [渝一中民初字] No. 603, 09 December 2005.
[127] The 1990 Copyright Act, Art. 10(5).

several rights (the rights to reproduce, perform, play, exhibit, distribute, make movies, TVs, videos, or the rights to adapt, translate, annotate, and edit) without providing specific definitions. Moreover, the right of obtaining remuneration is defined as being entitled to remuneration in return for permitting others to act according to relevant rights of exploitation.[128] These provisions regarding A2R are, however, very general and difficult to apply in judicial practice, which could leave plenty of leeway for courts to define copyright owners' interest in favour of the government's interest in conducting a content review.

For example, in the 1999 *Wang* case,[129] the defendant downloaded the plaintiffs' works for commercial use without permission. Facing a copyright infringement charge, the defendant argued that the 1990 Copyright Act did not require permission in online downloading. The Court found the defendant liable for copyright infringement in making the plaintiffs' copyright-protected works available online, although this was not a right provided for under the 1990 Copyright Act. This case is also important in that the Court ruled that online content provider must be responsible for reviewing the origin of the content. From then on, online content review became a prevalent practice. In 2000, the SPC issued the Interpretation on Several Issues Concerning the Application of Law in the Trial of Cases Involving Copyright Disputes Relating to Computer Networks Copyright (Networks Copyright Interpretation) [《最高人民法院关于审理涉及计算机网络著作权纠纷案件适用法律若干问题的解释》], mandating the online content provider to review the content on its website for copyright infringement.

2.3.3. Specific Access Rules Based on Proprietary Considerations

A second type of access rules in the 1990 Copyright Act derives from proprietary considerations, but is linked to the traditional Chinese ideology of restricting copyright owners' commercial interests. Although these rules seem to contribute to strengthening the public interest in A2K at reasonable costs, they may also help legitimise the government's interest in maintaining a censorship system. For one thing, although the international standards for subject matter are assimilated into Chinese

---

[128] Ibid.

[129] *Wang et al. v. Cenpok Telecommunication Technology Co. Ltd* [王蒙等六位作家诉世纪互联通信技术有限公司], Beijing Haidian District People's Court, (1999) Hai Zhi Chu Zi [海知初字] No. 57, 18 September 1999.

copyright law, they may serve the government's anti-A2R approach, albeit indirectly. Furthermore, the framework of free use caters to such an approach more directly.

2.3.3.1.   Subject matter: the double-edged principle of originality

The subject matter of copyright defines the border between copyrightable works and the public domain. Under Chinese copyright law, a copyrightable work of intellectual creation in literary, artistic, and scientific fields must be original and capable of being reproduced in a tangible medium.[130] The 1990 Chinese Copyright Act outlines nine categories of works including (1) written works; (2) oral works; (3) musical, dramatic, folk art, and choreographic works; (4) works of fine art and photographic works; (5) film, television, and video works; (6) drawings of engineering designs, product design blueprints, and related explanations; (7) maps, sketches, and other graphic works; (8) computer software; and (9) other works stipulated by laws and regulations.[131] Further, Article 5 precludes the protection of certain works, such as laws and regulations, resolutions, calendars, and numerical works.

In this regard, Chinese copyright law seems to be in line with international standards. In contrast, an earlier draft of the Chinese Copyright Act did not require creativity for copyright protection.[132] This was probably because some proponents feared that higher standards for originality would result in fewer chances for acquiring A2R and dampen the incentive to create. According to other scholars, however, the requirement for originality of the works was necessary because a copyrightable work must be a self-created rather than a copied one, while such a work represents the expression of an idea essentially and can be recorded in tangible medium for communication and reproduction.[133] Such a view reflects conventional Chinese doctrines about intellectual works. In traditional Chinese society, creating intellectual works was not regarded as an economic act, but as an act of bringing about moral values and life knowledge for the general public. Thus, a work that might be identified as

---

[130] The Regulations for the Implementation of the Copyright Act of the PRC, Art. 2, 24 May 1991.

[131] The 1990 Copyright Act, Art. 3.

[132] C. Zheng [郑成思], *On Intellectual Property* [《知识产权法学》] (北京: 法律出版社, 2003), p. 223.

[133] Q. Huang [黄勤南] (ed.), *The New Textbook of Intellectual Property Law* [《新编知识产权法教程》] (北京: 中国政法大学出版社, 1995), p. 391.

a valuable intellectual creation must assume a considerable degree of creativity. This adopted provision might have substantiated and facilitated the contemporary understanding of many Chinese about the high standards for a work that can be qualified for copyright protection. As a result, one might feel less guilty in "pirating" those works that are less creative.

On the surface, such a view could also be justified by the underlying public interest of the Chinese society in A2K at reasonable costs. This was corroborated by judicial practice in China in the 1990s, where courts applied a very strict approach of interpreting the criterion of originality. For example, in the case of *Guangxi Radio and Television Guide*,[134] the Court held that a TV timetable was not copyrightable because it lacked originality as required by copyright law. Although the producer invested a lot in producing the timetable, the timetable itself contained no explanation and merely served to show the existing TV program arrangements. Thus, the Court found it difficult to take such works as original and creative knowledge in the interest of the general public.

Indeed, there is no uniform practice on whether or not copyrightable subject matter should assume a certain degree of originality.[135] The Chinese courts' strict attitude toward the copyrightability of the subject matter, however, seems to be more akin to the traditional Chinese approach that laid down a high standard for intellectual works but a rather low standard for awarding authors with commercial gains. In practice, the subject matter determines the scope of speech/information the government may control legitimately. As such, Article 3(9) is a catchall provision that leaves it open to define any other works that should (and should not) be protected. This flexible framework allows the government to exercise its anti-A2R approach indirectly. In fact, the nature and scope of the subject matter under Chinese copyright law focus more on the nonproprietary than the proprietary functions of intellectual works.

[134] See *Guangxi Radio and Television Guide* v. *Guangxi Coal Miners Daily* [广西广播电视报诉广西煤矿工人报社预告表使用权纠纷案], Heshan People's Court (1991) He Fa Min Pan Zi [合法民判字] No. 46, 25 December 1991; Guangxi Liuzhou District Intermediate People's Court, (1994) Liu Di Fa Min Zhong Zi [柳地法民终字] No. 127 (25 November 1994), in *Gazette of the SPC of the PRC* [《中华人民共和国最高人民法院公报》], 1996, vol. 1, p. 50.

[135] Civil law countries tend to impose stricter standards on originality. See, e.g., BGH, *Inkassoprogram*, [1985] GRUR 1041 (9 May 1985). In contrast, common law countries tend to have a more relaxed view on this issue. See, e.g., *CCH Canadian Co. Ltd* v. *Law Society of Upper Canada* [2004] 1 SCR 339, 2004 SCC 13.

2.3.3.2.   Free use: restricting A2R in a milieu
dominated by the State

The 1990 Copyright Act allows twelve circumstances of "free use," where materials protected by copyright can be accessed without authorisation by or remuneration to copyright owners, as long as the name of the author of relevant works is indicated. They include (1) private use such as study, research, or self-entertainment; (2) quotation for the purposes of illustration or comments; (3) citation of media works for the purposes of reporting; (4) reprint of articles on current issues relating to politics, economics, or religion; (5) publication of a speech delivered at a public gathering, except where the author has explicitly forbidden such use; (6) translation or reproduction in small quantities for education and research; (7) free use by the government for fulfilling its official duties; (8) library/museum use; (9) free-of-charge live performance of published works; (10) self-copying of artistic works exhibited in the public; (11) translation of works from the Han language into any minority nationality language for distribution; and (12) transliteration of published works into Braille for publication.[136]

Thus, the 1990 Copyright Act endorses the regime of limitation/ exception rules on the basis of the BC. The particular importance of these rules in Chinese society is obvious: the traditional Chinese culture already stresses the moral value of intellectual works for the general public, and the value did not fade out in the contemporary milieu. At the beginning of the 1990s, copyright protection was being challenged by the rapid development of science and technology and widespread use of modern communication equipment in China. Apparently, an imminent task was to expand free access by the public to products of intellectual creations, which legitimises the restriction of A2R. The 1990 Copyright Act deals with this question through limitation and exception rules under Article 22, which takes conventional public interests into account, such as education, library use, and the use for minority and handicapped groups.

In fact, the pro-A2K tinge of the law covers up its anti-A2R and censorship-oriented nature. For instance, Article 22 allows free use by the government without permission from or remuneration to copyright owners. Moreover, the 1990 Copyright Act sets forth restrictions of neighbouring rights. A radio station or television station may broadcast

---

[136] The 1990 Copyright Act, Art. 22(1)–(12).

a published sound recording without permission from or paying remuneration to the copyright owner, performer, or sound recorder, if such broadcasting is carried out for noncommercial purposes.[137] Although these exceptions are not meant to prejudice against any prima facie infringement, most radio/television stations in China are state-owned. In the name of granting a wide scope of A2K to the general public for free, these access rules represent a more direct anti-A2R approach in favour of government censorship.

2.3.4. Specific Access Rules Based on Nonproprietary Considerations

Still other access rules in the 1990 Copyright Act serve to subject the private interest in A2R to the government's policy of controlling free speech in the name of protecting the public interest in affordable A2K, but they are, in fact, often based more on nonproprietary considerations. Before the 1990s when communication technology was still not prevalent in China, it was more important for the government to control the production than the dissemination of free speech. Thus, a more convenient approach was to dampen authors' incentive to make profits from producing literary and artistic works.

2.3.4.1. The compulsory license: an alternative means of media control

The 1990 Copyright Act was unique with its regime of compulsory licensing, which allows a work to be used without permission from the copyright owner, but requires remuneration to be paid. First, where a work is published in a newspaper or a periodical, another newspaper or periodical publisher may reprint the work, print an abstract of it, or print it as reference material.[138] Second, the law grants a compulsory license to a producer of sound recordings who, in producing sound recordings, may use works that another person has published.[139] Finally, a radio or television station may broadcast published works created by another person.[140] Certainly these access rules also seem to allow the general public to have A2K at ease (through modern technological facilities). However, there is an important reason for entertaining A2K at reasonable costs in this context. From the end of the 1980s to the beginning of the 1990s, such technological facilities were almost completely

---

[137] Ibid., Art. 43.   [138] Ibid., Art. 32.   [139] Ibid., Art. 37.   [140] Ibid., Art. 40.

monopolised by the State and were the sole instrument through which the State could communicate its ruling ideology to the general public in a prompt and convenient way. Because the government controls the entire media and cultural products through censorship, it becomes a necessity to grant compulsory licensing for the use of certain copyright-protected works.

2.3.4.2.   The censorship provision: a token of compromise

Apparently, a most cumbersome and kernel issue in drafting the first Copyright Act was the extent to which works protected by copyright should be subject to the government's control of publication (and dissemination of publications). Considering the anti-A2R structure of this Act, it is not difficult to understand why a censorship provision like Article 4 was written into the Copyright Act. Article 4 provides that works lawfully banned from publication and dissemination were not protected by copyright law. In that sense, Article 4 becomes a special access rule in Chinese copyright law, according to which both A2R and A2K will be subject to the government's control of free speech (censorship).

Presumably, Article 4 seems to be supported by the traditional Chinese culture and Article 17 of the BC.[141] According to Article 4, copyright owners can only claim copyright protection if their works conform to China's public policies. A famous case in China, which concerns a book entitled *The Inside Story* published in *Yanhuang Chunqiu* [《炎黄春秋》] in 1994, well illustrates the relationship between copyright and censorship. This magazine is a political publication in China, which is widely known for its intimacy with liberalism. The book was allowed to be published only on its review and approval by the Sichuan Provincial Communist Party Committee. According to a subsequent opinion issued by the SPC, the copyright over that story shall be protected because the content review revealed no violation of any laws.[142]

Nevertheless, this provision is easily vulnerable to criticism. Above all, it virtually denies copyright as a naturally born right because depriving the enforcement of copyright protection of certain works is equivalent to

---

[141] For a detailed analysis, see Section 2.4.3.

[142] See SPC, Letter from the Supreme People's Court to the Hunan Province Higher People's Court in *Zheng Haijin v. Xu Zheng Xiong and Tianjin People's Publishing House* [《最高人民法院关于郑海金与许正雄、天津人民出版社等著作权侵权纠纷案的函》], Zhi Jian Zi (1998) [知监字] No. 33, 9 March 2000.

denying the existence of copyright to the copyright owners of such works. In contrast, the Chinese Constitution recognises property rights including copyright as a basic right. In this regard, copyright as a constitutional right cannot be denied generally through a legal provision under civil law. Further, censorship itself aims not only at thwarting free speech, but also at impeding the free flow of information (A2K) by the general public. As analysed earlier, however, many access rules under the 1990 Copyright Act that impose an anti-A2R structure on Chinese copyright law could only be justified in the name of providing for affordable A2K to the public. A censorship provision in the Copyright Act would militate against and contradict such a seemingly legitimate title. Article 4, thus, becomes a most controversial and problematic provision under the 1990 Copyright Act.

Indeed, at the beginning of the 1980s, it was still widely held that the government's control was essential for the development of a planned economy and political and ideological education in a socialist country like China. Thus, while drafting the first Copyright Act, legislation proponents found it difficult to convince those government officials who were in charge of propaganda and culture that copyright protection would not interfere with their power to conduct censorship, but that there would be an alternative mode of control.[143] Throughout the 1980s, however, no one dared to openly cast doubt on the economic reforms led by Deng, which backed up the establishment of a copyright system. After the 1989 Tiananmen Movement, there was an overwhelming resurgence of Leftist political movements all over the country, which brought any "Rightist" ideologies to account. As a result, there must be an explicit compromise between private proprietorship and the State control, in order for the Copyright Act to be enacted safely. As a token of compromise, Article 4 might have lent political legitimacy to the 1990 Copyright Act at a sensitive juncture.

2.4. An Evaluation of the Access Rules Under the 1990 Copyright Act against the BC and the UCC

The international IP negotiations led China to make its national copyright law that was supposed to conform to international standards for

---

[143] R. Shen [沈仁干], 'The Making of the Copyright Law and Its Legislative Spirit' ['著作权法的制定和立法精神'], in the SPC (eds.), *Lectures on the Copyright Law of the PRC* [《著作权法讲座》] (北京: 法律出版社, 1991), p. 109.

copyright protection. As a result, China started to rely on international copyright law as the major source for copyright law making. Certainly, the Chinese government was aware that copyright law might facilitate A2K: many Chinese intellectuals viewed copyright law as a dynamic source of legitimising their free speech and made efforts to promote the establishment of a national copyright system. In the eyes of propaganda officials, this might create trouble for reining in "Bourgeois liberalisation." Luckily for such officials, while copyright owners may demand A2R for their works, there is no absolute copyright protection. Restriction of copyright in China, however, has a different dimension than in most Western countries: the socialist state has an interest in controlling free speech so that the government needs to conduct censorship in the publication of works and establish this control of free speech as a public interest.

The Chinese government often defines such a public interest in terms of the need to maintain public order in a socialist state.[144] As far as copyright law is concerned, this would also mean thwarting free speech by suppressing the private interest of copyright owners in claiming A2R through copyright. To justify its restriction on copyright, the government needs to uphold a general understanding of the public interest in promoting A2K at reasonable costs. These considerations make it necessary to establish a framework of access rules, which not only grants protection to copyright owners in terms of the BC and the UCC, but also empowers the State, "on behalf of the whole Chinese people,"[145] to impose restrictions on A2R. Compared with the legal framework of the BC and the UCC, such an anti-A2R structure of the 1990 Copyright Act can be better understood in several dimensions.

2.4.1.   Different Treatments of Domestic and Foreign Works

The 1990 Copyright Act came into effect before the PRC undertook negotiations toward acceding to the BC and the UCC. Compared with the subsequent regulations that followed China's accession to both treaties, in particular, the RIICC (which regulates the copyright protection of

---

[144] P. Drahos, *A Philosophy of Intellectual Property* (Aldershot: Dartmouth Publishing Co., 1996), p. 54.

[145] K. Hu [胡开忠], 'On the Philosophical Ground of Theory Concerning the Limitations to Copyright' ['著作权限制与反限制的法哲学基础研究'] (1996) 1 *Journal of Law and Business* [《法商研究》] 21.

foreign works), the 1990 Copyright Act fails to live up entirely to international standards. Whereas the overall framework of access rules under the 1990 Copyright Act is largely consistent with that of the BC and the UCC, several "access rules" under the 1990 Copyright Act, which were derived from international rules, restrict A2R in an excessive manner. In conclusion, the anti-A2R structure of Chinese copyright law is directed more at domestic than at foreign copyright owners. Such a "discriminatory" practice reveals the nonproprietary objective of such an anti-A2R structure of the Copyright Act, which aims at controlling those (Chinese) publications that might have greater potential in affecting China's political and social stability.

First of all, considering the national treatment under the BC and the UCC, a number of access rules under the 1990 Copyright Act provide different treatment of foreign copyright owners and their works. At first, the 1990 Copyright Act fails to protect unpublished foreign works. After China acceded to the BC and the UCC, however, the 1992 RIICC mends up this lacuna by granting foreign copyright owners more A2R than domestic copyright owners. For instance, one of the free use doctrines under the Copyright Act allows "translation of a published work from the Han language into minority nationality languages for publication and distribution within the country" without any authorisation or remuneration.[146] In contrast, the RIICC provides different treatment to a foreigner, who has created and published a work in the language of the Han nationality, by requiring prior authorisation of the copyright owner for "the publication and distribution of a translation of such works into the language of a minority nationality."[147] Further, Article 43 of the Copyright Act grants broadcasting and television stations free use of domestic works, performances, and sound recordings in nonbusiness broadcasting. However, Articles 11 and 12 of the RIICC deny such free use of foreign works. Similar inconsistencies exist between Article 37(1) of the Copyright Act and Article 9 of the RIICC with regard to the use of sound recordings.

Second, concerning the subject matter and the formalities, domestic and foreign works are also treated differently. Take the protection of software for example. The RPCS makes it practically possible for a Chinese copyright owner to file a complaint with an administrative authority or pursue civil litigation regarding copyright infringement of

---

[146] The 1990 Copyright Act, Art. 22(11).   [147] RIICC, Art. 10.

domestic computer software only on the condition that the software is registered with the software registration office.[148] In contrast, the RIICC grants copyright protection to foreign software without requiring the formality of registration.[149] Moreover, the RIICC protects the applied artistic works of foreign authors,[150] as is provided for under the BC. It even grants protection to compilation of those materials that are not protected under the 1990 Copyright Act, as long as such compilation is deemed "original/creative."[151] On the one hand, these access rules fail to guarantee the same level of A2R to domestic and foreign authors. On the other hand, the general public at home may have A2K through foreign works at higher costs than through domestic works.

Third, application of the compulsory license, under the 1990 Copyright Act, is vulnerable to similar criticism. The Berne Appendix allows the use of copyright-protected materials only on the condition of paying remuneration to authors, unless they have made a prior statement forbidding such use. The 1990 Copyright Act contains similar access rules under the Berne Appendix. Nevertheless, domestic authors and foreign authors are treated differently. For example, Article 32(2) of the 1990 Copyright Act allows domestic works in newspapers and periodicals to be reprinted without permission from the authors. Article 13 of the RIICC, however, requires newspaper or periodical publishers to obtain permission of the right holder before they can reprint foreign works.

Obviously, different considerations were underlying these general access rules, as China was starting its process of copyright internationalisation. Most of the aforementioned provisions reflect the government's initial anti-A2R policy in favouring the public interest in affordable A2K. By contrast, the RIICC, enacted shortly after the Sino–US IP negotiations and China's accession to the BC and the UCC, embrace international copyright standards. Such a practice of according different copyright owners with different dimensions of A2R is inconsistent with the national treatment. Unequal treatment of domestic and foreign works constitutes discrimination against Chinese authors and their works, which reveals the Chinese government's strategy of transforming international standards into national laws without weakening the government's power to control free speech at home.

---

[148] RPCS, Art. 7.   [149] RIICC, Art. 7.   [150] Ibid., Art. 6(1).   [151] Ibid., Art. 8.

2.4.2. *Vague Standards that Restrict A2R*

In a sense, the Copyright Act reflects the situation prior to 1990, in which China imposed more stringent restrictions on A2R than on A2K. Authors were rewarded only humbly at this stage because the social value of intellectual creations was deemed more important and the public should be encouraged to have A2K at little cost in a socialist planned economy. Although the law starts to recognise the private interest in A2R, which had been almost deprived of intellectuals for a long time, the need to render A2K affordable to the wide public in a planned remuneration system overrides A2R because it could justify the government's measures of conducting censorship. This may be why Chinese copyright law implements the minimum standards through such access rules as the limitation and exception rules (such as free use or compulsory license), which are, however, often defined rather vaguely.

Take the concept of authorship for example. Article 11 of the 1990 Copyright Act allows "legal persons and non-legal-persons" to be treated as authors, whereas Article 16 provides that "works created by citizens in the fulfilment of tasks assigned to him by a legal entity or other organisation shall be deemed a work created in the course of employment." This provision, which seems to grant copyright to individuals, must be interpreted in a narrow sense. In a socialist country, where a planned economy still prevailed and authors were traditionally seen as intellectual working class, their "working unit" to which they belong may always assume priority in exercising copyright.[152] In fact, such an approach allows the "working unit" to conduct self-censorship, and renders the collective unit responsible for the production and dissemination of certain working results. Therefore, "access rules" regarding authorship do not provide authors with complete protection of A2R.

There is a similar case with important access rules such as "free use," which fail to be clearly defined. For example, Article 10 of the 1990 Copyright Act refers to reproduction rights, where certain specific acts of reproducing works are enumerated. There is, however, no general limitation rule for reproduction rights, such as the three-step test under Article 9(2) of the BC. Therefore, it remains unclear how the "legitimate" interests of the author, as under Article 9(2) of the BC, could be weighed against the public interest in A2K at reasonable costs, or even the government's interest in maintaining control of free speech. Free use

---

[152] Alford, *To Steal a Book Is an Elegant Offence*, pp. 156–7.

for comments, for example, has long been a reasonable practice in Chinese culture, which allows someone to reproduce certain works for criticism without remuneration to the authors. There is, however, no precise definition as to the quantity of copies that can be reproduced in such circumstances.

In sum, vaguely defined access rules impose considerable restrictions on copyright owners' proprietary interests, especially considering the economic and social realities in China. Even though the 1990 Copyright Act recognises remuneration, the conventional remuneration system in the PRC granted authors only a humble and symbolic payment, which would cut them off from any further opportunity of being rewarded. In contrast, the government's interest in controlling free expression prevailed as a result of often vaguely and broadly defined provisions such as Article 22(7), which allows government authorities to reproduce works without permission. The open-ended feature of this free use rule, reined in only by a general warning against infringement, renders it easy for government authorities to make unauthorised use of copyright-protected materials in the name of fulfilling their official duties. Against the background of China's international negotiations toward copyright internationalisation, such an anti-A2R framework of access rules fails to reach international standards.

2.4.3.   The Question of the Legitimacy of Censorship in Copyright Law

By treating domestic and foreign works differently and by restrictions on A2R, access rules under the 1990 Copyright Act deny absolute protection of private intellectual creations. Although most access rules restrict the private interest of copyright owners largely out of proprietary considerations, the nonproprietary considerations that were underlying these rules are more fundamental. Because Chinese copyright law is established on the basis of the socialist legal theories, it caters to a given economic and social pattern and is guided by the prevalent sociopolitical values. Such a copyright law-making pattern aims to subjugate different interests to the socialist ideology. Therefore, as illustrated earlier, government officials were concerned whether copyright law would potentially loosen their control of publication, media, and the Chinese society.

In this sense, international negotiators' attempt to facilitate more stringent adherence to copyright protection seemed to give way to the Chinese government's anti-A2R law-making strategies. For China, the ultimate objective of copyright law making was to reassure the government's control over free speech and transform such control into access rules under Chinese copyright law. As such, Article 4 of the 1990 Copyright Act became the core "public interest" provision geared to China's censorship regime: works that are banned from publication and dissemination "in accordance with the law" and, particularly, works that prejudice against the government's interest will not enjoy copyright protection. As ambiguous and controversial as it is, Article 4 denies, rather than degrades, copyright protection for certain works. Such an approach, however, has no basis in the international sources, from which China's access rules may be derived.

Although the 1990 Copyright Act offers no further explanation, it is not difficult to understand that, in the Chinese sociopolitical context, a number of laws, regulations, and even the policies of the CCP require explicitly that some works be banned from publication and dissemination. Thus, Article 4 prescribes the doctrine that copyright protection must be subject to the outcome of censorship conducted by the government. The only legal basis in the international copyright framework, against which Article 4 of the 1990 Copyright Act could be measured, is Article 17 of the BC that allows the government to control and prohibit the dissemination of works for the purpose of protecting the public interest. A closer examination against the BC, however, would reveal that Article 4 of the Copyright Act is unwarranted.

First, if interpreted systematically, Article 17 of the BC must be subject to the national treatment as the most fundamental principle of the BC. Basically, Article 2 of the 1990 Copyright Act recognises and reiterates this principle, mandating that works of foreigners shall enjoy copyright protection under bilateral agreements or international treaties. After China's international IP negotiations and accession to the BC and the UCC, such foreign works shall, certainly, enjoy copyright protection under Chinese copyright law, regardless of whether the contents of such works are treated as violating the public interest in China or not. Therefore, by potentially denying the existence of copyright protection over certain foreign works, Article 4 of the Copyright Act comes into conflict with the principle of national treatment under the BC.

Second, Article 17 of the BC itself must be construed as being subject to the minimum standards of the BC. Because the BC is an international copyright treaty that aims at copyright protection, Article 17 does not deny the copyrightability of a work with regard to any subject matter. Article 4 of the 1990 Copyright Act, however, presupposes that the copyrightability of a work depends not only on the conditions for copyrightable subject matter as under Article 2 of the BC, but also on whether the Chinese government will approve the content of the work. Even if Article 17 could be invoked to support a state's action to control and prohibit the circulation of certain works, it does not mean that the copyright of a work can be denied. Under such circumstance, copyright of such works could only be seen as being withheld.

Third, Article 17 of the BC must also be subject to the principle of automatic protection. As illustrated earlier, Article 5(2) of the BC prescribes that no formalities be imposed on the copyrightability of works. In other words, once authors complete their works, they shall enjoy automatic protection immediately. As an exception to the entire legal framework of the BC, Article 17 allows the public interest to prevail only if the works are recognised as copyrightable works. Otherwise (if the existence of copyright is not recognised), Article 17 shall not be applicable. In this sense, granting copyright protection to works only on the condition that they survive the test of censorship is also incompatible with the requirement of disposal of formalities under Article 5(2) of the BC.

2.5.   Conclusion

Copyright legislation in the PRC prior to the end of the Cultural Revolution was basically featured by China's socialist planned economy and its censorship-oriented cultural policies. To a large extent, copyright was seen as contradictory to the public proprietorship as a cornerstone of the socialist state: many ordinary Chinese, as inculcated by a powerful propaganda machine of the CCP, believed that copyright abetted the intellectuals in developing an easy and independent life, which was hazardous to the rule of the Party-state. This led to disastrous political movements that witnessed numerous tragedies of the works and even personal lives of Chinese intellectuals. Copyright was, from the beginning of the Communist regime, treated as a legal instrument of controlling free expression and ordinary intellectuals.

After the policy of Reform and Opening was adopted, China had a new chance of developing copyright protection thanks to the overwhelming economic reforms that left a political vacuum behind (even for a short period of time). Most people set aside the debate about the legitimacy of private proprietorship so that the intellectuals could enjoy A2R again, even though most of them were not able to earn an independent living on their works. Although they were assigned to different stereotypes of the "working class," Confucianism, which requires intellectuals to assume a conventional sense of sociopolitical responsibilities, revived. To the advantage of copyright, Chinese intellectuals saw copyright protection as a seed of legitimising their freedom of speech, albeit in a clandestine manner. Shrouded by the aegis of economic reforms, many intellectuals called for an overall protection of their publications and works. To some extent, A2R provided a safe reason to justify their demand for respect of their intellectual work.

Seeing some danger of political instability after the initial stage of economic reforms, the communist state was reluctant to give away its control of production and dissemination of free speech and tried to justify its power to do so through copyright law making. This led the government to adopt a dualistic approach of imposing restrictions on the private interest in A2R by giving prima facie favour to the public interest in having A2K at reasonable costs. In other words, the Chinese government was ambivalent in facilitating copyright protection in line with the economic reforms and the international copyright standards. Copyright law making, at this stage, involved sophisticated strategies and was meant primarily as an instrument to serve the "public interest" as defined by the State.

International commercial negotiations, however, started to play an important role after the Cultural Revolution and, especially, after China's policy of Reform and Opening was put in place. Several rounds of Sino–US trade negotiations prompted China to draft its national Copyright Act to protect the private interests of individual creators. Since then, the PRC began seriously to learn how to create a refined framework of access rules. At this stage, the United States relied on unilateral mechanisms such as trade sanctions to force China to take legislative steps toward copyright protection. While drafting the 1990 Copyright Act, China was also having negotiations with WIPO and the United States on acceding to the BC and the UCC to align the national copyright system of the PRC with international standards. Under such international pressure, China established its initial modern copyright system on the basis of a Copyright Act and a few ancillary regulations that complement this Act.

In this sense, the 1990 Copyright Act was largely a result of a compromise between the need toward copyright internationalisation and the need to control free speech at home, especially after the 1989 Tiananmen Movement. More seemingly balance-oriented access rules were designed on the basis of international sources not only to ensure A2K at reasonable costs in the Chinese society, but also to justify the government's restrictions on authors and publishers, as well as its control over free speech. In this regard, it is not difficult to understand why quite a few access rules under the 1990 Copyright Act were inconsistent with the standards set forth in the international copyright treaties. In particular, the censorship provision is inconsistent with the BC. In fact, at a time when copyright-protected knowledge products are becoming an integral part of the globalising trade process, censorship would only increase, rather than lower, the economic and social costs for A2K.

3

Power Is Knowledge

In an incrementally integrated global system that encompasses knowledge as a fundamental engine of economic development, a nation's cultural and social policies can be largely assimilated into its trade interests through the IP laws. Since the end of the 1980s, China has been an indispensable player in the process of economic globalisation. So far, bilateral and multilateral trade negotiations have continued to exert influence on the copyright system of the PRC. After China became a member of the WTO, China could no longer dodge its obligations under TRIPS to enforce international copyright rules when implementing its economic, cultural, and social policies. In that connection, international copyright law has been able to infiltrate China's copyright system, which poses challenges to the chilling effects of China's censorship regime.

The external pressure to enforce copyright standards attenuated China's seemingly legitimate efforts to restrain A2R that might discourage author-ial interests in producing free-speech-oriented knowledge products. The booming enthusiasm of intellectuals at home for pursuing free speech and the concomitant commercial interests in producing creative works further backed up the trend to boost domestic copyright standards. Throughout the 1990s, China hailed a flourishing publication industry and an outburst of knowledge products of both domestic and international origins. Although China was witnessing a transitional period between the end of a planned economy and the onset of an overall market economy, it is no longer the A2R, which covers up the pursuit of free speech, but the A2K, which buttresses the free flow of information, that poses a genuine threat to the censorship regime.

Therefore, China relies on the negative correlation between A2R (which is an incentive for free speech) and A2K at reasonable costs (which underlies the free flow of information) to pursue China's policy goal of controlling free expression. Thus, the focus of China's intransigent cen-sorship regime shifts from the control of production of intellectual works to the control of dissemination of works. At this stage, international trade negotiations consolidate the role of WTO law in securing China's enforcement of copyright standards under TRIPS. Literally, the imminent issue was how to enforce the existing standards for copyright protection. China amended its copyright system by reshaping the contours of authorial protection, which seems to have enhanced their economic status and encouraged free speech. However, the amendment creates a unique pro-A2R mechanism of administrative enforcement, which enables the government to exert political power to maintain its intransigent control of knowledge dissemination through an anti-A2K practice of IP enforcement.

3.1. The Need to Enforce Universal Copyright Standards: Furthering the Compromise of China's Censorship-Oriented Copyright Law in the International Trade Negotiations toward China's Accession to the WTO

3.1.1. *The Dawn of Knowledge Economy: Copyright Development in the PRC Pending the Beginning of the Twenty-First Century*

3.1.1.1. The significance of the policy of establishing a market economy for copyright development

The development of copyright protection after China's accession to the BC and the UCC was interrelated to the new policy of establishing a market economy. After the 1989 Tiananmen Movement, the CCP remoulded its economic and social policies by advocating a money-driven life philosophy and paralysing the political consciousness that was starting to grow among the ordinary Chinese. As Deng stated earlier, the most fundamental key to socialism was to "develop productivity" [发展生产力]. The Leftist factions within the CCP, however, took advantage of the political aftermath of the Tiananmen Movement and intended to impose a conservative policy that might have reverted China to its status before the economic reforms.[1] At this time, Deng, who had already given up all his formal positions, saw the danger of getting China back onto a wrong road. As he was still able to rely on his unparalleled political influence, Deng decided to move in 1992 when he made a pontifical "Inspection Tour to the South" [南巡], which reinvigorated China's economic reforms.

---

[1] Z. Liu [刘政], 'Jiyun Tian in the Great Reforms' ['改革风云中的田纪云'], *Southern Weekly* [《南方周末》], 07 January 2009.

The views about China's economic and social development that Deng brought out during this trip were compiled into the famous "Southern Tour Speech." In his talk, Deng reiterated the need to further the policy of Reform and Opening Up, stating that "development is the absolute principle" [发展是硬道理] and "it is glorious to be rich." Therefore, China should set aside the unnecessary debate on the distinction between socialism and capitalism. Most important, Deng denounced the "abominable impacts" of the Leftist wing and clarified that whoever stands in the way of the reforms must "get away from power." Featured as "wading across the river by feeling the stones" [摸着石头过河], Deng's rhetoric soon won widespread support within the leadership of the CCP, which unleashed a new tide of economic reforms that were supposed to lead to the establishment of what Zemin Jiang [江泽民] described as a "socialist market economy."

Under the tide of globalisation in the 1990s, Jiang, aided by premier Rongji Zhu [朱镕基], continued the economic policies adopted by Ziyang Zhao [赵紫阳], their predecessor, so that China underwent a relatively stable phase of economic development and attained an astonishing annual growth of 8 percent GDP on average. All this was attributable to the legacy of Deng's support for a market economy, or, in other words, capitalism. However, as a result of Deng's "crippled reforms" [跛脚改革],[2] a "socialist market economy with Chinese characteristics" was criticised as being identical with "crony capitalism" [权贵资本主义],[3] in which egregious corruption, class polarisation, environment pollution, and social injustice were embedded. Such a path of economic development was almost destructive for a nation that had no serious religious tradition and had undergone a complete political and cultural vandalism under the earlier Communist rule: everyone was encouraged to worship and look to the pursuit of great wealth through whatever means [一切向钱看]. In a famous press conference where he reprimanded some journalists, Jiang himself even endorsed a philosophy of "making big money in silence" [闷声大发财].[4]

---

[2] This word is often used to refer to China's economic reforms without corresponding political reforms.

[3] See, e.g., J. Wu [吴敬琏], 'We Can Safeguard the Extreme Leftism Only by Curbing Crony Capitalism' ['遏制权贵资本主义才能防极左'] *Beijing Daily* [《北京日报》], 05 May 2009.

[4] R. L. Kuhn, 'American Scholar Reveals Zemin Jiang's Seldom Anger and Criticism of Hong Kong Journalists' ['美学者披露江泽民少见发火并批评香港记者始末'], news.ifeng .com [凤凰网历史], 24 December 2013, at http://news.ifeng.com/history/zhongguoxian daishi/detail_2013_12/24/32417303_0.shtml.

Certainly, all this had considerable influence on China's copyright policies. There was no reason to prevent Chinese intellectuals from craving for wealth while everyone else was getting into the arena of capitalism. Apparently, an anti-A2R copyright policy was not even logical, not to mention it was unfeasible. The publication industry alone had colossal commercial interests and witnessed a historical growth of published titles from 96,761 to 190,391 with a gross price growth from 13.7 billion Yuan to 56.2 billion Yuan within the decade from 1993 to 2003.[5] After the concept of "knowledge-based economy" came into being, Jiang soon endorsed this novelty and embraced the advent of knowledge economy in China. Up to 2004, China proclaimed that more than 12 million patents had been granted, that over 2 million trademarks had been registered, and that around 350 million pirated copies had been confiscated.[6] One might be tempted to envisage a new epoch of IP-related economy, an overall protection of copyright, and, certainly, at least some perceivable progress in free speech in China. Was this really the case?

3.1.1.2.   The enhanced status of Chinese intellectuals and the quandary of copyright

It is true that Chinese intellectuals also benefited from the flourishing market economy. Many writers became rich from their royalties, and for some of them, copyright became a vital instrument to make a living. After the China Copyright Protection Centre (CCPC) was established in 1998, the NCB entrusted the CCPC and the Chinese Writers Association to organise an association of the copyright of literary works. A number of famous copyright scholars, writers, and artists took the initiative to launch this association. Among them was Qiuyu Yu [余秋雨], for instance, who wrote several books about his personal journeys to different parts of the world that became very popular and went to the top of the bestsellers throughout the 1990s. Although there was no ranking in this regard during that time, Yu was reported to be the richest writer in

---

[5] D. Zhong, [钟鼎文], 'The Publication Industry in China: A Decade towards the Market' ['中国出版业: 走向市场化的10年'], *China Reading News* [《中华读书报》], 13 August 2004.

[6] The News Office of the State Council, 'The New Progress of Intellectual Property Protection in China' [《中国知识产权保护的新进展》], 21 April 1994, at http://politics.people.com.cn/GB/1026/3338425.html.

China in 2006 with 14 million Yuan annual royalties.[7] Indeed, Chinese intellectuals were now making use of copyright to pursue considerable commercial interests. The State also affirmed the "irreplaceable" role of intellectuals in "the construction of socialism" openly and advocated the respect for knowledge and intellectuals.[8] In the 2003 Report on the Work of the Government, Premier Zhu highlighted the protection of intellectuals and IP.

It is, however, important to differentiate A2R from A2K. While Jiang was reigning over the country, he adopted a more stringent policy of controlling free expression compared with that in the 1980s. The focus of control at this time was directed more at the free flow of information (especially through the media) than at individual free speech. In fact, up to 2001, China was reported to be the leading country that jailed its journalists,[9] while a vast sum of state budget was invested on building the "Great Firewall" in the Internet to block the international mainstream websites from being accessible in China.[10] A2K became a thorn in the flesh for the propaganda departments of the CCP. Indeed, it was not the production of certain information but the wide dissemination of such information (which might result in a collective action among the civil society) that poses a real threat to the rule of the CCP. Considering the trend of wide use of digital technologies toward the end of the 1990s, it must be a more urgent political task to control A2K in the civil society.

Yet, it was equally important for the propaganda officials not to ignore the potential challenges that copyright protection and A2R might bring about for the control of free speech. In that connection, the government employed a policy of "*divide et impera*" in treating Chinese intellectuals. On the one hand, the government provided a multitude of alluring academic titles and material benefits to buy over most intellectuals who were willing to become the "throat and tongue" [喉舌] of the government.[11]

---

[7] Z. Peng [彭志平], 'YU Qiuyu Tops the Ranking of the Richest Writers from the Mainland' ['大陆富豪作家排行　余秋雨占鳌头'], *China Times* [《中国时报》], 17 December 2006.

[8] Z. Jiang. [江泽民], *On Science and Technology* [《论科学技术》](北京: 中央文献出版社, 2001), pp. 13 and 35.

[9] Committee to Protect Journalists, '2001 Prison Census: 118 Journalists Jailed', 26 March 2002, at https://cpj.org/imprisoned/attacks-on-the-press-in-2001-journalists-in-prison.php.

[10] The Economist, 'The Great Firewall: The Art of Concealment', Special Report: China and the Internet, 6 April 2013, at www.economist.com/news/special-report/21574631-chinese-screening-online-material-abroad-becoming-ever-more-sophisticated.

[11] Q. He. [何清涟], 'The Status Quo and Prospects of China under Authoritarian Rule' ['威权统治下的中国现状与前景'](2004) 2 *Modern China Studies* [《当代中国研究》]5.

On the other hand, the government adopted draconian measures to cope with those few intellectuals who were not willing to be subordinate to the pressure and even dared to speak up freely.[12] The consequences were severe: their works were banned from publication or circulation, they would be dismissed by their relevant "working units" in which they were pigeonholed, or they could be under direct supervision or personal prosecution until they gave up or left China. As a result, most Chinese intellectuals held a cynical and detached life attitude and indulged themselves in matters that were remote from politics. From the beginning of the 1990s, the whole class of Chinese intellectuals were getting used to self-censorship, if they did not become "morally depraved."[13]

Thus, copyright development was trapped in a quandary. Throughout the 1990s, the publication industry was dubbed one of the most profitable industries in China. However, the annual gross volume of nationwide publications in 2003 (6.67 billion) equalled only that in 1986 and witnessed little growth:[14] only the market price per volume soared. This means that the growth of the publication industry in that decade was not based on the availability of more useful works, but on the increase of the costs for A2K. Moreover, the number of publishing houses only went up from 505 in 1993 to 535 in 2003, while the number of journals and newspapers increased only by less than 3 percent.[15] These statistics were consistent with the fact that the Chinese government started to carry out a policy of improvement and rectification [治理整顿] in the publication industry after the 1989 Tiananmen Movement.[16] Indeed, in 2001 when the amendments of the Copyright Act came into force, the APP/NCB, which used to be a subordinate organ of the MOC, turned into the General Administration of Publication and Press (GAPP)/NCB [新闻出版总署], a "ministry unit" that enjoys the same administrative rank as the MOC. A2K, as a functionality of copyright, became an enemy of censorship.

---

[12] Ibid.
[13] S. Han [韩少功], 'The Depravation of Chinese Intellectuals in the 1990s' ['90年代中国知识分子的堕落'], *Tencent Da Jia* [腾讯大家], 26 April 2015, at http://dajia.qq.com/blog/478612012821892.html.
[14] Zhong, 'The Publication Industry in China'.   [15] Ibid.
[16] The 5th Plenary Conference of the 13th Central Committee of the CCP, Resolutions on Further Improvement and Rectification and Deepening the Reforms [《关于进一步治理整顿和深化改革的决定》], 9 November 1990.

3.1.1.3.   Lack of effective IP enforcement and piracy: a perverted channel of information flow?

After the Sino–US IP negotiations and its accession to the BC and the UCC, China started to review its national copyright system in accordance with its obligations under the MOU. For one thing, computer software began to be protected as literary works so that software was no longer required to be registered.[17] The RIICC ensured the priority of international copyright standards, which applied to the protection of foreign works. For instance, the Chinese government allowed free use of American works, for certain purposes, to continue, as long as such works were in use prior to 17 March 1992, when the bilateral treaty started to take effect, subject to the condition that such use may not prejudice the legitimate interests of copyright owners.[18]

At this time, IP protection, especially the enforcement of IP standards, became a key issue in China. A number of courts at the intermediary and advanced levels in Beijing, Shanghai, and other special economic zones established special chambers for dealing with IP disputes. Between 1986 and 1993 about 3,505 IP-related civil disputes were accepted around the country, of which 468 were related to copyright.[19] It is noteworthy that in China, an important system of IP enforcement exists in the executive branch, which runs parallel to judicial enforcement. Within two years after China's accession to the BC and the UCC, Chinese copyright administration at all levels brought some 150 tort cases under control, and illegal materials were confiscated.[20] In 1994, the Chinese government even organised relevant departments to crack down on illegal reproduction of audiovisual products and illegal printing in the publishing industry.[21] All these measures taken by the Chinese government largely alleviated the tension between China and the United States in the bilateral IP/copyright-related trade relationship.

In practice, however, copyright was far from being understood and accepted by ordinary Chinese citizens, most of whom lacked a consciousness of copyright protection. A significant number of studies attribute

---

[17] Regulations on the Protection of Computer Software, Art. 15, 29 December 2001 (RPCS).
[18] The NCB, the Notice on Implementing the Bilateral Copyright Clauses under the Memorandum of Understanding Concerning the Protection of Intellectual Property Rights between the Government of the US and the PRC [《国家版权局关于执行中美知识产权谅解备忘录双边著作权保护条款的通知》], Arts. 5–6, 29 February 1992.
[19] 'Intellectual Property Protection- Presence and Prospect' ['知识产权保护'], *Law & Order Daily* [《法制日报》], 30 June 1994, p. 2.
[20] Ibid.   [21] Ibid.

this to the cultural differences,[22] economic growth,[23] political control,[24] legislative flaws,[25] and judicial weakness in China.[26] Put more precisely, the victims of copyright infringement cases did not lack a consciousness of protecting their own rights and interests, as can be seen from the great number of copyright disputes. Nevertheless, the remedies that they could expect from a lawsuit were barely enough to cover the costs they spent on the legal proceedings.[27] Thus, it seems that Chinese copyright law was featured by a bundle of rights that could by no means be enforced. Even after China enacted the 1990 Copyright Act and other regulations that helped to implement that Act, there was, on the whole, no effective remedy to combat piracy in copyright goods.

More recent studies on the ineffectiveness of enforcing IP protection in China, though they are also based on the starting point of the needs for economic and social development in China, have come to more illuminating conclusions. These studies indicate that piracy results from an imbalanced IP regime, which fails to take development needs into account sufficiently.[28] Whereas it might be too bold to underplay the role of IP in China's economic growth generally, piracy is often perceived as an insurmountable stage considering the unbalanced development in different regions and population layers in China.[29] For this reason, China lacks a profound incentive to enforce IP protection and

[22] B. W. Husted, 'The Impact of National Culture on Software Piracy' (2000) 26 *JBE* 197, at 200.

[23] G. R. Butterton, 'Pirates, Dragons and US Intellectual Property Rights in China: Problems and Prospects of Chinese Enforcement' (1996) 38 *Ariz L Rev* 1081, at 1116.

[24] P. K. Yu, 'Causes of Piracy and Counterfeiting in China' (2007) *Guanxi: The China Letter*, at www.peteryu.com/guanxi.pdf.

[25] WTO, Panel Report, *China–Measures Affecting the Protection and Enforcement of Intellectual Property Rights*, WT/DS362/R, paras. 7.1–7.144, 26 January 2009.

[26] S. E. Miller, 'The Posse is Coming to Town . . . Maybe: the Role of United States Non-Governmental Organisations in Software Anti-Piracy Initiatives as China Seeks WTO Accession' (2000) 7 *ILSA J Int'l Comp L* 111, at 120.

[27] E.g., a report in 2007 shows that the losses from piracy increased while the software piracy rate decreased. Business Software Alliance, 'Fifth Annual BSA and IDC Global Software Piracy Study' (2007), at http://globalstudy.bsa.org/2007.

[28] See, e.g., A. Wechsler, 'Spotlight on China: Piracy, Enforcement, and the Balance Dilemma in Intellectual Property Law', in A. Kur (ed.), *Intellectual Property Rights in a Fair World Trade System: Proposals for Reform of TRIPS* (Cheltenham: Edward Elgar, 2011), p. 61.

[29] P. K. Yu, 'Intellectual Property, Economic Development, and the China Puzzle', in D. J. Gervais (ed.), *Intellectual Property, Trade and Development: Strategies to Optimize Economic Development in a TRIPS Plus Era* (Oxford: Oxford University Press, 2007), p. 173, at 202.

eliminate piracy at home. Although some copyright owners may not necessarily suffer as substantial a loss as they claim, piracy will continue to be rampant unless it stops contributing to the social welfare, in particular, by providing A2K to the general public at considerably lower costs. As such, piracy, in conjunction with the lack of effective IP enforcement, constitutes a perverted, yet significant, channel of the free flow of information in China.

3.1.2. The 1995 and 1996 Sino–US IP Negotiations on IPR Enforcement and the Resulting Agreements

3.1.2.1. The conflicts between China and the US in IPR enforcement

Anyway, copyright infringement in China remained rampant, even after those important international IP negotiations and in the midst of soaring legal disputes. According to US industries, in 1994 alone, they suffered a loss of 800 million US dollars from piracy in China, and in 1995 the statistic was an estimated 866 million US dollars.[30] In October 1993, the US International Intellectual Property League pointed out that China had not complied with the MOU in 1992 and failed to undertake its obligations in enforcing IP protection. Therefore, the USTR placed China on the watch list in its 1992 Special 301 Annual Report. China remained on the priority watch list in 1993 and became a priority foreign country in 1994.[31] At this time, the USTR was no longer focusing on copyright legislation, but stressed the problem of IP enforcement and the importance of an IP enforcement mechanism in China.

In fact, a number of flaws and lacunas existed in China's national copyright system, which resulted in the failure to enforce copyright protection. Concerning the legislation, there were inconsistencies between various legal provisions, insufficient protection of the existing works, and overbroad provisions on free use and compulsory license. With respect to the executive branch, there was a lack of transparency and responsibilities of the administrative organs. As for the judicial practice, there were inconsistencies in interpreting the laws and regulations and a lack of explicit and effective criminal sanctions. In view of these flaws, the USTR

[30] USTR, 1995 National Trade Estimate – People' Republic of China.
[31] 'China Claims Success in Copyright Crackdown', *Reuter Bus Rep*, 3 August 1994.

complained about a lack of equal and fair market access that would have been available under a sound IP/copyright system.

Consequently, while the USTR launched in June 1994 a six-month investigative process under the "Super 301" of the Omnibus Trade and Competitiveness Act of 1988,[32] the United States and China started their second round of IP negotiations simultaneously. So far as IP protection and market access were concerned, the United States raised three requests. First, China must set up an administrative team of IP enforcement to fight against IP infringement, seize and destroy infringing products, and bring the infringers to litigation. Second, China must intensify its judicial institution-building with regard to IP enforcement, that is, set up a court system that really works. Third, China must allow US IP products to enter the Chinese market.[33]

China, however, argued that IP legislation and enforcement were internal affairs of the PRC, that any decisions must be made by China itself, and that the investigation the United States carried out on China, based on its Special 301 Section, was not legitimate but outrageous.[34] Such a gap resulted in a stalemate of the negotiations. In July 1994, the United States announced that it would designate China again as a priority foreign country under its 301 Section.[35] After the investigative period was closed, the United States issued, in February 1995, a trade retaliation list amounting to 280 million US dollars,[36] and the USTR even threatened to impose 100 percent duties on Chinese imports equivalent to the estimated losses to US companies caused by China's failure to enforce the agreed IP standards.[37] While China issued an antiretaliation list against the United States in return, the spokesperson of the Ministry of Foreign Trade and Economic Cooperation of the PRC requested that the United States give up its stance and cooperate with China in finding a solution through active negotiations.

---

[32] Omnibus Trade and Competitiveness Act of 1988, Pub L No. 100–418, sec. 1302(a), 102 Stat. 1176 (1988).

[33] B. K. Lim, 'China Court Favours Disney in Key Copyright Suit', *Reuter Asia-Pac Bus Rep*, 4 August 1994.

[34] Ibid.

[35] See, e.g., Butterton, 'Pirates, Dragons and US Intellectual Property Rights in China', 1104–5.

[36] See, e.g., J. A. Massey, 'The Emperor Is Far Away: China's Enforcement of Intellectual Property Rights Protection 1986–2006' (2006) 7 *Chi J Int'l L* 231, at 235.

[37] See, US, 'China Edging Back to Table', *Chicago Tribune*, 7 February 1995, 3.

3.1.2.2.   The second Sino–US IP negotiations and
the 1995 IPR Agreement

When both sides came back to the negotiation table, China made some compromises. China took active measures to crack down on IP infringement, such as closing factories, destroying infringing products, or confiscating infringing products in retail.[38] In addition, China promised to enforce the existing IP laws and regulations to curb infringement and protect the incentives of individual creators and enterprises. After nine rounds of negotiations, the second Sino–US IP dispute was resolved on 26 February 1995, when China and the United States reached an unprecedentedly detailed Sino–US bilateral memorandum of understanding under the 1995 Agreement regarding IPR protection (1995 IPR Agreement).[39] When both sides exchanged protocols, China submitted an "Action Plan for Effective Protection and Implementation of Intellectual Property Rights" as an Appendix to the 1995 IPR Agreement.

Under the 1995, IPR Agreement China made some important promises. First, China promised to protect and enforce IPR and render such protection and enforcement available to US nationals. The SPC would guide all levels of courts to deal with IP disputes, especially those related to the IPR of foreigners, as soon as possible. Second, the Action Plan, as made by the State Council, would come into effect immediately and become an enforcement mechanism in the long run. Third, China promised to allow US citizens and entities to set up joint ventures in China to produce and reproduce audiovisual products without imposing quotas, import licenses, or other restrictions on such products. Fourth, China would require public entities to use only legal computer software rather than copies of unauthorised software. Finally, from 1 June 1995 on, China and the United States would exchange information on IP enforcement regularly, which shall clarify the protection of US-related IPRs in China in great details. In a word, China was going to comply with the US's request regarding administration and enforcement of IP protection and market access of foreign IP products.[40] In return, the US government promised to withdraw its confirmation of the PRC as a

---

[38] 'Trade War Averted: Chinese Officials, Individuals Welcome Sino–US Copyright Accord', BBC Summary of World Broadcasts, Feb 28, 1995, part 3.

[39] PRC-US: Agreement Regarding Intellectual Property Rights, 26 February 1995, 34 *ILM* 881(1995).

[40] D. E. Sanger, 'Japan's Ghost in China Pact: US Tries to Avoid Old Trade Mistakes', *NYT*, 27 February 1995, Dl.

priority foreign country, terminate its investigation against China under the Special 301 Section, and lift the order of charging high customs on products exported from China.[41]

3.1.2.3.   The third Sino–US IP negotiations and the 1996 IPR Agreement

To a certain extent, the second Sino–US IP negotiations and the 1995 IPR Agreement pacified the dispute between China and the United States, as the Chinese government made positive attempts to improve its IP regime and protect the IPRs of US citizens. After a certain period of time, however, the United States maintained that China failed to carry out the substantial promises under the 1995 IPR Agreement, such as closing CD factories and delivering enforcement through Customs and the market access of IP products. Essentially, the measures that China had promised turned out again to be totally ineffective.[42] On 30 April 1996, the United States designated China again as a priority foreign country for its failure to protect IPRs[43] and threatened to impose approximately 2 billion US dollars' worth of trade sanctions on products exported from China.[44]

In return, China announced immediately a retaliatory sanction of a similar amount on American products.[45] At this time, China was taking active steps to close down infringing markets and products while expanding its market access for foreign IPRs.[46] As a result, in 1996, China and the United States held the third set of IP negotiations on how to implement the 1995 IPR Agreement. On 17 June 1996, both sides reached the third "eleventh-hour" Sino–US IP agreement,[47] whereupon

---

[41] S. Faison, 'US and China Sign Accord to End Piracy of Software Music Recordings and Film', *NYT*, 27 February 1995, A1.

[42] Massey, 'The Emperor Is Far Away', 235.

[43] R. W. Stevenson, 'US Cites China for Failing to Curb Piracy in Trade', *NYT*, 1 May 1996, D4.

[44] H. Cooper and K. Chen, 'US and China Announce Tariff Targets as Both Nations Step Up Trade Rhetoric', *Wall Str J*, 16 May 1996, A3.

[45] Ibid.

[46] K. Chen and H. Cooper, 'US and China Reach an Agreement, Averting Trade Sanctions by Both Sides', Wall St J, 18 June 1996, A2. S Faison, 'US China Agree on Pact to Fight Piracy', *NYT*, 18 June 1996, A1.

[47] PRC-US, China Implementation of the 1995 Intellectual Property Rights Agreement, 17 June 1996, at http://tcc.export.gov/Trade_Agreements/All_Trade_Agreements/exp_005361.asp.

both the United States and China gave up their trade retaliation plans.[48] At this time, the United States seemed to divert from its continuing coercive and strong-arm unilateral measures in the bilateral IP negotiation process. The United States, however, still placed China on its supervision list under Section 306.[49] Accordingly, if China was not strict in implementing the 1996 Sino–US IP agreement, the USTR could have directly imposed trade sanctions without launching a new round of investigative procedures.

3.1.3.   The Multilateral Trade Negotiations toward Acceding to the WTO

3.1.3.1.   China's earlier pursuit of the GATT membership

While negotiating with the United States on IP disputes, China was also trying to become a member of the WTO. In fact, China's pursuit of its membership in the global trade regime dated back to 1947 when the ROC acceded to the GATT, as one of the first signatories to the GATT, the predecessor of the WTO.[50] In March 1950, the Nationalist Regime of the ROC in Taiwan withdrew from the GATT.[51] China had no connection with the GATT until 1982, when the PRC was granted observer status in the GATT.[52] In 1984, China became a member of the Multi-fibre Agreement, which was unique in GATT-administered trade agreements and allowed membership to non-GATT members.[53] Meanwhile, China argued that the withdrawal of the Taiwan authority from the GATT was null and void because the Nationalist Regime ceased to be the legitimate government of China, and the government of the PRC had never consented to the withdrawal.[54]

As a result of its policy of Opening and Reforms, China formally filed an application to request "reinstatement" of its status as a Contracting

---

[48] Office of the USTR, Statement by Ambassador Barshefsky (17 June 1996), at www.clintonlibrary.gov/assets/storage/Research%20-%20Digital%20Library/ClintonAdmin HistoryProject/101–111/Box%20101/1756308-history-ustr-press-releases-june-august-1996.pdf.

[49] Office of the USTR, Special 301 Report Section 306, China, 05 January 2003, at www.ustr.gov/archive/document_Library/Reports_Publications/2003/2003_Special_301_ Report/Special_301_Report_Section_306.html.

[50] Q. Kong, *China and the World Trade Organization: A Legal Perspective* (Singapore: World Scientific Publishing, 2002), p. 4.

[51] Ibid.   [52] Ibid., p. 5.

[53] C. Li, 'Resumption of China's GATT Membership' (1987) 21 *JWT* 4, at 25–48.

[54] Ibid.

State of the GATT in 1986.[55] In accordance with the general accession guidelines, the GATT established a Working Party to deal with China's application and deliver a report with recommendations to the General Council in respect of China's accession protocols.[56] The General Council was then supposed to vote on China's accession: with an approval by two-thirds majority China would be able to accede to the GATT. However, this turned out to be a difficult process for China primarily on two grounds. First, China still embraced a socialist planned economy and a socialist legal system while declining a capitalist economy before 1992.[57] Second, the Tiananmen Movement in 1989 made the Working Party more cautious about China's political stability. Most important, as is illustrated earlier, the United States was very concerned with China's lack of effective IPR protection and was negotiating with China on the establishment of a sound copyright/IP system.

3.1.3.2.   The negotiations on China's WTO membership

This negotiation process was so long that China eventually failed to accede to the GATT before 1 January 1995, when the GATT was formally replaced by the WTO. Nevertheless, China required acceding to the WTO immediately, and a new Working Party on China's accession to the WTO was established, which was composed of the same members as the former Working Party during China's accession to the GATT.[58] At this time, accession to the WTO meant a series of bilateral negotiations with thirty-seven Member States of the WTO.[59] In a sense, the Sino–US IP negotiations as well as the agreement reached between them provided a precedent of finding solutions for many important issues that would have been obstacles to China's accession to the WTO. Further, the Sino–US IP negotiations also provided a prominent model for subsequent negotiations between China and other important Member States of the WTO, such as Canada and the EU.

Thus, although the Sino–US IP relationship dominated China's negotiations toward acceding to the GATT, a series of multilateral trade negotiations between China and the developed countries, including the

---

[55] Ibid.
[56] WTO, *Handbook on Accession to the WTO*, 'Chapter 4: The Accession Process — the Procedures and How They Have Been Applied', at www.wto.org/english/thewto_e/acc_e/cbt_course_e/c4s1p1_e.htm.
[57] P. K. Yu, 'From Pirates to Partners: Protecting Intellectual Property in China in the Twenty-First Century' (2000) 50 *Am U L Rev* 131, at 136–7.
[58] Kong, *China and the World Trade Organization*, pp. 6–7.   [59] Ibid., p. 7.

United States, the EU, Japan, and Canada, which aimed at China's accession to the WTO, were underway. As China was becoming one of the world's largest economic powers, China's accession would benefit all of the WTO Members, in that China's exploding economy would find its outlet through access to the global trade market. Mindful of the unpredictable economic and political impact of China's accession, the United States and the EU demanded that China take on WTO-plus obligations beyond those of other WTO members, while requesting China to adopt WTO-minus provisions, which prevented China from being entitled to certain rights granted to other WTO members.[60] The developed countries' protectionism was based on the perception that only such additional obligations could "level the playing field for their domestic industries in their home markets, as well as improve their access to the Chinese market."[61] This was exactly the underlying ground for extensive negotiations and disputes, as China fought against such WTO-plus and WTO-minus commitments. A central issue in this negotiation process was whether China could accede to the WTO as a developing country.

Why did China want so desperately to accede to the WTO as a developing country? Above all, the TRIPS Agreement, while mandating strict IP enforcement, gives developing countries certain privileges and flexibilities in implementing international minimum standards. For example, under Articles 7 and 8 of TRIPS, WTO dispute settlement bodies (DSB) are supposed to interpret TRIPS provisions in a way that allows Member States to better carry out their public policies and balance domestic interests. Articles 66 and 67 also impose obligations on developed countries to provide "technical assistance" to developing countries and require that developed countries provide incentives to encourage the transfer of necessary technology to developing countries.

There is, however, no uniform definition of developing countries under the WTO. In fact, although a country applying for accession may define itself as a developing country, other countries are entitled to make a counterargument and deny that country's request for developing country status.[62] Understandably, this tends to generate a complicated political

---

[60] J. Y. Qin, 'WTO-Plus Obligations and Their Implications for the World Trade Organization Legal System: An Appraisal of the China Accession Protocol' (2003) 37(3) *JWT* 483.

[61] M. D. Harpaz, 'China and the WTO: New Kid on the Developing Bloc?', Hebrew University of Jerusalem, Faculty of Law, Research Paper No. 2–07, 2007, p. 68, at www.ssrn.com/abstractid=961768.

[62] Harpaz, 'China and the WTO: New Kid on the Developing Bloc?', 5.

negotiation process that involves diverse interest balancing and bargaining. It was exactly the case when China endeavoured to negotiate with the existing members of the WTO, in particular with the United States and the EU, on its claim to be accorded the same treatment as other developing countries.[63] Whereas China relied on its per capita income to support its status as a developing country,[64] its negotiation partners disagreed on the basis of many contradictory facts such as China's overall economic scale, trading capacity, and foreign investment volume.[65]

Finally, after numerous rounds of harsh negotiations, China made some concessions and accepted a mixed result. On the consensus of all existing members, the PRC acceded to the WTO on 11 December 2001. In certain major areas, China was taken as a developing country, while in other areas including IP protection China was virtually treated as a developed country.[66] As China's chief negotiator said, in such areas China "had the capability to implement obligations as all WTO Members" so that it was "not necessary for China to enjoy preferential treatments to the developing countries."[67] Thus, China committed itself both to the substantive obligations to enforce the global IP standards and to the procedural obligations to be subjected to the WTO dispute settlement proceedings.

3.1.3.3. China's international law obligation of IP enforcement at the WTO

Ultimately, the undeniable economic potential of acceding to the WTO prompted China to accept the negotiation terms and fulfil some prerequisites before its accession. For instance, apart from accepting a number of WTO-plus commitments in agriculture, industrial subsidies, investment, or national treatment, China gave up the WTO-minus rights in areas such as antidumping and countervailing duties.[68] So far as IP was concerned, such conditions were even far beyond those that could

---

[63] GATT, China's Status as a Contracting Party: Communication from the People's Republic of China, L/6017 (14 July 1986).

[64] J. Nzelibe, 'The Case against Reforming the WTO's Enforcement Mechanism', Northwestern School of Law, Pub Law & Legal Theory, Series No. 07–12 2007, p. 32, at http://ssrn.com/abstracts=9801002.

[65] Harpaz, 'China and the WTO: New Kid on the Developing Bloc?', 71.   [66] Ibid., 14.

[67] Vice Minister Y. Long, Head of the Chinese Delegation, 'Address at the Sixteenth Session of the Working Party on China', 4 July 2001, at www.china-un.ch/eng/qtzz/wtothsm/t85632.htm.

[68] WTO, Accession Protocol of the People's Republic of China to the WFO, part I, sec. 10 (3), paras. 3, 7(3), and 12, WT/L/432 (10 November 2001) (Accession Protocol).

normally be imposed on a developing country. For one thing, in the negotiations China agreed not to enjoy the five-year grace period normally granted to developing countries – rather, China was required to implement and enforce IP laws immediately.[69] Moreover, in consideration of protection of undisclosed information under Article 39 of TRIPS, China accepted a TRIPS-plus obligation of providing a six-year period of such protection.

As a member of the WTO, China would have to comply with the fundamental WTO trade rules that encompass any requirements and conditions, as agreed on between members of the WTO. With regard to IP, China must conform to TRIPS in implementing its IP law. Thus, under international law China was obliged to revamp its national IP system, including its copyright laws, to be better adapted to the WTO system.[70] Whereas China had to overcome many difficulties in doing so, such a process of legal reforms was supposed to bring China's national copyright laws into harmony with the international copyright system.

In fact, as IP commitments are written into the WTO law, global IP topics moved from WIPO to the WTO, where more effective enforcement is expected. Although international copyright treaties prior to the TRIPS Agreement contained no enforcement provisions, the United States was able to rely on trade mechanisms such as agriculture, textiles, and tariff rate quotas in its trade negotiations with China to safeguard stronger copyright protection and ensure adoption of IP-related enforcement measures.[71] Although the initial Chinese national copyright system did not work well in enforcing the standards under the BC, TRIPS, which largely reproduces the substantive provisions of the BC and is backed by the WTO enforcement mechanism, was expected to be much more effective in obliging China to adopt stringent IP/copyright laws. As illustrated earlier, the United States employed unilateral trade measures and a coercive strategy under the Special 301 against China in the 1990s, which produced mixed results. By contrast, after China's accession to the WTO, more peaceful and rule-based negotiations took the upper hand because China would have to subject itself to the WTO's dispute settlement mechanism (DSM) which the United States had used extensively and effectively.

---

[69] Ibid., part I, § 2(A) (2), at 2.   [70] Ibid., Annex 1A, VI.

[71] D. E. Long, 'Copyright and the Uruguay Round Agreements: A New Era of Protection or an Illusory Promise?' (1994) 22 *AIPLA Q J* 531, at 534 n 4.

3.2. TRIPS as the New International Copyright Source for Advancing a Framework of National Access Rules toward the Free Flow of Information

Most of the substantive provisions of the BC are incorporated into TRIPS. These rules are, however, subject to the new guiding principles and treaty interpretation approaches under TRIPS. Notably, TRIPS crystallises certain efforts to facilitate A2K at more reasonable costs through a number of new balance-oriented, copyright-related provisions. These rules generate a bunch of flexibilities that WTO members may rely on to facilitate different interests, such as A2K at reasonable costs and the free flow of information. The following part will, therefore, focus on those A2K-oriented rules that may be most important for advancing a nation's existing framework of access rules.

3.2.1. *Principles Affecting Members' Pro-A2K Copyright Policy*

3.2.1.1. The principle for interpreting substantive provisions

Article 7 of TRIPS defines the objective of IPRs as contributing to knowledge transfer and "a balance of rights and obligations." Notable, what is enshrined in the provision is no longer a hortatory statement that the balance between the private interest in A2R and the public interest in A2K at reasonable costs "should" be an objective of the copyright system. Rather, this has turned into a peremptory norm and an interpretative approach that cannot be disregarded when applying the other provisions of TRIPS.[72] Yet, whereas the overriding part of TRIPS is composed of provisions that compel a mandatory application, a positivistic reading of this "should" provision renders its effect somewhat inferior to those of other "shall" provisions. This is well palpable in the WTO jurisprudence. In a patent-related dispute, the WTO Panel, which referred explicitly to Article 7, has decided against its interrelatedness with, and priority over, other relevant provisions.[73] Nevertheless, Article 7 has the full potential of being interwoven into the interpretative texture of copyright protection in the DSM, once the border between the private interest and the public interest under Article 7 is defined clearly.

---

[72] C. M. Correa, *Trade Related Aspects of Intellectual Property Rights: A Commentary on TRIPS* (Oxford: Oxford University Press, 2007), p. 94.
[73] WTO, Panel Report, *Canada–Patent Protection of Pharmaceutical Products*, WT/DS114/R, paras. 7.51–2, 17 March 2000 (*Canada–Pharmaceutical*).

Although the Doha Declaration refers to Article 7 of TRIPS only in the context of public health and patent law, the effect of Article 7 should not be confined to that dimension but be expanded to copyright as well.[74] It is true that the influence of Article 7 is expanding into the copyright scenario, as the WCT explicitly recognises the need for balance between the private interest and the public interest.[75] The normative framework of Article 7 complies with the most fundamental policy of copyright law in finding equilibrium between copyright owners' private interest in A2R for their contribution and the needs of the public for lowering the costs for A2K through copyright-protected works. Article 7, thus, betrays the effort to limit the *ultra vires* effect of strong copyright protection and an over-road approach in "renegotiate the overall balance of the Agreement."[76]

3.2.1.2.   The principle for creating procedural provisions

Article 8 of TRIPS further establishes the principles of the public interest and prevention of abuse of IPRs. Whereas Article 7 has an interpretative value in generating substantive provisions, Article 8 assumes procedural implications, which authorise members to realise those objectives through appropriate legal measures. Indeed, Article 8 is a "may" provision that deserves more emphasis in interpreting other provisions of TRIPS. It trumps, at least theoretically, any interpretation of TRIPS rules that aims to prevent members from framing national IP laws of favoring the public interest defined by Article 7.[77] Moreover, it provides the legal basis for members to adopt such policies that best fit with the local socioeconomic conditions.

According to Article 8, members are entitled to formulate or amend their copyright laws, where they deem necessary and where such laws are consistent with TRIPS.[78] Practically, this seems to leave members broad discretionary leeway in facilitating A2K at reasonable costs.[79] Further,

---

[74] M. Chon, 'Intellectual Property and the Development Divide' (2006) 27(6) *Cardozo L Rev* 2813, at 2895–901.

[75] WIPO Copyright Treaty, Pmbl., 20 December 1996, 36 *ILM* 65 (1997) (WCT).

[76] *Canada-Pharmaceutical*, paras. 7.25–6.

[77] WTO, Council for TRIPS, Submission by the Africa Group, Barbados, Bolivia, Brazil, Dominican Republic, Ecuador, Honduras, India, Indonesia, Jamaica, Pakistan, Paraguay, Philippines, Peru, Sri Lanka, Thailand and Venezuela on TRIPS and Public Health, IP/C/W/296 (19 June 2001).

[78] Agreement on Trade-Related Aspects of Intellectual Property Rights, Art. 8.1, footnote 3, Marrakesh, 15 April 1994, 33 *ILM* 1197 (1994) (TRIPS).

[79] Correa, *Trade Related Aspects of Intellectual Property Rights*, pp. 106–8.

members may take "appropriate measures" against abuse of authorial rights, unreasonable trade-restrictive practices, or acts that could adversely affect international technology transfer.[80] Indeed, both clauses reflect the substantive implications of the "objectives" as set forth in Article 7. This principle can be transformed into any enforcement mechanisms of the national copyright system where new access rules are needed.

3.2.2. The Idea/Expression Dichotomy as an A2K-Oriented Rule

Article 9(2) of TRIPS codifies, for the first time in the history of international copyright treaties, the idea/expression dichotomy, which determines the scope of human intelligence to be protected by copyright. In fact, the idea/expression dichotomy has transcended its own a priori intent of protecting computer programs and morphed into a universal principle that clarifies the question of copyrightability.[81] Accordingly, the substance of any copyrightable works is the "ordered expression of thought," whereas the idea encapsulated in the works that exist in any form of tangible medium (such as books or software) will not be protected.[82] This doctrine is engrained in the philosophy that the cost incurred by the dissemination of ideas is higher than that incurred by developing ideas.[83] It has served to draw the line between the subject matter eligible for copyright protection and the matter that will be left in the public domain.[84] Therefore, the idea/expression dichotomy represents an important rule for facilitating A2K. However, because it is difficult to differentiate unprotected ideas, procedures, methods, or mathematical concepts uniformly from the expressive form that shall be protected, members assume considerable latitudes in defining the border between the intellectual work eligible for protection and the material form of expression.[85]

---

[80] TRIPS, Art. 8.2.
[81] D. Gervais, *TRIPS: Drafting History and Analysis*, 3rd edn, (London: Sweet & Maxwell, 2008), p. 213.
[82] J. A. L. Sterling, *World Copyright Law*, 3rd edn (London: Sweet & Maxwell, 2008), pp. 248–9.
[83] W. M. Landes and R. A. Posner, 'An Economic Analysis of Copyright Law' (1989) 18 *J Legal Stud* 325, at 349–50.
[84] J. E. Cohen et al., *Copyright in a Global Information Economy* (New York: Aspen Publishers, 2006), p. 72.
[85] J. T. Füller, 'Art. 9.2', in P.-T. Stoll, J. Busche, and K. Arend (eds.), *WTO-Trade-Related Aspects of Intellectual Property Rights* (Leiden: Martinus Nijhoff, 2009), p. 250, at 250–1.

3.2.3. The Three-Step Test as a Pro-A2K Rule

3.2.3.1. A pro-A2K reading

Dwelling on Article 9(2) of the BC, Article 13 of TRIPS provides for a general exception rule to all exclusive rights under the BC that are incorporated into TRIPS, as well as to the new substantive rights under TRIPS. In that sense, Article 13 establishes a core framework for redistributing knowledge goods and restriking the balance between A2R and A2K. Certainly, the exception and limitation rules under TRIPS are merely permissible and optional, whereas TRIPS emphasises members' general obligation not to deviate from their obligations under the BC.[86] Indeed, Article 20 of the BC seems to have spawned the Berne-plus tenet that any subsequent copyright agreement must "grant more extensive rights" and may not be "contrary to" the BC. In this light, Article 13 of TRIPS qualifies members' power to establish statutory limitations and exceptions that could curtail A2R under national legislation.[87]

Practically, however, Article 13 allows for exceptions that cover the "entire *acquis*" of the incorporated Berne clauses, as the three-step test does not seek to impose additional restrictions to the existing limitation/exception rules under the BC.[88] On the contrary, the three-step test could justify those "implicit exceptions" of the aforementioned rights of translation, public performance, broadcasting and other communications, public recitation and adaptation under the BC, including the "minor exceptions."[89] Besides, one should not ignore the legislative intent behind a variety of Berne exceptions or the recent thriving appeal for promoting pro-A2K interests.[90] Even the WTO Panel referred to a systematic reading of Article 10 of the WCT, which suggests that the three-step test shall in no way restrict the existing Berne limitations and exceptions.[91] Such a flexible interpretative approach may contribute to facilitating A2K.

---

[86] TRIPS, Art. 2.2.
[87] WTO, Panel Report, *United States–Section 110(5) of the US Copyright Act*, WT/DS160/R, para. 6.97 (27 July 2000) (*US-Copyright*).
[88] Cf. M. Senftleben, *Copyright, Limitations and the Three-Step Test: An Analysis of the Three-Step Test in International and EC Copyright Law* (The Hague: Kluwer Law International, 2004), p. 88.
[89] *US–Copyright*, para. 6.63.   [90] Correa, pp. 139–42.
[91] WCT, Art. 10, agreed statements.

3.2.3.2.   "Certain special circumstances"

Regarding the first condition that the limitations and exceptions must be confined to "certain special cases," the WTO Panel of the dispute on *US–Copyright* supported a broad and literal threshold of "legal certainty,"[92] obviating the need to identify a public policy at this stage and deferring it to the other two steps.[93] The Panel adopted a case-by-case approach on the basis of "counting rights,"[94] as it did in other TRIPS-related disputes. Accordingly, the "quantity" of copies to be made was a decisive factor for determining whether it is a special case.[95] Thus, the Panel avoided examining the "quality" of such copies by rejecting any "special purpose" that might emanate from domestic public policies.[96] Such an interpretative approach, however, relied entirely on favouring A2R without taking A2K at reasonable costs into account.

3.2.3.3.   "Conflict with normal exploitation"

The second condition is that the limitations and exceptions may not "conflict with a normal exploitation" of the works. The *US–Copyright* Panel seems to endorse both an empirical and a normative approach,[97] though the Panel report subscribes more to the empirical approach on a purely economic basis.[98] In doing so, the Panel counted losses in terms of the number of works and potentially infringing acts[99] and embraces the need for compensation.[100] In fact, this interpretative approach still pertains to the quantity test and is consistent with the preparatory works of the 1967 Stockholm Conference,[101] in which case the normal use is gauged against any form of present and potential deprival of an author's income.[102] In contrast, a normative approach would have pinpointed the quality standards for such normal exploitation. Such an approach would go beyond that historical view and follow an "evolutive"

---

[92]   *US–Copyright*, para. 6.108.

[93]   S. Ricketson and J. C. Ginsburg, *International Copyright and Neighbouring Rights: The Berne Convention and Beyond*, 2nd edn (Oxford: Oxford University Press, 2006), p. 767.

[94]   G. B. Dinwoodie and R. C. Dreyfuss, *A Neofederalist Vision of TRIPS: The Resilience of the International Intellectual Property Regime* (Oxford: Oxford University Press, 2012), pp. 61–2.

[95]   WIPO, Records of the Intellectual Property Conference of Stockholm, Report of Main Committee I, 11 June to 14 July 1967, (2nd vol.), Doc. S/162, 1146 (1971) (Records 1967).

[96]   *US–Copyright*, para. 6.108.

[97]   Ricketson and Ginsburg, *International Copyright and Neighbouring Rights*, pp. 769–73.

[98]   *US–Copyright*, para. 6.183.   [99]   Ibid., paras. 6.180, 6.187 and 6.208.

[100]   Ibid., para. 6.166.   [101]   Records 1967, Doc. S/1, 112.

[102]   Senftleben, *Copyright, Limitations and the Three-Step Test*, p. 177.

approach,[103] that is, it would question whether certain kinds of copying acts *should* be treated as an exception to normal exploitation.[104] Where the *US-Copyright* Panel approach prevails, "a normal exploitation" of works would underpin A2R more than affordable A2K.

3.2.3.4.   "Unreasonable prejudice to legitimate interests"

The final condition that the limitation and exceptions do "not unreasonably prejudice the legitimate interests of the right holder" seems to leave still more flexibilities for members. Although Article 9(2) of the BC covers both pecuniary and nonpecuniary interests of the right holder, Article 13 of TRIPS may not cover the latter, that is, a copyright owner's personality interests.[105] The term *legitimate* should assume normative significance in restricting copyright protection to a certain extent,[106] which is in turn tempered by the term *reasonable*. The scope of any such restrictions, however, must be clarified. Whereas the original intent of the drafters of the term *legitimate* at the Stockholm Conference was to establish the principle of equitable remuneration,[107] it is submitted that "unreasonably prejudice" should be interpreted to follow the contemporary pro-A2K development in international copyright law.

In sum, the three-step test under Article 13 renders it possible to adopt a pro-A2K interpretative approach without prejudice to A2R. Even though the wording of Article 13 of TRIPS is different from that of Article 30 that refers to "the legitimate interests of third parties" in the protection of a patent, it does not preclude the protection of A2K at reasonable costs.[108] Dwelling on a rigid textual understanding of the provision would simply lead to a calculation of authorial interests in mathematic terms, which the Panel in *US–Copyright* also acknowledged to be "incomplete and thus conservative."[109] In fact, Articles 7 and 8 of TRIPS, which refer explicitly to the public interest in IP protection, do

---

[103] S. I. Štrba, *International Copyright Law and Access to Education in Developing Countries* (Leiden: Martinus Nijhoff, 2012), p. 74.

[104] J. C. Ginsburg, 'Toward Supranational Copyright Law? The WTO Panel Decision and the "Three Step Test" for Copyright Exemptions' (2001) 187 *RIDA* 3, at 17.

[105] Ricketson and Ginsburg, *International Copyright and Neighbouring Rights*, p. 774.

[106] Gervais, *TRIPS: Drafting History and Analysis*, pp. 240–1.

[107] This view was attributable to the Professor Ulmer and adopted by the Main Committee I. Records 1967, 1145–6.

[108] See, e.g., H. Sun, 'Overcoming the Achilles Heel of Copyright Law' (2007) 5 *Northwestern J Tech IP* 265, at 302.

[109] *US–Copyright*, para. 6.227.

not preclude such pro-A2K considerations in copyright-related interest balancing. Alone the titles of Articles 7 and 8, "objectives" and "principles," suggest that they should be applicable to the remaining TRIPS rules including the three-step test.

3.3. Controlling the Free Flow of Information: The Anti-A2K Enforcement of TRIPS through Access Rules under the 2001 Copyright Act

3.3.1. Enforcing New Copyright Standards in the Chinese Copyright System

3.3.1.1. Controlling A2K: the new balance needs at home

China's accession to the WTO highlighted a further deepening of the imbalance between the protection of domestic works and that of foreign works under the existing Chinese copyright system. As analysed earlier, the 1990 Copyright Act reflects legislators' purpose to dampen domestic authors' incentive to exercise their freedom of speech. Thus, for a period of time, double standards for the protection of domestic works and foreign works prevailed in China. The protection of foreign works was superior to that of domestic works, as most restrictions to copyright did not apply to foreigners. Prominent examples of such stark contrast lie in the free use of reprinting articles in other newspapers and periodicals, compulsory license for performing published works, broadcasting published recordings by broadcasting and television stations for nonbusiness purposes, most of which concern media control.

After China acceded to the WTO, however, the standards for IP protection granted to any member of the WTO must be accorded to nationals of all the other members as well according to the national treatment principle and the MFN treatment under TRIPS. This would mean that the aforementioned privileges in copyright protection of foreign works should be accorded to residents of Taiwan, Hong Kong, and Macao after they have acceded to the WTO with China together. If the 1990 Copyright Act still prevailed, then two different types of standards would be accorded to two different types of Chinese, which would definitely prejudice against the legitimacy of China's national copyright system. More important, the consciousness of ordinary Chinese citizens about copyright protection was enhanced considerably after two decades of economic reforms, as ordinary authors were trying to articulate their claims for being remunerated for producing intellectual works.

Moreover, rampant piracy activities reflected the lack of appropriate legal measures such as interlocutory injunctions or legal compensation for infringement. As a result, China was frequently accused of not complying with international copyright standards and had difficulties in its negotiations with foreign countries. Facing the challenges of enforcing TRIPS, it became essential for China to find out and smooth out the inconsistencies between the 1990 Copyright Act (and other supplementary regulations) and the international copyright treaties. Further, there was wide dissemination of unauthorised materials, including politically sensitive information in the rampant piracy activities. China tolerated piracy activities that contributed to A2K at lower costs for most Chinese before the middle of the 1990s because media control was more effective in the traditional technological and legal environment. In fact, an anti-A2R structure of the copyright law worked well to curb the proliferation of undesirable works. The situation changed, however, with the advent of new technologies such as the database, multimedia, and the Internet, which posed great challenges to the regulation and control of copyright industries ranging from journalism and publication to entertainment enterprises in China. Consequently, China made a shift from controlling free speech to controlling the free flow of information. This was done by a shift from suppressing copyright owners' A2R to heightening the cost of A2K by the general public.

3.3.1.2.   The drafting process of the 2001 amendment of the Copyright Act

The thorny task of drafting a new amendment of the Copyright Act was outstanding in China's legislative agenda. In 1996, the State Council of the PRC placed the task in its legislative plans and, under the support of a renowned team of copyright experts, started to draft the amendment. In 1998, the State Council submitted a proposal to the SCNPC concerning the amendment of the 1990 Copyright Act. While the proposal was being reviewed, two issues caused wide concern and debates. One was whether a broadcasting organisation should enjoy the free use of recordings without paying the right holder under Article 43 of the 1990 Copyright Act.[110] The other was whether transmitting works through the Internet should be protected as a copyright.[111] Both issues were related to the

---

[110]   M. Li et al. [李明山 等], *The Contemporary Chinese History of Copyright* [《中国当代版权史》](北京: 知识产权出版社, 2007), pp. 295–9.

[111]   Ibid., pp. 304–8.

question of disseminating information and media control in face of the development of new technologies.

There was, however, no precise answer to these questions at that time. In 1999, the State Council withdrew the proposal from the SCNPC to discuss the proposal further and clarify some technical questions.[112] At this time, the United States and China reached agreement on China's accession to the WTO after hard negotiations, and it became imminent for China to carry out its obligation under the WTO law to revise its IP laws and regulations thoroughly in accordance with TRIPS. This would require China to modify its former anti-A2R legislation that largely restricted copyright protection. Finally, at the 33rd Meeting of the State Council held on 22 November 2000, a formal draft for amending the 1990 Copyright Act was formulated and submitted to the SCNPC. Having been examined twice at the 19th and 21st Sessions of the SCNPC, respectively (in December 2000 and April 2001), the final draft was adopted at the 24th Session of the 9th SCNPC on 27 October 2001.

3.3.1.3.   The new national copyright system after the 2001 amendment

Although China's major task was to bring the Copyright Act in line with TRIPS, the substantive copyright provisions of the BC – except for the moral right under Article 6(2) – are incorporated into TRIPS. Certainly, such a revision was driven, in essence, by China's WTO obligation to enforce TRIPS and, ultimately, by the potential application of the DSM under TRIPS. On the surface, China's major challenge was how to balance A2R against A2K at reasonable costs, or how to correct the anti-A2R structure of the laws and regulations. The real concern, however, was how to carry on with the control of free expression as defined by the Chinese government through copyright law. The SCNPC, thus, endorsed certain principles for amending the 1990 Copyright Act.[113]

Accordingly, the amendment must cater to the "socialist market economy." China understood that copyright law is designed to protect the legitimate interests of creators in copyright-related economic activities

---

[112] Ibid., p. 293.
[113] NCB, Illustration to the Revision Draft of the Copyright Act of the PRC [《关于＜中华人民共和国著作权法修正案(草案)＞的说明》], 22 December 2000.

and that copyright legislation and enforcement would have a direct impact on the development of the cultural, publication, and software industries. However, the amendment must cater to the requirements embedded in the "socialist" market economy. Moreover, the amendment must facilitate "copyright internationalisation." Above all, the new amendment must address the enforcement issue, whereas the SCNPC stressed that the local needs of balancing different interests must be taken into account. Finally, the amendment must address the challenges arising from digital technology. As there were no laws and regulations that address these new communication technologies, it was an essential task for copyright law to do so.

To better implement the first amendment of the 1990 Copyright Act, the RICA was also revised and took effect on 15 September 2001.[114] For the same reason, the revision was done to the RPCS, which took effect on 1 January 2002. The copyright administration departments also had a clearer guide on how to impose administrative sanctions, after the NCB amended the MICAP in 2003 and 2009, respectively. Concerning the judicial protection of copyright, the SPC issued its Interpretation Concerning the Application of Laws in the Trial of Civil Disputes over Copyright [《最高人民法院关于审理著作权民事纠纷案件适用法律若干问题的解释》] in October 2002.

Due to the importance of digital technology and its effect on online copyright protection, China took active steps to adapt its national copyright system to the new technology. Although the 2001 amendment introduced merely one new provision for online protection, online copyright disputes multiplied prior to the amendment. In this regard, the SPC issued the Networks Copyright Interpretation as early as in December 2000, which was amended in 2003 and 2006, respectively. With respect to the administrative protection of online copyright, the NCB and the Ministry of Information Industry issued Measures for the Administrative Protection of Internet Copyright (MAPIC) [《互联网著作权行政保护办法》] on 30 April 2005. In May 2006 the State Council issued the Regulation on the Protection of the Right of Communication of Information on Networks [《信息网络传播权保护条例》/Information Network Regulation],[115] which was amended in 2013.

---

[114] Regulations for the Implementation of the Copyright Act of the PRC, 14 August 2002 (RICA).
[115] Regulations on the Protection of the Right of Communication of Information on Networks, 18 May 2006 (Information Network Regulation).

3.3.2.　General Access Rules that Reinforce A2R

The 2001 Copyright Act contains important amendments in terms of the principle of national treatment. First, whereas the 1990 Copyright Act allows "legal entities without legal personality" to enjoy copyright protection, the new amendments extend the scope to "other organisations" as a whole.[116] Second, so far as the protection of foreign works is concerned, the new amendments have taken "person without nationality" into account.[117] Third, foreign works not published in the PRC, which are not protected explicitly under the 1990 Copyright Act, enjoy protection under the amendments subject to certain agreements between China and the countries of which authors of such works are nationals.[118] Finally, the new amendments protect works of those who cannot be identified as one of the aforementioned categories (such as stateless person) subject to the conditions of a relevant international treaty with China.[119] In this sense, the new amendment has no more discrimination of nationalities with regard to A2R, but provides for national treatment in a way very close to that under the international copyright treaties.

As illustrated earlier, the 1990 Copyright Act provides an ambiguous and general definition of five categories of copyright. In contrast, the 2001 Copyright Act has made a major revision and improvement in this respect by advancing an all-rounded and nuanced definition of rights including: (l) the right of reproduction, (2) the right of distribution, (3) the right of rental, (4) the right of exhibition, (5) the right of performance, (6) the right of showing, (7) the right of broadcasting, (8) the right of communication of information on networks, (9) the right of making cinematographic work, (10) the right of adaptation, (11) the right of translation, (12) the right of compilation, and (13) any other rights a copyright owner is entitled to enjoy.[120] Article 10 of the new amendments also clarifies that those rights were economic rights, under which the right holder may authorise another person to exercise or assign, partially or entirely, to another person and are under both circumstances entitled to remuneration. The expanded palette of economic rights inoculate copyright owners against potential infringement in a legislative sense.

---

[116]　The Copyright Act of the PRC, Art. 2(1), adopted 7 September 1990, revised 27 October 2001 (2001 Copyright Act).
[117]　Ibid., Art. 2(2) and (3). 　　[118]　Ibid., Art. 2(2). 　　[119]　Ibid. 　　[120]　Ibid., Art. 10.

3.3.3.   Access Rules with the Potential of Restricting A2K

3.3.3.1.   The neighbouring rights burdened by media control

The ideas in intellectual works cannot reach the public unless such works are disseminated as knowledge goods. Professional individuals and entities, such as publishers, performers, broadcasters, and producers of films, readily do so, while their works are protected, respectively, to allow them to have A2R. The rights granted to them, as illustrated earlier, are often referred to as neighbouring rights, which may have considerable implications for A2K and affect the dissemination of works (and, thus, freedom of the media). Although A2R has been strengthened under the 2001 amendments, the neighbouring rights are burdened by the government's policy of media control.

3.3.3.1.1.   The performer's right   In respect of the performer's right, the 2001 Copyright Act has reinforced the protection of A2R in comparison with the 1990 Copyright Act. Indeed, the amendments have strengthened the protection of authors' remuneration because performers and performing organisations shall obtain permission from and pay remuneration to the author not only in the case of commercial performance but also in any case where a performance is carried out on the basis of the author's works.[121] However, because the government controls the circulation of traditional works in terms of Article 4 of the Copyright Act, performance is only a derivative means of disseminating such works. Based on this logic, the amendments safely expanded the scope of the performer's economic rights. For example, the performers are entitled to receive remuneration in the case of authorising others to make live broadcasts and public transmission, to make audio and video recordings, to reproduce or distribute such recordings, and to communicate the performance to the public on information network.[122]

3.3.3.1.2.   The recorder's right   Moreover, the 2001 Copyright Act has also enhanced the protection of the recorder's right. Notably, the recorder may affect potential A2K by the general public in a more influential dimension than the performer, in which case social control is more urgent. Originally, Article 37 of the 1990 Copyright Act allows the recorder who produces a video recording to record published works without asking for permission from the right holder. In contrast, the

---

[121] Ibid., Art. 36(1).   [122] Ibid., Art. 37(2).

2001 Copyright Act confines this privilege only to the circumstance where music works that have been duly made into a sound recording are used.[123] Thus, whereas the protection of published works and copyright owners' interest in A2R are strengthened, the revision ensures, practically, that only those works that have survived censorship can be used freely.

3.3.3.1.3. The broadcaster's right   By the end of the 1990s, broadcasters such as radio or TV stations had played an essential role in affecting A2K by the public in a most influential way in China. The 2001 amendments have rendered different types of broadcasters' rights more distinct. For instance, Article 43 of the 1990 Copyright Act is, virtually, equivalent to a compulsory license that grants free use to the broadcaster for facilitating the public interest at home. To align this provision with China's obligation under TRIPS, the 2001 Copyright Act alleviates the restriction in the former provision by removing the wording "for non-commercial purposes" and requiring the payment of remuneration to the copyright owner.[124] However, although the revision seems to extend copyright owners' A2R in this respect, the remuneration is subject to the specific regulation set forth by the State Council.[125] Indeed, the remuneration of copyright owners makes part of the system of administrative IP enforcement, where there are already a number of censorship regulations in place.[126]

In fact, the amendments in the 2001 Copyright Act have tightened the control of A2K by restricting the dissemination of copyright-protected works at the broadcaster's level. Article 42 of the 1990 Copyright Act grants radio or television stations the right to receive remuneration for authorising others to use the programs produced by the station itself. The 2001 Copyright Act, however, simply allows such broadcasters to prohibit the use of their programs (not necessarily produced by themselves) without their consent,[127] but fails to provide explicitly for their right to receive remuneration. This provision curbs broadcasters' incentive to make profits by disseminating information products and fits into relevant censorship regulations, which require

---

[123] Ibid., Art. 39(3).   [124] Ibid., Art. 43.
[125] See, e.g., Regulations on Broadcasting and Television Administration of the PRC, done on 1 August 1997, revised on 7 December 2013 [RBTA].
[126] The 2001 Copyright Act, Art. 43.   [127] Ibid., Art. 44(1).

media actors to conduct censorship and prohibit dissemination of certain information on request by state organs.[128]

Further, the protection of cinematographic works is geared to the censorship regime as well. By the end of the 1990s, the use of cinematographic, television, or videographic works had been widely in use in China. As such, the Chinese government issued relevant censorship regulations in the field of movies in 2001.[129] For this reason, it was necessary to make corresponding revisions in copyright law. In comparison with Article 44 of the 1990 Copyright Act, the 2001 amendments take into account the protection of a new subject matter, that is, "works created by virtue of an analogous method of film production and video graphic works," and clarifies the obligation to pay remuneration to the right holder of videographic works.[130] Although the protection of these works ensures A2R, the circulation of these works is subject to Article 4 of the Copyright Act, which justifies the application of the censorship regulations in the case of movie works.

3.3.3.2. Free use overshadowed by media control

By granting free use without permission from or remuneration to the right holder, some of the limitation and exception rules under Article 22 of the 1990 Copyright Act derogate so much from the standards under the BC that the doctrine of free use could be interpreted only in a vague and almost unlimited manner. These extensive and vague definitions of free use aim to impose restrictions on publication more than to protect copyright. The 2001 amendments no longer adopt such an anti-A2R structure of copyright law, but bring forth changes to align the fair practice with the international copyright treaties by limiting the scope and extent of the doctrine of free use. These rules, however, are overshadowed by the policy of media control and assume anti-A2K potential.

On the one hand, the doctrine of free use seems to endorse the practice relating to freedom of the media. Article 22(3) of the 1990 Copyright Act allows free "use of published works in newspapers, periodicals, radio programs, television programs or newsreels for the purpose of reporting current events." Indeed, Article 10*bis* (2) of the BC allows for pro-A2K

---

[128] For regulations on censorship and self-censorship in broadcasting and television stations, see, e.g., RBTA, Arts. 33 and 43.

[129] Regulations on the Administration of Movies [《电影管理条例》], Art. 25, 12 December 2001 [RAM].

[130] The 2001 Copyright Act, Art. 45.

practices, as long as they are justified by "informatory purposes." Nevertheless, the new amendments permit only "reuse or citation, for any unavoidable reason" of such works for the purpose of reporting.[131] Moreover, Article 22(4) of the 1990 Copyright Act allows "reprinting by newspapers or periodicals, or rebroadcasting by radio stations or television stations, of editorials or commentators' articles published by other newspapers, periodicals, radio stations or television stations." This seems to be justified by Article 10bis (1) of the BC. The new amendments now allow such reproduction of "articles on current issues relating to politics, economics or religion" published by other media only if the author has not forbidden the reprinting and rebroadcasting.[132]

On the other hand, the doctrine of free use is still largely subject to the government's policy of maintaining social control. By the end of the twentieth century (before the Internet became really a universal device), almost all the media facilities in China were state-owned and subject to strict control of censorship. Thus, free use of copyright-protected materials for journalism may not help facilitate the freedom of media considerably. Further, the need to maintain social control through the suppression of A2R is still palpable, though it may be checked to some extent by the need to strengthen the protection of A2R. Indeed, while Article 22(7) and (9) of the 1990 Copyright Act allows free use by government institutions simply "for the purpose of fulfilling official duties," the new amendments have qualified such use "within a reasonable scope."[133]

It is, however, often hard to differentiate commercial use from non-commercial use of such copyright-protected works. In the 2007 *Hu* case,[134] a journalist brought an action against a government institution at the Beijing Haidian District People's Court for copyright infringement relating to the "public interest" under Article 22(7). The defendant used one of the plaintiff's published articles as reading material in a national examination without permission from the author or referring to the author's name. The Court confirmed the plaintiff's authorship, but held that the defendant can exploit a work without permission from or paying remuneration to the copyright owner because the defendant used the plaintiff's work for noncommercial purposes. The Court also found that

---

[131] Ibid., Art. 22(3).   [132] Ibid., Art. 22(4).   [133] Ibid., Art. 22(7).
[134] *Hu v. National Examination Centre of the Ministry of Education* [胡浩波诉教育部国家考试中心侵犯著作权纠纷案], Beijing Haidian District People's Court, (2007) Hai Min Chu Zi [海民初字] No. 16761, 20 November 2007.

the public interest is more important than the private interest, so that the government may use such works in a way as it deems necessary. By contrast, in the 2007 *Hu* case,[135] the same plaintiff sued several publishers for compiling the examination materials that contained the same copyright-protected article at the Beijing Xicheng District People's Court. The Court found that the defendants infringed the plaintiff's copyright on the ground that the defendants were conducting commercial activities.

Further, media control through copyright regulation concerns China's policy of minority nationalities. Article 22(11) of the 1990 Copyright Act allows "translation of published works from the Han language into minority nationality languages for publication and distribution within the country." This represents the government's goal of infusing the mainstream ideologies to the ethnic nationalities in China. Certainly, this provision is not applicable to foreign works but addresses the special situation in China. Therefore, this provision has been retained in the new amendments, though it is slightly modified as permitting such translation of such works by a "Chinese citizen, legal entity or any other organisation."[136]

3.3.3.3.   The compulsory license: A2K beyond commercial purposes?

Based on the model of the Berne Appendix, the 2001 amendments have established two types of compulsory license. The first type concerns traditional copyright. In particular, Article 23 provides for the rules regarding the public interest of education, allowing certain works to "be compiled into textbooks without the authorisation from the authors" subject to other conditions such as ensuring the authors' A2R. Further, the amendments allow newspaper or periodical publishers to reprint a work published in another newspaper or periodical on the condition of paying remuneration to the copyright owner.[137] The second type of compulsory license concerns neighbouring rights. The amendments grant compulsory license to producers of sound recordings to exploit music works that another person has duly made into a sound recording,[138] while allowing radio or television stations to broadcast published works created

---

[135] *Hu v. Yanbian Publishing House et al.* [胡浩波诉延边大学出版社等侵犯著作权纠纷案], Beijing Xicheng District People's Court, (2007) Xi Min Chu Zi [西民初字] No. 0962, 10 December 2007.
[136] The 2001 Copyright Act, Art. 22(11).   [137] Ibid., Art. 32(2).   [138] Ibid., Art. 39(3).

by another person or a published sound recording.[139] In such circumstances, users do not have to seek permission from, but shall pay remuneration to, the copyright owner, unless the copyright owner has explicitly
forbidden such exploitation.

It must be noted, however, that the establishment of compulsory license
does not amount to buttressing free speech or the free flow of information
in a real sense, even though the compulsory license seems to ensure A2R.
The compulsory license involves both published works in traditional forms
and media products in the entertainment industry, which concern, to a
large extent, the commercial use of copyright-protected works. In China,
however, the border between commercial and noncommercial use of
works is blurred not only by the vague definition in legislative acts, but
also by the practice of reusing commercial works for noncommercial
purposes. For this reason, China has imposed an even stricter censorship
regime that sorts out potentially offensive works, regardless of their commercial nature.

For instance, the Provisions on the Administration of Movies provide
for an overall censorship system in the charge of the SARFT.[140] Over the
decades, the SARFT has banned the dissemination and circulation of
numerous films that seemed to be directed at the commercial markets for
fear of causing irritating consequences to the Party-state. Such films,
though with commercial titles, were, *inter alia*, suspected of containing
elements that criticise the political, judicial, or social system of the PRC;
allude to sensitive historical events, such as the Cultural Revolution, the
Tiananmen Movement, or other political movements in the PRC; portray
the democratic events or movements of other countries; smear the image
of the Chinese or decorate that of the Japanese; or reflect a critical view of
the current educational system or any miserable existence in the Chinese
society. In such practice of regulating the free flow of information in the
cultural market, China's copyright policy is attuned to the censorship
regime. Copyright protection, at this stage, appears to be pro-A2R, but
anti-A2K.

3.3.4.   The Anti-A2K Mechanism of Administrative
Copyright Enforcement

The seemingly pro-A2R amendments are incompatible with the Chinese
government's former policy of suppressing the incentive to produce and

---

[139] Ibid., Arts. 42(2) and 43.   [140] RAM, Art. 23.

disseminate ideas freely. To maintain the control of free expression, a balance can be reached only by thwarting the public interest in affordable A2K. Whereas the legislation aims to enforce the international copyright standards, only by imposing an anti-A2K structure on access rules would the government be able to effectuate censorship. This is done, above all, by empowering the copyright administrative departments at various levels to enforce copyright protection in terms of the public interest. The administrative enforcement, together with copyright enforcement by the judicial authorities, envisions a dualistic system of copyright enforcement in the PRC.

3.3.4.1. The public interest provision

Since the beginning of its copyright law making, China has been issuing a number of administrative regulations concerning copyright protection. Article 46 of the 1990 Copyright Act grants copyright administrative departments the authority to enforce copyright protection by imposing on copyright infringers administrative penalties, such as confiscating unlawful income and imposing a fine. In a sense, administrative sanctions may be even more effective in enforcing copyright protection than judicial decisions, considering China's long tradition that the executive branch assumed quasi-judicial functions. Moreover, the spontaneous campaigns launched by administrative authorities, which aim to crack down on piracy activities, provide an expedient instrument of addressing the international pressure for China to improve copyright protection. Thus, administrative enforcement represents a specific approach in Chinese copyright law that endorses both quasi-judicial and campaign-oriented functions of administrative authorities.

Article 47 of the 2001 amendments upgrades such an important regime that allows copyright administrative departments to adopt more influential measures of administrative enforcement. Copyright administrative enforcement is triggered by the fact that the infringer(s) have violated both the private interest and the public interest [同时损害公共利益].[141] The 2001 Copyright Act, however, does not clarify what will be classified as the "public interest." Presumably, it may not only refer to A2K at reasonable costs, but also cover up censorship as implied in Article 4 of the Copyright Act, as one could deduce reasonably that the government will enforce this provision. Although the 2001 Copyright Act

---

[141] The 2001 Copyright Act, Art. 47(1). The Copyright Act of the PRC, Art. 48, revised 26 February 2010.

must correct the anti-A2R practice under the 1990 Copyright Act that burdens copyright protection with overdue restrictions, the government's interest in controlling the dissemination of ideas (A2K) through censorship has remained intact. As China was obliged to introduce more effective enforcement measures to facilitate copyright protection, it would have to find alternative legitimate bases to shelter and justify censorship in copyright law to inhibit the free flow of information effectively. This task would now be supported by the public interest enforcement provision.

In addition to the equivocal definitions of the public interest under Article 47 of the Copyright Act, the law confers power on local authorities to take actions against any copyright infringement.[142] The MICAP seems to confine such power to those circumstances where "the public interest" is violated without defining it.[143] So it is with Article 11 of the MAPIC. Besides, other laws and regulations can define such illegal copyright-related acts,[144] which could further add to the power of copyright administrative authorities in cracking down on "piracy activities." Notably, the major authorities, which are empowered to carry out copyright administrative enforcement,[145] are also the authorities that oversee the duty of censorship at various levels of the government. The GAPP/NCB, for example, is in charge of publication, copyright, and news reporting.[146] Thus, these administrative departments will follow the censorship regulations when enforcing copyright protection.

The mechanism of copyright administrative enforcement makes it more convenient for government authorities to carry out censorship and prevent those censored works from being disseminated. Because relevant government departments are all placed in the censorship-dominating framework, such a regime ensures the materialisation of censorship before any meaningful administrative or judicial enforcement measures are carried out. This is even corroborated by the SPC, the highest judicial authority of the PRC, which ruled on the relationship between censorship and the copyrightability of a work. The SPC confirmed that courts should

---

[142] Ibid., Arts. 47 and 48. RICA, Arts. 36 and 37.
[143] NCB, Measures for the Implementation of Copyright Administrative Punishment, Art. 3 (1), 7 May 2009 (MICAP).
[144] Ibid., Art. 3(2) and (3).
[145] Other government authorities that conduct administrative enforcement include the MOC and the SARFT. M. Dimitrov, *Piracy and the State: the Politics of Intellectual Property Rights in China* (Cambridge: Cambridge University Press, 2012), pp. 126–9.
[146] Ibid., p. 127.

grant copyright protection to the work in question only on the condition that the relevant censorship department had conducted content review and approved the publication of the work.[147] In other words, the SPC clarified that the prerequisite for any enforcement of copyright protection is that the work survives censorship by relevant institutions of the State. Obviously, the administrative copyright enforcement must be subject to censorship, whose purpose is to prevent the free flow of information to the public (A2K).

3.3.4.2.   The anti-A2K quasi-judicial interpretation of the public interest in copyright enforcement

Such an anti-A2K approach underlies the practice of the copyright administrative authorities in exercising its quasi-judicial functions, where the public interest under Article 47 of the 2001 Copyright Act remains a vaguely defined concept. In 2001, Tenai Textile Decoration Trade Co. Ltd [特耐纺织装饰贸易有限公司]] filed a case to the Guangdong Copyright Bureau, claiming that Xiqiao Henghui Printing Factory [西樵恒辉印花厂] made copies of their artwork "Tingting Yuli" [亭亭玉立] in decorating the textile for commercial purpose without Tenai's permission. The Guangdong Copyright Bureau then ordered Xiqiao to cease infringement and destroy the textiles with infringing copies, while confiscating its illegitimate profits.[148] Xiqiao brought an action against the Bureau, arguing that the administration was not entitled to intervene because there was no damage to the public interest as provided under Article 47 of the Copyright Act. Although Xiqiao admitted its infringing act that concerned Tenai's private interest on a small scale, the plaintiff questioned the impact of such acts on the public interest.

The defendant, Guangdong Copyright Bureau, claimed that Xiqiao's infringing act disturbed the fair competition, brought about chaos in the economic order, and discouraged cultural creativity. The defendant also tried to establish a link between copyright infringement and economic and social order, thus incorporating A2R into the public interest. The Guangzhou Dongshan District People's Court endorsed such a view.

---

[147] See SPC, Letter from the Supreme People's Court to the Hunan Province Higher People's Court in *Zheng Haijin* v. *Xu Zheng Xiong and Tianjin People's Publishing House* [《最高人民法院关于郑海金与许正雄、天津人民出版社等著作权侵权纠纷案的函》], Zhi Jian Zi (1998) [知监字] No. 33, 9 March 2000.

[148] Guangdong Copyright Bureau, Administrative Punishment Decision [行政处罚决定书], 粤权(案) [2002] No. 2.

Xiqiao, however, appealed to the Guangzhou Intermediate People's Court and argued that such reasoning was too general to be convincing. Indeed, following the logic of the defendant, almost all copyright infringements could bring damage to fair competition and the economic order. According to Xiqiao, the public interest was equivalent to the fundamental values of the public order and should be understood in terms of common rather than individual interests. Accordingly, administrative authorities are only entitled, under Article 47, to deal with large-scale copyright infringements that might affect the public interest. In contrast, the administration simply maintained that it was entitled to handle any copyright infringement cases regardless of the scale or amount of the infringements. Unfortunately, the intermediate court supported the defendant in this respect.

It is easy to cast doubt on the standpoint of the administration and the courts in linking the public interest under Article 47 with A2R.[149] The term of the public interest in the context of copyright law refers generally to the interest of the public in having A2K at reasonable costs. By contrast, the public interest invariably connotes "socialist values" in connection with state security, as long as the provision is subject to interpretation by Chinese government authorities in charge of both copyright protection and censorship. The courts' approach in *Xiqiao*, for instance, was to adopt an overbroad interpretation of the public interest and disregard its distinction from the private interest. Where the courts fail to differentiate between A2R and A2K, it becomes easier for the government to cover up its real intention to maintain censorship in enforcing copyright protection. Such is an anti-A2K approach that serves to offset the potential impact of reinforcing copyright owners' A2R and encouraging intellectuals to create free ideas.

3.3.4.3.   The anti-A2K campaigns of copyright enforcement

In carrying out administrative enforcement, relevant administrative authorities often deal with two situations. In the case of quasi-judicial enforcement, copyright owners may, with proof of ownership and evidence of copyright infringement, submit a request to the copyright administration authorities for administrative protection.[150] Alternatively, relevant administrative departments may launch piracy-directed campaigns and

---

[149] See, e.g., R. H. Yang [杨瑞华], 'The First Case on Harming the Public Interest' ['损害"公共利益"第一辩案']2004 (3) *Modern Towns* [《现代乡镇》] 24.

[150] MICAP, Art. 12.

detect copyright infringement on their own. In both cases, the authorities may require suspected infringers to provide evidence that they've been authorised lawfully to make copies or may give them a specific period of time to do so.[151] Where the suspected infringers fail to produce such evidence, or the authorities confirm such illegal acts, they may correct or put an end to such infringing acts, confiscate any infringing copies, investigate, or gather evidence.[152] In a word, these authorities may establish a prima facie case in carrying out the administrative enforcement of copyright protection.

Presumably, such a spontaneous means of administrative enforcement of copyright protection contributes to the government's anti-A2K practice in the name of the public interest. In particular, this is accomplished through the campaigns of "Anti-pornography and Anti-illegal Publications" [扫黄打非], which aim at eliminating certain pirated publications.[153] When such campaigns started in 1989, they were directed far less at piracy than at preserving the public interest of eliminating pornographic and politically offensive publications.[154] In the middle of the 1990s when China was under great pressure in its international trade negotiations (particularly with the United States), China relied more heavily on irregular campaigns and raids to combat piracy as well because most of such banned publications were pirated products.[155] Although their frequency, duration, and locations vary considerably, such campaigns, often dubbed different working titles, have continued to exist despite their capricious nature.

Although the role of such campaigns in combating piracy used to be ancillary (compared with the function of censorship), the situation has changed considerably. Since the end of the 1990s, the campaigns have become a major instrument of combating piracy.[156] However, the campaigns still play a substantial role in effectuating censorship, which may explain why public security departments, instead of copyright administrative authorities, are the dominant participator in enforcing such raids on piracy.[157] In fact, these campaigns are launched and organised by the "Anti-pornography and Anti-illegal Publications Working Office," an organ that is led jointly by dozens of institutions of the CCP and

---

[151] Ibid., Art. 16.   [152] Ibid., Art. 15.
[153] See China Anti-pornography and Anti-illegal Publications Net [全国扫黄打非网], at www.shdf.gov.cn/.
[154] Dimitrov, *Piracy and the State*, p. 228.   [155] Ibid., pp. 229–30.   [156] Ibid., p. 230.
[157] Ibid., p. 232.

government authorities, including the Publicity Department of the Central Committee of the CCP, the Commission of Politics and Law of the Central Committee of the CCP, the GAPP, the SARFT, the MOC, and so on.

Officially, the mission of this working office is to carry out the "ideological struggle,"[158] which contains profound implications of content review of the publications. By combining the censorship and the combat against piracy, such nationwide campaigns seem to assume a legitimate nature and provide China with a good bargaining chip in international IP negotiations. In that connection, the campaigns have become an important and effective instrument of exercising censorship in the name of combating piracy. This can be substantiated by a comparison of relevant statistics released recently by the said Working Office concerning the campaigns of anti-pornography and anti-illegal publications:

In 2014, the Working Office cooperated with other government authorities including the Ministry of Public Security and started to conduct a campaign of "Purifying the Internet 2014" [净网2014], which lasted for six months and covered campaigns on the Internet nationwide.[159] Around 8,300 cases of illegal publications were reported with about 2,700 copyright infringement cases and 840 cases of pornographic publications.[160] Although the nature of the rest of the cases of illegal publications is not revealed, the statistics released show that these "other cases" involve publications, such as religious materials produced on the basis of copies downloaded from foreign websites and sold around the country.[161] These cases of illegal publications can, however, by no means be neglected because they make up more than half of the entire cases of illegal publications.

In fact, it is widely reported that, during this campaign of "Purifying the Internet," a large number of websites that were suspected of

---

[158] GAPP, LIU Binjie: the Work of "Anti-pornography and Anti-illegal Publications" Must Follow Five Key Points Strictly ['柳斌杰: "扫黄打非"工作要严把"五个关口"'], 11 January 2012, at www.gov.cn/gzdt/2012-01/11/content_2042269.htm.

[159] See 'Anti-Pornographic and Anti-Illegal Publications, Purifying the Internet 2014' ['扫黄打非净网2014'], at www.xinhuanet.com/legal/shdf/.

[160] 'The Anti-Pornographic and Anti-Illegal Publications Working Office Releases Ten Significant Statistics of Anti-Pornographic and Anti-Illegal Publications in 2014' ['全国扫黄打非办公布2014扫黄打非十大数据'], Xinhua Net, 25 December 2015, at http://news.xinhuanet.com/legal/2014-12/25/c_1113778449.htm.

[161] The Case of Producing Illegal Religious Publications in Xinjiang Hetian on the 13th of March and Selling Them across Provinces [新疆和田"3·13"跨省区制贩非法宗教出版物案], see Ibid.

containing pornographic and illegal content were blocked.[162] Most influential Internet media facilities in China, such as *Sina*, *Baidu*, *Tencent,* and *Netease* were obliged to conduct content review of their websites.[163] Even the most widely used peer-to-peer software in China, including WeChat, launched self-censorship programmes among its users.[164] More recently, the Chinese government has declared that it is determined to continue to carry out this campaign in the following years.[165] Although piracy activities might facilitate A2K at lower costs in a totalitarian state, such copyright enforcement campaigns, under the cloak of Article 47 of the Copyright Act, provide the Chinese government with a legitimate basis to conduct censorship in the name of safeguarding the public interest.

3.4.   An Evaluation of the Access Rules under the 2001 Copyright Act against TRIPS

Whereas TRIPS recognises copyright/IPR as a private right, the 2001 amendments remain as silent about the nature of copyright as the 1990 Copyright Act. Clearly, this shows that, after so many international negotiations have taken place and bilateral/multilateral treaties have been signed, China is still reluctant to give up openly the socialist legal doctrine that copyright should not be privatised, even though China has embraced a market economy and claimed to undertake enforcement of international copyright standards. Accordingly, the right holder is entitled to "hold" certain categories of rights granted to them by the State, but cannot entirely "own" such rights. In other words, copyright is not recognised as a human right by nature in China, but endowed on Chinese citizens by the socialist state through its IP legislation. These

---

[162] 'In the Campaign of Purifying the Internet 1222 Pornographic Websites Have Been Dealt with' ['净网行动处理淫秽色情网站1222家'], *People's Daily* [《人民日报》], 21 June 2014.

[163] 'China Internet Association Advocates the Sharing of a Common Black List to Combat Online Pornographic Information' ['中国互联网协会倡议建立黑名单共享机制 抵制网络淫秽色情信息'], Xinhua Net, 23 April 2014, at http://news.xinhuanet.com/legal/2014-04/23/c_1110375964.htm.

[164] 'Seven Instantaneous Telecommunication Companies Launched Rectifying Measures to Echo the Specific Campaign of Regulating the Internet' ['全国七大移动即时通信商启动整顿措施响应移动互联网治理专项行动'], Xinhua Net, 30 May 2014, at http://news.xinhuanet.com/legal/2014-05/30/c_1110927841.htm.

[165] 'LIU Qibao: Building a Cleaner Cultural Domain in Online and Offline Environment' ['刘奇葆: 营造更加清朗的网上网下文化空间'], Xinhua Net, 19 January 2015, at http://news.xinhuanet.com/legal/2015-01/19/c_1114051457.htm.

doctrines are guaranteed by enforcing copyright protection through both judicial and administrative organs.

Based on these doctrines, the national copyright system of the PRC became the government's instrument of realising its social and cultural policies. Before the 2001 amendments were adopted, foreign and domestic works enjoyed different treatment. Whereas the law justified the need to prioritise the public interest in A2K at reasonable costs, more restrictions were imposed on the protection of domestic works than on that of foreign works. Nonetheless, as the public interest is defined by the government, it is not difficult, then, to prioritise censorship and impose restrictions on the dissemination of domestic works. This approach enabled the government to control the incentive to produce any ideas that were apt to be disseminated to the rest of the Chinese society.

After China acceded to TRIPS, however, China must enforce copyright protection as a rule-based trade principle and implement the most fundamental rules as incorporated into TRIPS, that is, the national treatment and the minimum standards under the BC, as well as those new provisions under TRIPS. This means that China must modify its previous anti-A2R legislative practice, which granted different treatment to foreign works and domestic works and imposed overdue restrictions on copyright owners' A2R. In other words, the government can no longer justify the priority of censorship in the name of favouring the public interest in rendering A2K at lower costs. Rather, China is not only obliged but also willing to enforce the standards for copyright protection in accordance with TRIPS to legitimise its restrictions on A2K in copyright law.

3.4.1. National Treatment in Place: The Starting Point for Reinforcing A2R

Concerning the guiding principles under TRIPS, the 2001 amendments endorse national treatment as a universal principle. The legal effect of Article 2 of the amendments even overlaps with the MFN treatment under Article 4 of TRIPS. The MFN treatment, though not a traditional copyright principle, mandates that favourable conditions granted to one member be extended to other members as well. Article 2 of the 2001 Copyright Act protects foreign works and ensures that their authors can equally claim copyright protection under Chinese law. Through such an overall revision, the previous unequal treatment regarding domestic and foreign works under the 1990 Copyright Act and the RIICC has been eliminated. In a word, national treatment is the starting point in the new amendments, which improves the status of domestic copyright owners in enjoying A2R at the same level as foreign copyright owners.

3.4.2. Enforcing the Minimum Standards: The Potential of Restricting A2K

In enforcing its obligations under TRIPS, China looked readily to the minimum standards and managed to render the amendments consistent with TRIPS. Thus, the 2001 Copyright Act turns out to impose fewer restrictions on copyright owners' A2R than the 1990 Copyright Act, whereas the real policy goal aims to suppress the free flow of information by enhancing the costs for A2K. Above all, the 2001 amendments specify a variety of economic rights formerly prescribed by the 1990 Copyright Act. As such, the new amendments adopt the definitions of some rights under the RICA and provide for a number of new rights, such as the rental right, the right to play, the right to broadcast, and the right to communicate through networks. Besides, Article 43 of the 1990 Copyright Act, which allows broadcasters and TV stations to use published recordings without permission from or remuneration to the copyright owner, has turned into a rule of compulsory license. In fact, Article 43 is based on the model of the Berne Appendix, which allows free use without permission from, but grants compensation to, the right holder. This represents a new access rule that aims to grant A2R to copyright owners. Nevertheless, considering the widespread use of telecommunication technology, these free use doctrines may also expand A2K that could run out of the government's control.

As for the neighbouring rights, the 2001 Copyright Act expands the scope of protection considerably and aims to reach the standards of TRIPS. Articles 36–45, which provide for the performer's rights, the recorder's rights, and the broadcaster's rights, have almost been rephrased to incorporate the standards set forth in Articles 11 and 14 of the BC, as well as Article 14 of TRIPS. Further, revisions have been made to the right to receive remuneration in each category of neighbouring rights and the term of protection of each of these rights. Notably, however, the emerging neighbouring rights may also generate pro-A2K potential in disseminating free ideas to the wide public, which could jeopardise the government's policy of maintaining social control. Thus, the law must impose restrictions on such rights.

As far as the limitation and exception rules are concerned, Article 22 of the 2001 amendments is much closer to the standards of Articles 9 and 10 of the BC and Article 13 of TRIPS. The three-step test presupposes special circumstances, no conflict with normal exploitation of works, and no unreasonable prejudice against the legitimate interests of the right holder. Basically, Article 22 conforms to these tests. First, the provision provides for a number of cases of free use explicitly, which are defined more clearly than those under Article 22 of the 1990 Copyright Act. Second, the provision mandates a "normal use" by requiring that the name of the author and the title of the work shall be mentioned. Third, the provision prohibits prejudice against the rights of the copyright owner. Whereas the vaguely defined free use in the 1990 Copyright Act may contradict the three-step test, the new amendments largely mend up this gap. The free use doctrines are, however, overshadowed by the censorship regime: as illustrated earlier, the scope of free use under Articles 22(3), (4), (7), (9), and (11) has been narrowed down, respectively.

3.4.3.   Administrative Enforcement as an Anti-A2K Approach

In prescribing the amendments, however, the government is wary of the risk of granting overprotection of A2K that may facilitate the free flow of information. Article 47 of the new amendment presents a highly interesting case of access rules under the Chinese national copyright system. Since 1994, China's international negotiations, in particular those with the United States, focused on the IP enforcement issue. After acceding to TRIPS, China endeavoured not only to render its substantive copyright standards consistent with the international copyright standards, but also to establish a set of more stringent measures to ensure enforcement of the TRIPS standards. One must, however, bear in mind that the acceptance of the mentality of copyright protection and the establishment of a copyright system in the PRC are not a spontaneous process but imported from, if not imposed by, the Western world. In China, the task of universalising copyright protection would have to be carried out by a powerful institution – the Chinese government. Thus, the mechanism of administrative enforcement seems to be more than reasonable in China.

A dualistic enforcement system, however, may not be consistent with prevalent international practice. As such, Article 47 of the 2001 Copyright Act restricts the administrative power of copyright administrative departments by stating that government authorities can only impose administrative penalties on copyright infringers when the latter also violate the public interest. Nevertheless, the public interest is not defined in the 2001 Copyright Act at all. It follows that this provision must be subject to the interpretation by relevant copyright administrative departments at various levels. In China, the major authorities that are in charge of copyright protection are also responsible for carrying out censorship. Confronted with the risk of encouraging A2K through the new amendments, the government would have to adopt an anti-A2K approach in interpreting the public interest. Thus, while guaranteeing an effective way of enforcing copyright protection in China, Article 47 of the 2001 Copyright Act leaves the government with considerable latitude in wielding its interest-balancing tools.

3.4.4. The Conflict between Censorship and Idea/Expression Dichotomy

Apparently, Article 4 of the 1990 Copyright Act remains intact under the 2001 amendments, which is still a troublesome provision. There is fundamental inconsistency between this provision and the BC, as analysed in Chapter 2. After China acceded to the WTO, this provision came into conflict with the idea/expression dichotomy under Article 9(2) of TRIPS because the latter mandates that copyright protects only the expression of ideas rather than the idea itself. The idea/expression dichotomy indicates that copyright exists and shall be protected regardless of whether the idea will be protected or forbidden by law. Under the tutelage of the public interest, however, the Chinese government feels it more legitimate to prohibit the publication and distribution of certain works to prevent the free flow of the ideas contained in certain works. Article 4, which denies protection to such works whose "publication or distribution is prohibited by law," ignores the idea/expression dichotomy and, thus, contradicts a fundamental principle under TRIPS.

3.5. Conclusion

To further its economic reforms, China spent about 15 years negotiating with its major trade partners to get into the GATT/WTO system. At the same time, China went a long way from its planned economy with almost no copyright legislation to what it called a socialist market economy with a modern copyright system. In this process, negotiations with trade partners were particularly important for China to get onto the track of aligning its national economic development with global standards. Also at this stage, China's trade partners were concerned more about the enforcement of copyright standards than about copyright legislation.

To compel China to enforce the international copyright standards, the United States, for instance, continued to avail itself of several unilateral measures, such as trade sanctions/wars, nonrenewal of the MFN status, and even a veto to allow China to enter the WTO. These IP and trade negotiations all led to China's prompt steps of adapting its national copyright laws to the international copyright system.

The domestic situation was, however, more than complicated. In fact, the Tiananmen Movement was a milestone for the ideological demise of a communist Utopia in China. From then on, China could no longer be labelled as a real communist country in terms of the traditional understanding, though the regime still claims that the legitimacy of its totalitarian rule is rooted in the theories of communism. The year 1989 marked a complete farewell to China's previous political economy, as the CCP gradually abandoned its policy of a planned economy and advocated indifference to the distinction between capitalism and socialism. Thanks to China's economic reforms, masses of parvenus, in particular a class of "communist upstart," sprang up in China. Thus, private proprietorship was no longer disdained but became a must. The CCP believed, however, that the wealth accumulated on the basis of a crony capitalism could only be safeguarded by an iron-fisted rule that must marginalise, if not eliminate, such personal freedom as free expression. Such an ambivalent policy was intertwined with the development of Chinese copyright law.

Under the call of a looming knowledge economy, more individual creators were engaged in a dynamic process of creating intellectual works and had a growing consciousness and incentive of receiving remuneration for their works. As such, legislators had to take into account copyright owners' claims for materialising their private interest in A2R. Although the Chinese government still intended to control free production of ideas in the name of defending the public interest, it may no longer do so by openly suppressing the private interest of Chinese intellectuals in claiming A2R for their creative works. As the development of new technologies began to promote A2K and the free flow of information in China, the new international copyright standards also posed challenges to China's copyright policies. In particular, TRIPS not only defines copyright as a private right but also nails down the idea/expression dichotomy as a principle of copyright law. Obviously, copyright law should facilitate both A2R and A2K rather than thwart either of the goals. However, both A2R and A2K, which may contribute to free expression, could run contrary to the government's policy goal of maintaining social control.

Although access rules under the 1990 Copyright Act impose more restrictions on copyright in the name of facilitating A2K at reasonable costs, the framework of access rules under the 2001 Copyright Act has been adapted considerably to comply with the standards of TRIPS, which helps to enhance the standards of copyright protection. All in all, the legal framework of access rules under the new amendments of the 2001 Copyright Act represent a positive turn from the traditional Chinese mentality about copyright to copyright internationalisation. The 2001 Copyright Act has largely accomplished the task of bringing the Chinese copyright system into harmony with not only the traditional regime of the BC/UCC, but also the new regime of TRIPS.

However, A2K remained a challenging task for China, although the pro-A2K doctrines prescribed by TRIPS are supposed to be transplanted into Chinese copyright law. The access rules under the 2001 Copyright Act have different regulatory objectives per se than those under the 1990 Copyright Act in that the focus turns from the control of individual speech to the control of the media. Thus, the potential tension that exists between A2R and A2K at reasonable costs becomes an instrument for the Chinese government to realise its underlying policy of controlling the free flow of information. Under this background, China adjusted its copyright policies through the 2001 amendments.

As a result, the access rules under the 2001 Copyright Act reflect China's international obligation of reinforcing the protection of A2R. Being obliged to do so, China would have to justify its dualistic enforcement system, especially its administrative copyright enforcement mechanism. Only in this way would the government find a more legitimate basis to regulate and exert control over the circulation of works. The "public interest" as a core factor in this mechanism can be defined not only in terms of A2K at reasonable costs but also in the light of an anti-A2K approach that might consolidate the entrenched censorship. Accordingly, a focus of the copyright policies in China turns from the restriction of A2R (which might dampen the incentive to create "expression") to the restriction of A2K (which aims to curb the dissemination of "ideas"). In a sense, the shift from control of expression to that of ideas represents a move from indirect conflict to direct conflict between censorship and free expression in copyright law.

4

Toward Free Expression?

The new century has witnessed a new round of China's structural economic reforms in the tide of globalisation and digitisation, which have a profound influence on China's copyright policies. Since China enacted its 2001 amendments, China has primarily positioned itself in international IP and trade negotiations within and beyond the context of WIPO and the WTO. Currently, there is an emerging new copyright milieu, as rendered by the overall regulation in the ACTA and the TPP. As such, China's stance in the new context prompts China to readjust its national copyright strategies, endorse digital copyright reforms, and ultimately, replace its censorship provision with a viable public order provision.

As the new domestic contingencies have added to the externalities of A2R and A2K, it is necessary to reconsider China's national copyright system with regard to the domestic policy of regulating free expression and recalibrate China's contemporary legal framework of access rules. The major concern remains whether China's national copyright system would adopt a pro-free-expression model under international influence. In addition, the recent process of revising the Copyright Act provides an opportunity to explore the leeway of free expression in Chinese copyright law. While China wields the policy instrument of circumventing A2R and A2K, respectively, in response to international copyright development, there is an irreversible trend of aligning copyright with free expression.

4.1. A Free-Expression-Oriented Copyright Taxonomy: China's IP and Trade Negotiations in the Twenty-First Century

4.1.1. Accession to the WIPO Internet Treaties: China's Multilateral IP Negotiations at WIPO

WIPO provides its Member States with a platform to negotiate, draft, and adopt multilateral IP treaties. Since China acceded to WIPO in 1980, a most influential event was the 1996 Diplomatic Conference on Certain Copyright and Neighbouring Rights Questions, which led to the "WIPO Internet Treaties," including the WCT and the WPPT.[1] The PRC participated in the 1996 Diplomatic Conference, but didn't accede to the WIPO Internet Treaties until 2007. In 2004, the Chinese government declared openly that China would accede to the WIPO Internet Treaties when it was appropriate to do so. In October 2006, the State Council submitted the protocol concerning China's accession to the WCT and the WPPT to the SCNPC.[2] On 29 December 2006, the tenth Session of the SCNPC approved China's bid to accede to the WCT and the WPPT.[3] In accordance with the decision, the Chinese government claimed to make reservations regarding the application of the two treaties in Hong Kong and Macau, as well as reservations concerning Article 15(1) of the WPPT. On 6 March 2007, the Chinese government submitted its protocol to WIPO. Within two days WIPO confirmed that it had received the protocol and stated that both treaties would take effect in China on 9 June 2007.[4]

Upon China's accession to the WIPO Internet Treaties, China may not have fully evaluated the potential impact of these treaties on its policy of controlling free expression in the digital environment. Before its accession to the WIPO Internet Treaties, China had no experience in domestic legislation or international negotiations regarding digital copyright protection. While the Internet industry in China was undergoing robust growth, Internet censorship has continued to exist since China's accession to the WIPO Internet Treaties and affected the commercial transactions of many transnational corporations. China's accession to the WIPO Internet Treaties is, however, a token of accepting international copyright standards and a sign of China's cooperative attitudes. Indeed, China did not expect that any access rules, which may be derived from the new copyright treaties, would ever affect its social control policies.

It must be noted that international treaties cannot be applied in China directly unless the standards have been transformed into

---

[1] WIPO Copyright Treaty, Art. 1(2), 20 December 1996, 36 ILM 65 (1997) (WCT). WIPO Performances and Phonograms Treaty, 20 December1996, 36 ILM 76 (WPPT).

[2] J. Feng [冯建华], 'From Beijing to Berne: China's Process of Copyright Protection' ['从北京到伯尔尼——中国版权保护历程'], *Beijing Weekly Review* [《北京周报》], 3 August 2007, at www.china.com.cn/book/zhuanti/qkjc/txt/2007-08/03/content_8624228.htm.

[3] Ibid.   [4] Ibid.

national laws. This means that neither the executive branch nor the judicial branch in China can enforce the WIPO Internet Treaties by invoking a provision of the WCT/WPPT. Instead, the legislators must readjust China's national copyright system to the WIPO Internet Treaties completely before the treaties can truly work. The creation of new national access rules may, in any case, generate new implications for regulating free expression under copyright law. Moreover, effective enforcement of both treaties would require knowledge and acceptance on the part of ordinary Chinese citizens, which may equally be a challenge.

4.1.2.   Censorship in Focus: The Sino–US Copyright Dispute at the WTO

Compared with WIPO, the WTO provides a completely new institutional platform for multilateral trade negotiations that involve IPR issues frequently. The WTO is also a double-edged instrument for its members, which would be bound by the entire bundle of WTO agreements including TRIPS. Because developed countries have played a major role in laying down the IP standards under TRIPS, most developing countries often bear greater pressure in complying with TRIPS and dealing with TRIPS-related complaints from developed countries. Where a member fails to fulfil its obligations under the WTO law, other members may resort to the DSM for a remedy. As a matter of fact, China has become increasingly involved in the WTO dispute settlement proceedings. Until 2015, China has had a profile of 13 cases as complainant and 33 cases as respondent, apart from 128 cases in which China has stood by as a third party.[5] In a sense, the DSM has become an extension of China's bilateral or multilateral negotiation process. Of all those disputes in which China is a major party, only one case is related to TRIPS and copyright: the *China–IPR* dispute.[6]

4.1.2.1.   Post-TRIPS Sino–US trade negotiations: the background of the China–IPR dispute

Within four years after China's accession to the WTO, there was no major harsh negotiation round going on between China and the United

---

[5] See WTO, Dispute Settlement, the Disputes, Disputes by country/territory, at www.wto .org/english/tratop_e/dispu_e/dispu_by_country_e.htm.

[6] WTO, Panel Report, *China–Measures Affecting the Protection and Enforcement of Intellectual Property Rights*, WT/DS362/R, para. 7.126, 26 January 2009 (*China–IPR*).

States. Indeed, the United States, as China's most important trade partner, gave China enough time to implement its obligations under TRIPS. Such a peaceful period, however, soon came to an end because of the unmitigated piracy in China. Despite the efforts of the Chinese government, China's enforcement record remained extremely poor. It is estimated generally that over 90 percent of IP products in China, such as computer software and phonograms, are counterfeiting products, causing a loss of some 1.4 billion US dollars to US copyright owners every year.[7] The loss resulting from copyright piracy in China amounted to an estimated 2.4 billion US dollars in 2006 and nearly 3 billion US dollars in 2007.[8] Moreover, downstream markets such as cinematic and home video industries were also affected.[9]

The Joint Commission on Commerce and Trade (JCCT), which was established in 1983 and has an IPR Working Group, is the primary forum for conducting Sino–US bilateral trade and commercial negotiations. At a meeting of the JCCT in April 2004, China made commitments to enforce certain IP-related obligations under TRIPS. In April 2005, however, the USTR released the results of its out-of-cycle review on China,[10] articulating its grave concern about China's lack of IP enforcement and the level of infringements. Meanwhile, the USTR placed China on its Priority Watch List again.[11] In October 2005, the United States, along with Japan and Switzerland,[12] invoked Article 63.3 of TRIPS to request clarifications regarding specific cases of IPR enforcement in China from 2001 to 2004. At this stage, however, the USTR was still reluctant to launch a formal WTO proceeding against

---

[7] D. E. Long and A. D'Amato, *A Coursebook in International Intellectual Property* (St. Paul, MN: West Group, 2000), p. 578.

[8] IIPA, IIPA's 2008 Special 301 Recommendations (2008) app. A 1, at www.iipa.com/pdf/2008SPEC301LOSSLEVEL.pdf.

[9] S. Ilias and I. F. Fergusson, Congressional Research Service Report for Congress, Intellectual Property Rights and International Trade, 20 December 2007, Congressional Research Service, Washington, DC, p. 12.

[10] Office of the USTR, Out-of-Cycle Review Results, 2005 Special 301 Report.

[11] Office of the USTR, Special 301 Report Finds Progress and Need for Significant Improvements: Results of China OCR Released, China Elevated to Priority Watch List (29 April 2005), at www.ustr.gov/archive/Document_Library/Press_Releases/2005/April/Special_301_Report_Finds_Progress_Need_for_Significant_Improvements.html.

[12] Office of the USTR, US–China Trade Relations: Entering a New Phase of Greater Accountability and Enforcement, Top-to-Bottom Review (February 2006) 14, at www.ustr.gov/sites/default/files/Top-to-Bottom%20Review%20FINAL.pdf.

China for several important reasons, such as lack of evidence and a relatively weak legal basis for such disputes.[13]

In February 2006, the USTR established the China Enforcement Task Force to prepare a WTO dispute against China. In reply, the SPC and the Supreme People's Procuratorate of the PRC (SPP) co-issued a judicial interpretation to lower the threshold of IPR-related prosecution and increase the penalties.[14] The United States held, however, that China had left a lacuna for a safe harbour regime.[15] Finally, the United States brought a WTO complaint against China on 10 April 2007. This was a watershed in Sino–US trade negotiations and their bilateral economic relationship because it marked an end to the US's unilateral sanctions and, for the first time in history, the continuance of the IP negotiations in the form of a multilateral DSM relating to China's IP/copyright enforcement. In a word, the United States levelled four allegations against China, one of which was that Chinese copyright law did not cover enough types of works owing to its strict content review system.[16] On 21 August 2007, the United States requested setting up a WTO panel to deal with the complaint.[17] Accordingly, the United States and China took steps to negotiate again to reach a compromise.[18] Although such efforts failed, the United States made a second request for establishing a panel on 25 September 2007, which resulted automatically in the establishment of a WTO panel by the WTO DSB on 13 December 2007. In addition, twelve members, including the European Communities, joined the dispute as third parties. In October 2008, the Panel released an interim report, and in January 2009, the final report was delivered.

---

[13] P. K. Yu, 'The US–China Dispute over TRIPS Enforcement', in C. Antons (ed.), *The Enforcement of Intellectual Property Rights: Comparative Perspectives from the Asia-Pacific Region* (Alphen: Kluwer Law International, 2011), p. 239, at 242–54.

[14] SPC and SPP, The Interpretation II of the Issues concerning the Specific Application of Law in Handling Criminal Cases of Infringement of Intellectual Property Rights [《最高人民法院、最高人民检察院关于办理侵犯知识产权刑事案件具体应用法律若干问题的解释(二)》], 5 April 2007.

[15] Office of the USTR, WTO Case Challenging Weakness in China's Legal Regime for Protection, Enforcement of Copyrights, Trademarks (April 2007), at www.ustr.gov/sites/default/files/uploads/factsheets/2007/asset_upload_file908_11061.pdf.

[16] WTO Dispute Settlement, Requests for Consultations by the United States, China-Measures Affecting the Protection and Enforcement of Intellectual Property Rights, WT/DS362/1 (10 April 2007).

[17] WTO Dispute Settlement, DSB Establishes a Panel on China's Protection of IPR and a Compliance Panel to Review US Implementation in "Zeroing" Case, WT/DS362/7 (21 Aug 2007).

[18] S. R. Weisman, 'China Talks Don't Resolve Major Issues', *NYT* (24 May 2007) C1.

4.1.2.2. The censorship provision in the Sino–US copyright dispute

As a corollary of China's increasing importance in international IP negotiations, the Sino–US copyright dispute (which refers to the part of the Sino–US IP dispute focusing on copyright) became the first litmus test for aligning China's national copyright system with the international copyright system, with particular regard to the role of China's censorship in balancing different interests under its national copyright system. In the Sino–US copyright dispute, China's public policies in copyright protection, as defined by its censorship regime, received more careful review through the lens of a global trade regime. In this dispute, the United States accused China of denying the "publication or distribution" of the works of certain authors which have not passed the "content review."[19] This review focused on Article 4 of the 2001 Copyright Act, the first sentence of which provides that "works the publication and/or dissemination of which are prohibited by law shall not be protected by this Law."[20] This provision received attention from foreign investors because it left the overseas owners of works – such as books and movies that had been legally published in other countries but were not approved for publication in China – with little recourse to act against copyright pirates in China. Now that the substantive provisions of the BC have been incorporated into TRIPS, any issue under national copyright law, including the censorship regime under Article 4 of the 2001 Copyright Act, can be investigated in the DSM of the global trade system.

Notably, the United States listed in its submission a few regulations that allow censorship of works explicitly and authorise prohibition of the publication or distribution thereof, which the WTO Panel reviewed carefully in its ruling.[21] A plethora of such laws and regulations, which empower public authorities to conduct content review, aroused concern about whether and to what extent the censorship system would affect global trade. Eventually, the Panel epitomised Article 4(1) of the 2001 Copyright Act encompassing the censorship system as producing "commercial uncertainty" with regard to copyright trade and dismissed China's defence thereof as unsubstantiated.[22] The Panel's finding that Article 4(1) is inconsistent with China's obligations under TRIPS rests on

---

[19] *China–IPR*, para. 7.16.
[20] The Copyright Act of the PRC, Art. 2(1), adopted 7 September 1990, revised 27 October 2001 (2001 Copyright Act).
[21] *China–IPR*, para. 7.73.   [22] Ibid., paras. 7.136–37.

three arguments: absence of copyright protection, lack of effective legal procedures, and the legitimacy of censorship in copyright law.

4.1.2.3.   The union treatment sensu stricto under Article 5 of the BC

The standards of the protection of substantive authorial rights have been enshrined in Article 5(1) of the BC as encompassed by TRIPS and are composed of the "twin pillars": national treatment in its classical meaning – rights prescribed by the existing and subsequent legislation may be granted to foreign authors, and "union treatment *sensu stricto*" – rights specially granted by the BC.[23] This means that even if the level of copyright protection required by the BC cannot be provided generally under domestic laws to nationals, the Member State must guarantee this level of protection to foreign works.

China has, however, demonstrated an ambivalent attitude between its willingness to comply with the WTO law and its stubborn-mindedness in defending the censorship system. On the one hand, China claimed that, under Chinese copyright law, "copyright" must be differentiated from "copyright protection," and that copyright cannot be enforced under certain circumstances even though copyright is conferred on all works principally.[24] On the other hand, China acknowledged explicitly that its censorship process operates independent of Article 4(1), and that the works, which failed content review, were not denied copyright protection but were virtually denied the "authority to publish" in accordance with Article 4(1).[25]

Accordingly, the panel reviewed a number of Chinese laws and regulations on censorship to ascertain whether works that have entirely or partially failed such review, works that are never submitted, or works that await the results of such review would be granted copyright protection.[26] The panel concluded, then, that any works that fail the content review in China would be denied "protection," in the substantial sense of the term.[27] Interestingly, the panel justified its conclusion by referring to the judicial practice in China that granted copyright protection of a book on being approved by political censorship organs.[28] Based on relevant

---

[23] S. Ricketson and J. C. Ginsburg, *International Copyright and Neighbouring Rights: The Berne Convention and Beyond*, 2nd edn (Oxford: Oxford University Press, 2006), pp. 302–3 and 309–10.

[24] *China–IPR*, para. 7.21.   [25] Ibid., paras. 7.21, 7.56.   [26] Ibid., paras. 7.72–103.

[27] Ibid., para. 7.103.   [28] Ibid.

judicial interpretations, the panel inferred that if, conversely, the content of that book were not endorsed during the political review by "the United Front Department of the Sichuan Provincial Communist Party Committee" owing to its illegal content, that is, if it were "reactionary, pornographic or superstitious," then it would "not be protected by the Copyright Law, and all the presses shall neither publish nor disseminate it. . . ."[29] Thereupon, the Panel found that the corollary policy engrained in Article 4(1), which granted enforcement of protection on the condition of successful fulfilment of criteria set forth by censorship, deprived a whole range of authors of their copyright because such a regime denied copyright protection under Article 5(1) of the BC to authors of all WTO members.[30] Thus, the cacophony of Article 4(1), as a result of the censorship, has not only been inconsistent with national treatment, but also violated the union treatment "specially granted" by the BC.[31]

4.1.2.4.   Lack of genuinely effective enforcement procedures under Chinese law

The practice of preconditioning copyright protection on successful conclusion of censorship is also incongruent with members' obligation to enforce copyright protection. As laid down in the first sentence of Article 41.1 of TRIPS, members must provide effective procedures to cope with infringement of copyright covered by TRIPS.[32] According to China, however, censorship was legitimate, as referred to in Article 4(1) of the Chinese Copyright Act. Thus, copyright enforcement would cease to be meaningful provided that unqualified works, which did not live up to the standards of censorship, were banned in all aspects.[33] In contrast, the panel endorsed the US's view that China's dichotomy between "copyright" and "copyright protection" was "artificial" and dismissed such dichotomy as irrelevant[34] because the vacuum of protection, after having been denied to relevant authors, betrays the specious state of copyright as a "phantom right."[35] The panel went on to point out that Part III of TRIPS, which specifies the availability of legal procedures, should not be intersected from Part II, which provides substantive protection. In that connection, Part III of TRIPS must be interpreted together with those provisions under Part II. Therefore, such omission of

---

[29] Ibid., paras. 7.51–7.   [30] Ibid., para. 7.50.   [31] Ibid., para. 7.107.
[32] TRIPS, art. 41(1).   [33] *China–IPR*, para. 7.134.   [34] Ibid., paras. 7.62–4.
[35] Ibid., para. 7.67.

remedies in the 2001 Copyright Act was incompatible with both the substantive and the procedural standards.[36]

Conspicuously, the panel didn't take the enforcement mechanism under Part III of TRIPS as an isolated regime, which would otherwise be vulnerable to any arbitrary deviation. Rather, the panel urged China to consider and face the legal consequence of its censorship regime in the scenario of copyright law. Certainly, authors whose works fail censorship should not also fall prey to an ostensible judicial system that provides feigned procedural fairness.[37] The panel also pointed out that the judicial authorities in China lacked such authority to make independent decisions in compliance with TRIPS, in case authors resorted to these authorities for remedies when censorship authorities denied copyright protection to them.[38]

4.1.2.5. The legitimacy of Article 4 under the lens of Article 17 of the BC

In consequence, the panel dispute focused on the legitimacy of censorship under the lens of copyright. Notably, the aforementioned dichotomy between copyright and copyright protection under Chinese law emanates from more profound legal backgrounds. It was, in fact, underpinned by the government's entrenched mentality of conducting censorship. Such mentality is also reflected in Article 17 of the BC concerning the authority of any state member "to permit, to control, or to prohibit, by legislation or regulation, the circulation, presentation, or exhibition of any work or production in regard to which the competent authority may find it necessary to exercise that right."[39] Indeed, this provision is also incorporated into TRIPS.[40] Overshadowed by such ideologies, China claimed that the power of governments to censor works must take precedence over all other rights granted by the BC, and that China could deny the WTO's jurisdiction in this respect.[41] By citing numerous resources in defence of its legitimacy to conduct censorship, China declared that the Chinese government was entitled, just as "many other countries in the world,"

---

[36] Ibid., para. 7.68.   [37] Ibid., paras. 7.164, 7.178.   [38] Ibid., paras. 7.86, 7.179.

[39] Berne Convention for the Protection of Literary and Artistic Works, Art. 17, Paris Act, revised on 24 July 1971, 1161 UNTS 30 (BC).

[40] Agreement on Trade-Related Aspects of Intellectual Property Rights, Art. 9.1, Marrakesh, 15 April 1994, 33 ILM 1197 (1994) (TRIPS).

[41] *China–IPR*, paras. 7.18, 7.120.

to ban any works that are labelled as "unconstitutional or immoral" for publication and dissemination.[42]

As the United States did not challenge China's right to conduct censorship, the panel agreed that Article 17 might entail the government's right to interfere with the exercise of certain rights by copyright owners,[43] and, thus, its findings did not affect China's right to do so.[44] The panel clarified, however, that this provision did not authorise the elimination of copyright protection in any work.[45] Therefore, the Panel was dissatisfied with the interference with copyright protection that must be secured by the trade regime. Indeed, Article 17 of the BC seems to allow states to conduct censorship without even qualifying the nature and scope of such kinds of censorship.[46] A historical interpretation of the provision would, however, confine the censorship to a partial curtailment, instead of denial, of an author's substantive copyright based on the principle of legality.[47] Precisely speaking, this provision remains indifferent to, rather than legitimises positively, an act of the sovereign state in maintaining the public order. In fact, it is only concerned with the restrictive effect of such acts on copyright protection.

4.1.3.   China's Bilateral IP-Related Trade Negotiations

4.1.3.1.   The subsequent Sino–US copyright-related negotiations

Because the Sino–US IP dispute was settled at the WTO, the most important Sino–US bilateral IP-related trade negotiations have continued to take place on an annual basis through the JCCT. In 2009, for the first time in history, three Cabinet officials in the Obama administration came together to the economic summit of the 20th JCCT. At this key negotiation round, the Chinese government agreed to take a series of measures in respect of copyright protection, such as imposing maximum administrative penalties on Internet infringers through a four-month campaign that aimed at cracking down Internet piracy. China also agreed to work with the United States regarding the US's concern about a new circular issued by the MOC of the PRC on online music distribution, which

---

[42] Ibid., para. 7.17.   [43] Ibid., paras. 7.131–2.   [44] Ibid., para. 7.144.
[45] Ibid., paras. 7.127, 7.132.
[46] Ricketson and Ginsburg, *International Copyright and Neighbouring Rights*, p. 844.
[47] Ibid., p. 843.

might have negative effects on the US music industry.[48] The outcome of this round of bilateral negotiation has continued to influence the following rounds of JCCT bilateral negotiations relating to online copyright protection in China.

At the JCCT in 2010, China announced that, in respect of combating online copyright infringement, the judiciary departments were conducting a study on drafting relevant Judicial Interpretations. Both sides signed agreements to hold a program jointly with public and private participants to discuss the issue of intermediary legal liability on the Internet.[49] At the JCCT in 2011, China briefed on setting up an organ at the level of the State Council to lead and coordinate IPR enforcement across China and enhance its crackdown regime regarding IPR infringement. China also ensured the legalisation of software in government and enterprise facilities all over the country. Besides, the two sides have agreed to use the JCCT IPR Working Group to study the link between government measures and IP and to hold government/industry roundtables to discuss online copyright protection and enforcement, including library copyright protection.[50]

At the JCCT in 2012, China confirmed that it required all of its state-owned enterprises to purchase and use legitimate software and announced that the SPC would issue a Judicial Interpretation on Internet Intermediary Liability before the end of 2012.[51] At the JCCT in 2013, China and the United States signed a memorandum of understanding in support of IPR training, which aims to enhance the capacity and commitment of the public authorities in China to protect IPR.[52] At the JCCT in 2014, China agreed to strengthen enforcement of online IP

---

[48] Office of the USTR, Fact Sheet: US–China Joint Commission on Commerce and Trade (29 October 2009), at www.commerce.gov/sites/default/files/documents/migrated/3FACT%20SHEET-JCCT.pdf.

[49] Office of the USTR, 21st US–China Joint Commission on Commerce and Trade Fact Sheet (15 December 2010), at www.ustr.gov/about-us/press-office/fact-sheets/2010/21st-us-china-joint-commission-commerce-and-trade.

[50] Office of the USTR, 2011 US-China Joint Commission on Commerce and Trade Outcomes (20–21 November 2011), at www.ustr.gov/about-us/press-office/fact-sheets/2011/november/2011-us-china-joint-commission-commerce-and-trade-ou.

[51] Office of the USTR, Fact Sheet: 23rd US-China Joint Commission on Commerce and Trade (19 December 2012), at www.commerce.gov/news/fact-sheets/2012/12/19/fact-sheet-23rd-us-china-joint-commission-commerce-and-trade.

[52] Office of the USTR, 24th US-China Joint Commission on Commerce and Trade Fact Sheet (19–20 December 2013), at www.ustr.gov/about-us/press-office/fact-sheets/2013/December/JCCT-outcomes.

infringement. Besides, China and the United States reaffirmed their commitment to implement the Sino–US Intellectual Property Cooperation Framework Agreement.[53] At the JCCT in 2015, China revealed its ongoing process of amending the Copyright Act, which would encapsulate the principles of digital copyright protection under the aforementioned judicial interpretation in 2012. [54]

4.1.3.2.   The Sino–EU IP-related trade negotiations

Just like the United States, the EU has been experiencing the same issues of copyright infringement in China.[55] In fact, a number of EU companies have been lobbying EU institutions to launch trade sanctions and file disputes against China. Compared with the United States, the EU has been taking a more realistic and soft approach in this respect. As the EU Ambassador to China once described, "the trade conflict between the EU and China is inappreciable, as of 'a small tree' in 'a dense forest', and a strengthened cooperation remains to be the mainstream."[56] Nevertheless, as the EU has urged China repeatedly to improve its IP enforcement in vain, the EU ran out of patience, too.[57] Soon after the EU articulated its dissatisfaction, it joined the United States along with other countries in the Sino–US IP dispute.

In contrast to the US's coercive negotiation approach, the EU perceives China's negotiation approaches and standpoints from a different perspective, as the EU has developed a more flexible and feasible position that ensures China's cooperative positions in the Sino–EU bilateral IP/ trade negotiations. Although the EU law takes a "one-size-fits-all" approach, the EU understands that this may not be the right approach in IP regulation in all countries of the world. Most important, the EU has

---

[53] Office of the USTR, US–China Joint Fact Sheet on the 25th US–China Joint Commission on Commerce and Trade (16 December 2014), at https://ustr.gov/about-us/policy-offices/ press-office/fact-sheets/2014/december/us-china-joint-fact-sheet-25th-us.

[54] Office of the USTR, US Fact Sheet: 26th US-China Joint Commission on Commerce and Trade (23 November 2015), at www.commerce.gov/news/fact-sheets/2015/11/us-fact-sheet-26th-us-china-joint-commission-commerce-and-trade.

[55] European Commission, EU Strategy to Enforce Intellectual Property Rights in Third Countries – Facts and Figures, Brussels, MEMO/04/255, 10 November 2004, p. 2, at http://europa.eu/rapid/press-release_MEMO-04-255_en.htm.

[56] W. Lu [陆文军], 'The EU Ambassador to China: Conflict is by No Means the Mainstream of EU–China Trade Relations' ['摩擦绝非中欧贸易主流'], *Xinhua News Net* (7 March 2007), at http://news.xinhuanet.com/fortune/2007-03/07/content_5814346.htm.

[57] 'Mandelson Urges China to Tackle Piracy, Hints at WTO Action', *EU Business*, 26 November 2007.

focused on China's continued integration into the economic and trade globalisation and its step toward becoming a country of "rule of law." Thus, the EU seems to be willing to help China deal with the development of its national IP/copyright system in the unprecedented economic and political reforms. As such, the EU's approach in bilateral IP and trade negotiations has often dwelled more on how China could refine its legal framework gradually. Thus, the Sino–EU IP and trade negotiations have been established on a framework composed of several institutional platforms.

4.1.3.2.1. The EU–China Economic and Trade Joint Committee Historically, the EU–China Economic and Trade Joint Committee (ECETJC) assumed the role of a trailblazer in initiating the bilateral IP-related negotiations between China and the EU. While the JCCT stands for the platform of Sino–US bilateral trade negotiation, there has been a regular platform for Sino–EU bilateral trade negotiations since 1985 when the ECETJC was established to hold high-level talks on bilateral trade issues.[58] At the Sino–EU bilateral summit in trade and economics, the ECETJC usually addresses economy and trade, bilateral agreements and dialogues between China and the EU, as well as other Sino–EU cooperation programs.[59] In 2005, representatives from the EU and China discussed important aspects of bilateral trade issues including IPR. The EU, for example, highlighted "the urgent need to correct the perception that IPRs are not properly enforced in China."[60] Thereupon, China and the EU agreed on the need to work more closely to ensure that IPR is protected effectively in China. After the Sino–US IP dispute, however, the IP-related negotiations at the ECETJC seemed to give precedence to those at the EU–China Annual Summit, a political negotiation platform at a higher rank.

4.1.3.2.2. The EU–China Annual Summit The EU–China Annual Summit, which was established in 1998, has become an overarching bilateral negotiation platform concerning the development and

---

[58] European Commission, Trade, China, at http://ec.europa.eu/trade/policy/countries-and-regions/countries/china/.
[59] Ibid.
[60] European Commission, EU–China Economic and Trade Joint Committee Debriefing, Brussels, 4 November 2005, at http://trade.ec.europa.eu/doclib/docs/2005/november/tra doc_125721.pdf.

enforcement of the Chinese IP/copyright laws. The leadership of the EU and the PRC have met annually to update important progress in various trade areas, including IPR protection. Further major bilateral submechanisms concerning IP issues have been derived from this mechanism. Generally, the Annual Summit differs from the platform of the ECETJC in that it provides overall political guidance to developing such negotiations between China and the EU. Most important, it has always encompassed commitments to mutual dialogues on human rights and rule of law with an aim of facilitating China's ratification of the ICCPR (which, certainly, includes freedom of expression),[61] apart from trade and IP issues.

As early as 2003, China and the EU agreed to set up the mechanism of EU–China IP Dialogue and IP working group,[62] which has turned into a concrete institutional framework for Sino–EU bilateral negotiations. In 2005, leaders from both sides recognised the importance of implementing and enforcing IP laws while safeguarding the interests of consumers.[63] In 2007, China and the EU reached consensus on establishing a high-level economic and trade dialogue on a broad range of bilateral trade issues including the IP protection.[64] Recently, at the 17th Summit in June 2015, China and the EU agreed on a new joint summit declaration,[65] reaffirming their commitment to reinforcing the cooperation on the protection and enforcement of IPR, along with several agreements on further facilitating bilateral trade relations.

4.1.3.2.3. The EU–China IP Dialogue The EU–China IP Dialogue represents a fundamental sub-mechanism of the EU–China Annual Summit concerning IP issues. At the EU–China Summit in October

---

[61] See, e.g., European Union External Action Service, Joint Statement of the 12th EU–China Summit, para. 8, 30 November 2009, at http://eeas.europa.eu/delegations/china/press_corner/all_news/news/2009/20091130_02_en.htm.

[62] EU-Asia Centre, EU–China Intellectual Property Dialogue, 30 October 2003, at http://eeas.europa.eu/china/docs/ipr_291003.pdf.

[63] See European Commission, Joint Statement of the 8th EU–China Summit, Art. 15, IP/05/1091, Brussels, 5 September 2005, at http://europa.eu/rapid/press-release_IP-05-1091_en.htm?locale=en.

[64] See Council of the European Union, 10th China–EU Summit, Beijing, 28 November 2007, Joint Statement, Art. 24, 16070/07 (Press 279), Brussels at www.gov.cn/misc/2007-12/03/content_824127.htm.

[65] EU–China Summit Joint Statement: the Way forward after Forty Years of EU–China Cooperation, 29 June 2015, Brussels, at www.consilium.europa.eu/en/meetings/international-summit/2015/06/150629-eu-china-joint-statement/.

2003, China and the EU agreed to launch a regular institutional platform for IP dialogues to discuss bilateral issues concerning the protection and enforcement of IPRs and set up joint efforts to combat piracy and counterfeiting. The subjects that attend these bilateral trade negotiations on both sides are led by the Ministry of Commerce of the PRC and Directorate General Trade of the European Commission, respectively. In 2005, these two departments agreed to set up an EU–China IP Working Group as a complementary component to the EU–China IP Dialogue.

The IP Dialogue was supposed to cover broad areas ranging from improvements in interagency coordination, institutional reforms, and enforcement of IPRs to international cooperation.[66] At the beginning, the Sino–EU bilateral IP dialogue remained at an initial stage of tentative plan without substantial and operational guidelines for the implementation of the agreements concluded between both parties. The decade following that summit, however, witnessed robust development of a reliable platform for both sides to conduct extensive discussions and cooperation on a wide range of IP-related issues with regard to promoting the mutual understanding of the IP systems and reducing potential trade frictions.

The development in IP Dialogue in recent years is of symbolic meaning. In 2013, China and the EU adopted the EU–China 2020 Strategic Agenda for Cooperation in which both sides agreed to reinforce the IP Dialogue Mechanism to strengthen cooperation for combating counterfeiting and piracy.[67] In 2015, the EU–China IP Dialogue Mechanism was further updated when both sides signed a memorandum of understanding concerning this mechanism of IP Dialogue.[68] The main objective of the mechanism is to improve the IP environment as one of the key conditions to promote creativity, innovation, and investment, and the deepening of mutual understanding and public awareness of IP issues in the EU and China. Besides, the memorandum also manifests the structure and content of the IP Dialogue, along with the mutual commitment to developing joint initiatives to support the protection and enforcement of IPR.

---

[66] Ibid., Art. 1(a)–(c).
[67] EU–China 2020 Strategic Agenda for Cooperation, Beijing, 21 November 2013, at http://eeas.europa.eu/china/docs/20131123_agenda_2020__en.pdf.
[68] Memorandum of Understanding on Reinforcing the EU–China IP Dialogue Mechanism, Brussels, 29 June 2015, at http://trade.ec.europa.eu/doclib/docs/2015/july/tradoc_153588.pdf.

4.1.3.2.4. The EU–China IP Cooperation Programme The EU–China IP Cooperation Programme is also an important by-product of the EU–China Summit and provides technical support to the improvement of China's IP system. As early as 1995, the European Commission and the Ministry of Foreign Trade and Economic Cooperation of the PRC signed an agreement on establishing the EU–China IPR cooperation program, which took place from 1998 to 2004.[69] The main objective of the program was to facilitate bilateral trade by supporting China's efforts to develop a modern and effective system for the protection of IPR.[70] The program covered training of judges and lawyers, administrative enforcement, border enforcement, public awareness building, academic institutions, technology transfer, legislative support, international study tours, and three specialised areas including copyright, patent, and trademark.[71] Various seminars, workshops, and conferences were organised at all levels.[72] After its termination in 2004, the programme was integrated into the EU–China Trade Project that spanned over 2004 to 2007, which was then replaced by the program of IPR II that spanned over 2007 to 2011.[73] At the EU–China Summit in 2012, China and the EU further agreed to develop the EU–China IPR Cooperation Project III actively.[74]

4.1.4. The ACTA and the TPP: China's Role in Recent Multilateral IP-Related Negotiations and the Prospects of a Free-Expression-Oriented Legal Framework

China's growing profile in the global economy and its increasing experiences in multilateral negotiations have made it possible for China to

---

[69] European Commission, EPO/Commission Cooperation in the Fields of IPR, MEMO/06/182, Brussels, 3 May 2006, at http://europa.eu/rapid/press-release_MEMO-06-182_en.pdf.

[70] European Commission, A Maturing Partnership – Shared Interests and Challenges in EU–China Relations, Commission Policy Paper for Transmission to the Council and the European Parliament, Brussels, 10/09/03, COM (2003), at http://eur-lex.europa.eu/Lex UriServ/LexUriServ.do?uri=COM:2003:0533:FIN:EN:PDF.

[71] European Commission, EU–China Relations: Chronology, European External Action Service, at http://eeas.europa.eu/china/docs/chronology_2012_en.pdf.

[72] Ibid.

[73] EU–China Project on the Protection of Intellectual Property Rights, at www.ipr2.org/index.php?option=com_content&view=section&layout=blog&id=12&Itemid=89.

[74] Council of the EU, Joint Press Communiqué of the 14th EU–China Summit, Beijing, 14 February 2012, 6474/12, Press 50, at http://eeas.europa.eu/china/summit/summit_docs/120214_joint_statement_14th_eu_china_summit_en.pdf.

influence the process and consequence of international IP-related negotiations significantly. WIPO does not pose serious questions about the
legitimacy of China's censorship regime. In the Sino–US copyright dispute, China was shrewd in relying on the law of public interests to thwart
any potential efforts to advance free expression. Also in bilateral copyright negotiations, China has learned to sidestep topics relating to free
expression and embrace the more specious and hortatory approach of
interest balancing in IP laws. Since the beginning of this century, however, a new international copyright milieu with more demanding implications for free expression is emerging.

Whereas contemporary copyright protection is rooted in an international system, recent development in digital technologies has necessitated more intensive regulation, which in turn has led to an increasingly
fragmented patchwork of digital copyright legislations. National legislators have developed different, and sometimes conflicting, laws and regulations for digital networks and digital means of production. At the global
level, the ACTA and the TPP represent two new regulatory systems of
digital communication, which aim to reinforce the existing global IP
standards and the traditional proprietary model. The legislative trends
that endorse the traditional legal framework for IP protection, however,
are confronted with a variety of challenges. These issues carry different,
often nonpecuniary, implications about the new mode of digital production around the world, such as free expression.

4.1.4.1.   The ACTA negotiations: the deficit of legitimacy

Initiated by Japan and the United States in 2006, the ACTA aimed to
enforce and complement IPR provisions in existing trade agreements
such as TRIPS. Virtually, this multilateral agreement was created because
major industrialised countries were dissatisfied with the extent to which
TRIPS could curb IP infringement. Throughout the ensuing years, a
number of countries such as the EU, Canada, Australia, South Korea,
and even the United Arab Emirates participated in the negotiations. In
2011 eight countries signed the finalised treaty text, and another 23 countries signed the ACTA in 2012. Among the 31 signatories, Japan remains
the single country that has ratified the ACTA so far, while the ACTA
would enter into force on ratification by six states.[75]

---

[75] The Anti-Counterfeiting Trade Agreement (ACTA), Art. 40, 3 December 2010, at
www.dfat.gov.au/trade/acta/Final-ACTA-text-following-legal-verification.pdf.

Notably, the ACTA aims to enhance the enforcement of IPR on a higher level than TRIPS, while encompassing more fundamental values such as free expression. For instance, the ACTA requires that member countries provide enforcement measures to permit effective actions against IP infringements in the digital environment, whereas such measures must preserve "fundamental principles such as freedom of expression."[76] Essentially, such rules manifest the relationship between IPR and freedom of expression, which provide international standards for states to follow in contemporary media regulation, for instance, when regulating the intermediary liabilities of ISPs for copyright infringement in the digital environment. These are commendable policy goals that help legitimise the principle of enforcing IPR or combating infringement in the Internet.

However, some of the rules in the ACTA may constitute serious barriers to fulfilling these fundamental values. For example, Article 27 of the ACTA allows monitoring or even blockading measures for supervising online infringing activities despite its requirement for deference to free expression. Moreover, the provision consolidates the universal trend of "TRIPS-plus" standards by allowing legal measures that set up electronic fences to copyrighted works. These new legal measures, once hallowed as global rules, might produce unexpected negative effects on free expression. Thus, Internet Service Providers (ISPs) may encroach on a person's expressive activities considerably.

In addition, the State would rely inevitably on processing a huge amount of personal information to fulfil its obligations to its citizens, say, ensuring national security, thus visualising a "national surveillance state."[77] Presumably, this multilateral agreement also jacks up the universal threshold of online copyright infringement by imposing pecuniary punishments in astronomical dimensions.[78] The ACTA becomes an object of public denunciation also because it seems to suffer from deficits of procedural legitimacy such as opaque negotiations, lack of consultation with the general public, or independence from international treaty bodies.[79]

---

[76] Ibid., Art. 27.2–4.

[77] J. M. Balkin, 'The Constitution in the National Surveillance State', in J. M. Balkin and R. B. Siegel (eds.), *The Constitution in 2020* (Oxford: Oxford University Press, 2009), p. 197.

[78] Foundation for a Free Information Infrastructure e.V., 'The world faces major challenges Introduction', at http://action.ffii.org/acta/Analysis.

[79] L. Floridi, ACTA – The Ethical Analysis of a Failure, and Its Lessons, ECIPE Occasional Paper, No. 4/2012, pp. 5–6.

As a result, an overwhelming audience has accused the ACTA of trampling the freedom that it promises to promote. Since the very beginning, developing country groups, nongovernmental organisations (NGOs), academicians, and grassroots activists have been criticising the ACTA for adding more obstacles to users' rights with vaguely and disproportionately defined copyright standards.[80] Even in leading developed countries, the ACTA has been branded as a "unilateral copyright treaty" and encountered widespread resistance.[81] In the tide of wide protests and petitions across Europe, the European Parliament voted against the ACTA in 2012. Clearly, the ACTA is not merely about copyright, but part of the most disputable ACTA-related debates so far perpetuates the fundamental issue of balance between copyright (A2R) and users' rights (A2K).

Being identified as the main target of piracy and counterfeiting activities, China was not invited to the negotiation table of ACTA. However, a treaty that aims to diminish such activities is of little significance without the major target being involved. Already at the WTO TRIPS Council meeting held from 26–27 October 2010, China articulated its standpoint against the ACTA, stating that the ACTA might conflict with TRIPS, encroach on the rights and flexibilities in the WTO agreements, undermine the government's freedom to interfere, and lack procedural legitimacy.[82] To be fair, as long as piracy and counterfeiting goods remain a significant part of the Chinese economy, there is little chance for China to accede to a treaty that is premised on the highest level of IP enforcement.

4.1.4.2.   The TPP negotiations: a potential breakthrough for Internet freedom

If, however, IP topics are dealt with in connection with more alluring topics, for example, where IP is linked to trade, China seems to be more active in getting involved. Currently, the TPP represents a proposed trade agreement reached between twelve countries in the

---

[80] Public Knowledge, 'Key Issues: The Anti-Counterfeiting Trade Agreement', at www.publicknowledge.org/issues/acta.

[81] See, e.g., Program on Information Justice and Intellectual Property, 'Over 75 Law Profs Call for Halt of ACTA', 28 October 2010, at www.wcl.american.edu/pijip/go/blog-post/academic-sign-on-letter-to-obama-on-acta.

[82] WTO Council for TRIPS, Excerpt from the Minutes of the Council's Meeting, WTO Doc. IP/C/M/64, 26–27 October 2010.

Asia-Pacific area concerning a variety of matters of economic policy.[83] Compared with the ACTA, the IP framework of the TPP not only consolidates the role of the BC, TRIPS, and the WIPO Internet Treaties in regulating copyright protection, but also endorses IP regulation in terms of an interest balancing approach. In compliance with TRIPS, the TPP stresses the need to "achieve an appropriate balance in its copyright and related rights system, among other things by means of limitations or exceptions ... including those for the digital environment, giving due consideration to legitimate purposes such as, but not limited to: criticism; comment; news reporting; teaching, scholarship, research, and other similar purposes; and facilitating access to published works ... ."[84] In a sense, this provision can be regarded as a free-expression-oriented principle for copyright law.

Originally, the TPP negotiations stemmed from the Trans-Pacific Strategic Economic Partnership Agreement (TPSEPA or "Pacific 4"), a comprehensive trade agreement signed by four countries in 2005.[85] In 2008, another eight Pacific Rim countries such as the United States and Vietnam became interested in the TPSEPA and joined the negotiation rounds covering a wide range of topics.[86] Due to the highly controversial nature of such topics as IP, the negotiation process lasted for seven years until the negotiating countries agreed on the final text in October 2015. During the negotiations prior to the final agreement, a number of countries (mainly members of the Asia-Pacific Economic Cooperation) with the potential of acceding to the TPP showed interest in this agreement.[87] Although China was not invited to join the negotiations, the TPP negotiations did not seem to be enticing enough for China at the moment.

There might be, however, some reasons for China to consider joining the TPP. With thirty chapters, the TPP is an all-in-one regime that would have significant impacts on the economic patterns in this region. Apart from the economic weight that the TPP members may have on the global scale, the TPP also requires a potential member to open its domestic market, including those sensitive parts such as

---

[83] The Trans-Pacific Partnership (TPP), at https://ustr.gov/tpp.   [84] Ibid., Art. 18.66.
[85] D. K. Elms and C. L. Lim, 'An Overview and Snapshot of the TPP Negotiations', in C. L. Lim, D. K. Elms, and P. Low (eds.), *The Trans-Pacific Partnership: A Quest for a Twenty-First-Century Trade Agreement* (Cambridge, Cambridge University Press, 2012), p. 21.
[86] Ibid., pp. 25–6.
[87] C. Kuriyama, 'APEC and the TPP: Are They Mutually Reinforcing?', in Lim, Elms, and Low (eds.), *The Trans-Pacific Partnership*, p. 242, at 254–7.

state-owned enterprises and to ensure Internet freedom.[88] These may, certainly, constitute serious challenges to China's structural reforms at home. China's absence from the TPP, however, would mean China's reluctance to cooperate with important trade partners in the region and even great economic losses at a time when the pace of China's economy is bound to slow down. Even if China rejects the TPP, the framework set by the TPP would be a model for future development that China can never circumvent. If the CCP further seeks to legitim- ise its rule by high-speed economic growth, the leadership would have to make a choice between economic failure and loosening its control on certain parts of the market such as the Internet, A2K, and the free flow of information.

Thus, the TPP surpasses the ACTA in that its standards will be of significance for China's future role in the economic development of Asia Pacific zone. Although China stood isolated outside the TPP negoti- ations, China seems to have overcome its hostility to the TPP after the agreement was reached in 2015. Already in 2014, China expressed its willingness to participate in the recent TPP negotiations.[89] Recently, China has also clarified that it remains open to participate in the TPP negotiations sometime later.[90] This is partly because such an IP approach may further enable China to enhance its participation in economic cooperation and add to its legitimacy in regulating IP affairs at home. In that case, the free-expression-oriented copyright rules under the TPP may well assume beacon effects on China and provoke a breakthrough in Chinese copyright law, which should be aligned with free expression.

4.1.4.3.   A taxonomy of new free-expression-oriented copyright rules

In an international community intertwined by common interests and agreed values, the sovereignty of national states to prioritise certain policy goals in domestic settings has been eroded by the need to comply

---

[88] The TPP recognises "the provision of unfair advantages to state-owned enterprises undermines fair and open trade and investment" and aims to promote "transparency, good governance and rule of law." See TPP, Pmbl.

[89] 'LI Keqiang, RCEP and TPP Can Go Hand in Hand and Benefit Mutually' ['李克强: RCEP 和 TPP 可并行不悖、相互促进'], *China News Service*, 10 April 2010, at www.chinanews.com/gn/2014/04-10/6048467.shtml.

[90] 'LI Keqiang: China Remains Open towards the US' Promotion of the TPP' ['李克强:中国 对美国推动 TPP 持开放态度'], *China Economy Weekly* [《中国经济周刊》], 19 October 2015, at http://finance.sina.com.cn/china/20151019/231423516298.shtml.

with duties that hinge on the principle of coexistence.[91] Thus, in copyright scenario, national legislations have been streaming into international legal regimes since the end of the nineteenth century. In essence, this is because copyright protects works that eventually render national borders meaningless, whereas legal "borders" – universal copyright standards – will return to the borderless world of works. Presumably, copyright protection has no inborn universal standards. National standards for copyright protection should conform to the economic and cultural conditions of relevant countries. The varying degrees and stages of economic and cultural development in different countries, therefore, have created tremendous problems for establishing universal standards for copyright protection in the global sphere.

In general, developed countries demand higher universal protection standards to stimulate innovation and creation at home, whereas developing countries whose large populations remain impoverished often regard lower levels of protection as more desirable to their economic and social development. Certainly, in an ideally set economic perspective, efficient universal IP standards will produce distributive effects for developing countries.[92] Unless this has turned into reality, applying uniformly high protection standards in these countries may produce uncertain results. As the role of these countries gradually shifts from mere recipients to robust producers of knowledge products, however, they are more likely to change their standpoints by moving toward higher IP protection standards. Therefore, the existence of a new free-expression-oriented copyright topology may have radiating effects on copyright laws of countries in transition such as China. The following section discusses those copyright provisions under the ACTA and the TPP, which are new in comparison with the former international copyright treaties and may affect free expression in one way or another.

4.1.4.3.1. The digital rights   The TPP summarises a palette of new rules concerning the substantive rights that are derived from the WIPO Internet Treaties. These digital rights are definitely in favour of copyright owners' interest in A2R. For example, the TPP provides that copyright

---

[91] A. Van Staden and H. Vollaard, 'The Erosion of State Sovereignty: Towards a Post-Territorial World?', in G. Kreijen et al. (eds.), *State, Sovereignty, and International Governance* (New York: New York University Press, 2002), p. 165, at 171–2.

[92] G. M. Grossman and E. L. C. Lai, 'International Protection of Intellectual Property' (2004) 94 *Am Econ Rev* 1635.

owners enjoy the exclusive right of authorising "direct or indirect" acts of duplication of their works "in any manner or form."[93] Further, it is made clear that any temporary "storage of a protected performance or phonogram in digital form in an electronic medium constitutes a reproduction."[94] Besides, the TPP allows the "making available to the public ... through sale or transfer of ownership,"[95] whereas the WIPO Internet Treaties subject this right to the exhaustion rule after initial consent by the author.[96] Nevertheless, a systematic interpretation would suggest that the scope of the right of distribution in this context is virtually smaller than that of the reproduction right because it involves merely "fixed copies that can be put into circulation as tangible objects."[97] Finally, the TPP, as the WIPO Internet Treaties, has established the full title of a "right of communication to the public" by making available to the public of their works (performances and phonograms) "in such a way that members of the public may access them from a place and at a time individually chosen by them."[98] Arguably, Member States have sufficient flexibilities in redefining direct and indirect modes of communication and determining whether or not to apply compulsory license where conducting wireless communications is treated as exercising the broadcasting and wireless diffusion rights.

4.1.4.3.2. Digital protective measures   The development of new technologies has led to two new models of formality rules for the purpose of strengthening the protection of copyright owners' interests in A2R in the digital environment. One is the technological protection measure (TPM) that enables right holders to protect their works with their own digital measures or facilities.[99] The other is the rights management information (RMI) that identifies all the information regarding the work and the right holder.[100] Both rules tend to consolidate the universal trend of "TRIPS-plus" standards by allowing legal measures that set up electronic fences to copyrighted works and have, thus, become frequently the target of proponents who argue for more consideration of A2K in copyright law.

---

[93] TPP, Art. 18.58. See also WPPT, Arts. 7 and 11.   [94] WPPT, note 6.
[95] TPP, Art. 18.60. WCT, Art. 6(1).   [96] WCT, Art. 6(2). WPPT, Arts. 8 and 12.
[97] Ricketson and Ginsburg, *International Copyright and Neighbouring Rights*, pp. 696–7.
[98] TPP, Art. 18.59. WCT, Art. 8. WPPT, Arts. 10 and 14.
[99] WCT, Art. 12. ACTA, Art. 27.5–6. TPP, Art. 18.68.
[100] WCT, Art. 12. ACTA, Art. 27.7. TPP, Art. 18.69.

4.1.4.3.3. The ISP safe harbour regime In Internet-focused economic models, right holders have frequently sought to hold large websites, rather than individual perpetrators, accountable for online copyright infringement. Yet, even if the right holders are eventually able to establish an ISP's intermediary liabilities, they may find it difficult to stop an illegal online act in a timely and effective manner. On the other hand, their efforts toward holding ISPs liable may be offset by powerful regimes that aim to limit or grant immunity from these liabilities. In the landmark *Sony* case,[101] the US Supreme Court developed the so-called safe harbour doctrine to protect ISPs from being held responsible for any direct infringements committed by a third party. The Court held that the establishment of secondary liabilities may not constitute an obstacle to users' access to information.

Virtually, the TPP reflects such a growing trend toward adapting relevant legal regimes to the age of the Internet and imposing more responsibility on corporate actors. Article 18.82 of the TPP summarises the existing safe harbour regime around the world such as those under the DMCA and the 2001 E-Commerce Directive.[102] This principle grants exemptions to ISPs provided that they do not collaborate with users in conducting illegal acts.[103] As a specific structure of the "notice and takedown" regime, this principle also imposes a general obligation that ISPs act "expeditiously to remove or to disable access" to any illegal information on "obtaining actual knowledge" or awareness of illegal activities.[104] Only on appropriate counternotice can such measures be reversed.[105] Although the TPP prevents members from requiring ISPs to monitor their services for illegal activities,[106] it allows them to provide information identifying the alleged copyright infringer.

Under these doctrines, ISPs can be ordered to take technical measures, such as filtering or blocking access to a specific website, to prevent further online copyright infringement. For legislators and courts, however, the underlying policy goal of the safe harbour doctrines is to strike the balance between copyright protection and freedom of expression. In

---

[101] *Sony Corporation of America et al.* v. *Universal City Studios Inc.*, 464 US 417 (1984).
[102] Digital Millennium Copyright Act, Pub L No. 105-304, 112 Stat. 2860, 17 USC § 512(a)–(d) (1998). Directive 2000/31/EC of the European Parliament and of the Council of 8 June 2000 on certain legal aspects of information society services, in particular electronic commerce, in the Internal Market (Directive on electronic commerce), OJ L 178, 17/07/2000, 1, arts 12-14.
[103] TPP, Art. 18.82(2).   [104] Ibid., Art. 18.82(3)(a).   [105] Ibid., Art. 18.82(4).
[106] Ibid., Art. 18.82(6).

the 2011 case of *Scarlet* v. *SABAM*,[107] for example, the Court of Justice of the European Union (CJEU) decided that an order sought against the ISP, which requires the installation of a filtering system to collect and identify the IP addresses of users without differentiating between lawful and unlawful contents, contravenes freedom of expression. In the 2014 case of *UPC* v. *Constantin and Wega*,[108] the CJEU reiterated the principle that the measure specified by the ISP must not affect Internet users' freedom to access information.

4.2.   Standing at the Crossroad: Reviewing China's Censorship-Oriented Copyright Law and Policies

4.2.1.   Free Expression as a Prerequisite for Further Economic and Social Development: The Externalities of A2R and A2K

After China became a WTO member, the country managed to maintain a breathtaking economic growth during the first decade of this century. Thanks to the low labour costs and large government investment in local infrastructure, China attained an admirable leading status in global manufacturing industry. This stunning achievement did not, however, enable China to step smoothly into the track of an advanced knowledge economy. Instead, the Chinese economy is featured by its labour-intensive and energy-consuming structure, and the reputation of a world factory is tainted by its flagrant counterfeiting and piracy market. Such a development model started to prove unsustainable after the global financial crisis in 2008, and China's economic growth has slowed down since the beginning of the 2010s.[109] At this crucial moment, it is essential for China to initiate structural reforms of its economy to catch up with the pace of the digitised knowledge economy.

Before the free flow of information, a fundamental prerequisite for developing knowledge economy, takes root in the Chinese society, China has witnessed another stunning growth of its e-commerce industry: up to

---

[107] CJEU, *Scarlet Extended SA* v. *Société belge des auteurs, compositeurs et éditeurs SCRL*, Case 70/10, Judgment of the Court (Third Chamber) (24 November 2011).

[108] CJEU, *UPC Telekabel Wien GmbH* v. *Constantin Film Verleih GmbH und Wega Filmproduktionsgesellschaft GmbH*, Case 314/12, Judgement of the Court (Fourth Chamber) (27 March 2014).

[109] P. Wiseman, 'Top Story in 2015: China's Sharp Economic Slowdown', The TandD.com, 26 December 2015, at http://thetandd.com/business/top-story-in-china-s-sharp-economic-slowdown/article_16a59d2f-69f6-5d54-a29e-8326b175a320.htm.

2015 the proliferation of online transactions has generated unravelled platforms such as Alipay owned by the Alibaba Group. Yu'E Bao (余额宝), for instance, a financial product platform designed by Alipay, ushers in an exchange instrument that represents a highly competitive alternative to the existing currency.[110] However, the Alibaba and its Taobao have been widely branded as a notorious fake supplier,[111] and the unmatured manufacturing industry in China is being marginalised by cheap and convenient online commodity. Recently, Alibaba is even reported to be engaged in buying several overseas Chinese media facilities,[112] which might enable Beijing to further monopolise its control of free expression in mainstream Chinese language media. It is, thus, largely uncertain whether this rapid development of e-commerce is a blessing or an ill omen for China.

Today, the role of the Chinese government in the economic development of China is becoming increasingly peripheral. In fact, China's economic growth in the past three decades is primarily attributable to the establishment of private proprietorship and the fact that the Chinese nation has been partly freed from the shackles that it was forced to wear.[113] It is hard to imagine that the CCP could ever bring China back to the old track of planned economy as in Mao's day. Now that the legitimacy of the CCP's grip on power seems to lie in the "development of the productivity,"[114] the only viable choice is to follow the mainstream economic path dependency that this nation is pursuing. Facing the challenges of upgrading the Chinese economy into knowledge economy, the CCP leadership discerned the importance of Chinese intellectuals and the protection of their IPR and upheld policies such as the strategy of "relying on science and education to rejuvenate the nation" [科教兴国].

China is, however, often ambivalent in carrying out its copyright-related science and education policies through its control of free expression. The embarrassing situation of A2R for intellectuals at universities

---

[110] 'Alibaba's Maturity Mismatch', *The Economist*, 24 July 2014, at www.economist.com/blogs/freeexchange/2014/07/chinese-finance.

[111] G. Wong and K. Chu, 'US Trade Group Seeks Relisting of Alibaba's Taobao as "Notorious"', *The Wall Str J*, 06 October 2015, at www.wsj.com/articles/u-s-trade-group-says-alibabas-taobao-should-be-relisted-as-notorious-for-fakes-1444096618.

[112] S. Yan, '3 Things about Alibaba's Move into Big Media', *CNN Money*, 13 December 2015, at http://money.cnn.com/2015/12/13/media/alibaba-scmp.

[113] Cf. R. Coase and N. Wang, *How China Became Capitalist* (Basingstoke: Palgrave Macmillan, 2012), pp. 171–4.

[114] Ibid., pp. 175–6.

may best explain the lack of a market of free ideas. In China, universities are invariably led, organised, and managed by different committees of the Party, a sophisticated architecture of the CCP, which supervises the exchange of ideas. These committees could virtually determine principles for awarding and promoting professors. For instance, the State Council has announced its agenda to "build the world's first class universities." A state-funded university ranking system in China, however, defines such "first class universities" as those that rank among the 100 top in its ranking list.[115] Presumably, the ranking of a university is determined largely by the quantity of articles published by academic staff of that university in a small number of academic journals selected in the light of commercial principles.[116]

As a result, professors and scholars, most of whom still receive a humble salary, are encouraged to publish only such journal articles. Although copyright owners do not usually benefit financially from their publications in academic journals, they will receive extra bonus from the government or the universities for such achievements and get promoted. By contrast, publications concerning "irrelevant" contents, or in any other form such as monographs and book chapters, or in a non-English language, are totally unrewarding and will not be considered even meaningful. Through such a system of manipulated A2R, the State succeeds in leading university elites to ignore a vast dimension of their freedom of expression and focus on a narrow field of producing and exchanging ideas for commercial purposes.

In addition, the "Great Firewall" aims to filter and block the dissemination of ideas that are seen as hazardous and harmful in the Internet. Notably, 2015 became a particularly traumatic year for A2K. In that year, the CCP issued new disciplines for Party members, forbidding any "reckless comment on the Central Committee of the Party" [妄议中央].[117] Besides, the ninth Amendment of the Criminal Act in 2015 criminalises an online act of "spreading rumours" in social media,[118] in

---

[115] Centre for World-Class Universities of Shanghai Jiao Tong University, the Academic Ranking of World Universities (ARWU), at www.shanghairanking.com.

[116] ARWU, Methodology, at www.shanghairanking.com/ARWU-Methodology-2013.html. See also J. Testa, The Thomson Reuters Journal Selection Process, at http://wokinfo.com/essays/journal-selection-process.

[117] Xinhua News Agency, Regulations on Disciplinary Punishments of the CCP [《中国共产党纪律处分条例》], Art. 46, 22 October 2015, People's Daily.

[118] The Criminal Act of the PRC, Art. 291(2), done on 14 March 1997, last revised on 29 August 2015.

addition to two statutes enacted earlier in 2015, which lay down concrete legal measures to thwart the free flow of information in the Internet in the name of safeguarding the national security. A2K can further be constrained because courts may sentence authors and publishers, who publish sensitive materials at their own costs, for committing a crime of "illegal business operation" [非法经营罪],[119] which sounds more legitimate than criminalising such publication for "instigating the subversion of or subverting the government."

Thus, an inherent demand for stronger protection of A2R and A2K in the Chinese economy and the society conflicts with the government's policy of controlling free expression. Currently, such conflicts are all the more palpable. On the one hand, the civil society is thriving with sharp consciousness of private proprietorship, individual freedom, participation in politics, and public media. On the other hand, the previous administration led by Jintao Hu [胡锦涛] and Jiabao Wen [温家宝] was unable to deal effectively with the complicated situation after China entered into the WTO, though the leadership took advantage of a free ride on the initial benefits of the global trade system. At this critical juncture, what China needs imminently is political reforms that bring forth ideological pluralism.

Compared with the predecessors, however, the administration presided over by Jinping Xi [习近平] has taken a less mediocre, but more scathing, cultural policy. Accordingly, "neither the first three decades nor the recent three decades of the PRC can be negated" [不否定两个三十年] of the PRC.[120] Practically, this means that what really matters is the monopolised rule of the CCP at any costs. Indeed, Xi even lamented that there was no "single real man" [竟无一人是男儿] to save the socialist country when the former Soviet Union collapsed.[121] To avoid a similar situation in China, the current administration took more draconian measures against free expression. In 2014, 72 years after Mao delivered a famous speech at the 1942 Yan'an Forum on Literature and Art, Xi convened a Forum on Literature

---

[119] See, e.g., J. Chen [陈家俊], 'Journalists from Hong Kong Accused of the Crime of Illegal Business Operation' ['港传媒人在深圳被控非法经营罪'], Deutsche Welle, 06 November 2015, at www.dw.com/zh/港传媒人在深圳被控非法经营罪/a-18832754.

[120] Y. Wu [吴雨], 'XI Jinping: We Can't Say No. to Our History of the First 30 Years' ['习近平:不能否定前30年历史'], Deutsche Welle, 05 January 2013, at www.dw.com/zh/习近平不能否定前30年历史/a-16500930.

[121] B. Chu [储百亮], 'XI Jinping Admonishes the CCP to Remember the Lessons of the Former Soviet Union' ['习近平警告中共记取前苏联教训'], The NYT, 15 February 2013, at http://cn.nytimes.com/world/20130215/c15xi/.

and Art, in which the 72 most famous Chinese writers and artists took part, and admonished that literature and art should not follow the market.[122] Such a cultural policy could pose serious challenges to the perspective of a free-expression-oriented copyright system in China.

4.2.2. The Need to Readjust Copyright Strategies in Terms of International Negotiations and the Domestic Economic and Social Development

4.2.2.1. The 2008 national IP strategy of the PRC

After decades of constantly facing the pressure from international negotiations, China has learned to appreciate the value of its national IP/copyright system. Admittedly, a sound national IP/copyright system is an indispensable condition for ensuring the market economy and international exchange in various areas. Further, in several rounds of post-TRIPS negotiations, China has gathered experience in settling international trade disputes. As such, designing an overall national IP strategy became necessary for China, as it is a global trend to incorporate innovative strategies into a comprehensive national IP framework.[123]

In August 2004, the Chinese government set up a working group of national IP protection to intensify the overall coordination of IP protection at various levels of governments around the country.[124] In 2005, the Chinese government launched the work of drafting an outline of national IP strategy with the goal of "building an innovative country."[125] It took three years to complete this work by more than a hundred experts from thirty-three government departments.[126] The outline consists of a general overview and twenty subtopics, which focus on the creation, management, protection, and operation of IP. In June 2008, the State Council published the Outline of National IP Strategy [《国家知识产权战略纲要》].[127]

---

[122] XinhuaNet.com, 'XI Jinping: Literature and Art Should Not Get Lost in the Tide of Market Economy' ['习近平:文艺不能在市场经济大潮中迷失方向'], 15 October 2014, at http://news.xinhuanet.com/politics/2014-10/15/c_1112840544.htm.

[123] See WIPO, National IP Strategies, at www.wipo.int/ipstrategies/en/.

[124] Y. Guan [管育鹰], 'Development of the Chinese Intellectual Property System in Globalisation' ['全球化背景下中国知识产权法律制度的发展'], at www.iolaw.org.cn/show Article.asp?id=2774.

[125] Ibid.   [126] Ibid.

[127] The State Council of the PRC, the Outline of the National IP Strategies [《国家知识产权战略纲要》], 5 June 2008, at http://english.gov.cn/2008-06/21/content_1023471.htm.

The Outline articulates a five-year plan with the goal of building China into a country "with a comparatively high level of the creation, utilisation, protection, and administration of IPRs."[128] Moreover, the Outline embraces five fundamental strategies covering IP protection. Accordingly, China shall carry out its obligations under the international copyright treaties, improve its copyright law in accordance with the economic and social development at home, and establish a sound enforcement and administrative system. Ultimately, such an improved national copyright system shall serve as one of the basis for making economic, social, and cultural policies in China.

In effect, the Outline works at the administrative level. As improving the IP regime becomes a keynote strategy, the NCB and many other departments of the government have been issuing a number of regulations and rules to promote copyright protection. The Outline has also been playing an important role in enhancing the consciousness of ordinary Chinese citizens and inculcating the importance of copyright protection. For instance, within one year after the Outline was published, the application for software copyright registration topped a historical record of 29,804, a 112.9 percent increase compared to the statistic in 2008, while 28,748 applications were approved, a 100.4 percent increase of the 2008 statistic.[129]

4.2.2.2. The digital copyright reforms: consolidating A2R

One of the fundamental pillars of the national copyright strategy is to consolidate A2R. While the RCSP represents one of China's earlier efforts to regulate computer-based copyright, the SPC has taken a leading role in carrying out digital copyright reforms. As early as 2000, the SPC issued the Networks Copyright Interpretation,[130] which deals with issues such as jurisdiction, the right holder's communication right, online reprint and excerpts, and the ISP's liability. Accordingly, the 1990 Copyright Act would apply to the Internet,[131] so that online newspaper/

---

[128] Ibid.
[129] See State Intellectual Property Office of the PRC, 'The Volume of Registration of Copyrighted Software in Our Country Multiplied in the First Half of 2009' ['2009 年上半年我国软件著作权登记量同比成倍增长'], at www.sipo.gov.cn/yw/2009/200907/t20090708_467794.html.
[130] The Interpretation on Several Issues Concerning the Application of Law in the Trial of Cases Involving Copyright Disputes relating to Computer Networks, 22 November 2000 (Networks Copyright Interpretation).
[131] Ibid. Art. 2.

periodicals publishers may enjoy the freedom of online reprint and excerpts in terms of the compulsory license.[132]

In the 2001 amendments, China introduced the "right of communication via information networks" as a new exclusive right for copyright owners, before acceding to the WIPO Internet Treaties. Although the 2001 Copyright Act did not provide specific guidance on how to apply the law to Internet copyright disputes, the State Council may issue separate regulations for the protection of computer software and the right of communication of information on networks.[133] Before the State Council took any steps, however, the SPC updated the Networks Copyright Interpretation in December 2003 by summarising its judicial practice, which represented a further step of the digital copyright reforms in China. The updated interpretation addresses copyright protection in the digital environment and deletes the original provision that provided for a maximum amount of 500 000 Yuan RMB as compensation for online copyright infringement.[134] It also lays down civil liabilities for circumventing TPM, another important legal measure under the WIPO Internet Treaties.[135]

In 2004, the SPC and the SPP jointly released the Interpretations on Several Specific Issues Concerning the Applicable Laws for Handling Criminal Cases relating to Intellectual Property Right Infringement [《关于办理侵犯知识产权刑事案件具体应用法律若干问题的解释》].[136] The Criminal IP Case Interpretations impose more stringent punishments on online copyright infringements with criminal measures, so that the communication of works through the Internet could be treated as "illegal publishing and distributing," in the sense of criminal law.[137] Notably, such development in judicial practice reflects China's response to the pressure from the United States in the bilateral trade negotiations during that period.

---

[132] Ibid. Art. 3.   [133] The 2001 Copyright Act, Art. 58.

[134] Networks Copyright Interpretation, Art. 10.

[135] The Interpretation on Several Issues Concerning the Application of Law in the Trial of Cases Involving Copyright Disputes relating to Computer Networks, Art. 7, done on 22 November 2000, amended on 23 December 2003 (Networks Copyright Interpretation 2003).

[136] The Interpretation on Several Specific Issues Concerning the Applicable Laws for Handling Criminal Cases Relating to Intellectual Property Right Infringement, 2 November 2004.

[137] Ibid., Arts. 5 and 11.

It was only in 2006 that the State Council issued the Information Network Regulation.[138] This regulation, however, is a milestone in China's digital copyright reforms. It specifies the right of making available to the public through the Internet, the TPM, and the RMI as prescribed by the WIPO Internet Treaties.[139] In addition, it extends the applicability of most of the free use doctrines and the educational compulsory license under the 2001 Copyright Act to the digital environment.[140] Further, the regulation also contains detailed provisions on the liabilities of the ISP.[141] Because the regulation does not allow for certain other compulsory licenses (such as that concerning the reprint and excerpts of online newspaper/periodical articles) in the digital environment, the SPC revised its Networks Copyright Interpretation in 2006 and deleted Article 3, which encompassed such compulsory licenses.

Following the aforementioned reforms of substantive digital copyright rules, China has further refined the protection of A2R by improving the enforcement mechanism. On 26 November 2012, the SPC promulgated the "Rules on Several Issues Concerning the Application of Law in the Trial of Civil Disputes Involving the Right of Communication of Information on Networks" [《最高人民法院关于审理侵害信息网络传播权民事纠纷案件适用法律若干问题的规定》].[142] Thus, the Networks Copyright Interpretation is replaced by a more detailed and specific regime of dealing with civil liabilities for online copyright infringement.[143] On 30 January 2013, the State Council revised the Information Network Regulation by raising the sum of administrative fines considerably.[144]

4.2.2.3.   The aftermath of the 2010 revision: prospects of A2K

The other key issue in China's national copyright strategy is A2K. Indeed, the challenge that digital copyright reforms have brought about to the Chinese government is not the heightened incentive in producing free speech but the difficulties in controlling A2K in the Internet. Can copyright law, under the influence of global negotiation process and

---

[138] Regulations on the Protection of the Right of Communication of Information on Networks of the PRC, 18 May 2006 (Information Network Regulation).

[139] Ibid., Arts. 2–5.   [140] Ibid., Arts. 6–8.   [141] Ibid., Arts. 13–17.

[142] SPC of the PRC, Rules on Several Issues Concerning the Application of Law in the Trial of Civil Disputes Involving the Right of Communication of Information on Networks, 17 December 2012 (Information Network Rules).

[143] Ibid., Art. 16.

[144] Information Network Regulation, revised 30 January 2013, Arts. 18–19.

the digital technology, promote A2K in China? To what extent will China's censorship regime hinder the emancipation of free expression by the development of an increasingly sound copyright system? Before any meaningful legislative proposal came up, however, the Sino–US IP dispute, as an outcome of China's international negotiations, brought China to the brink of preupdating its copyright law. China reacted promptly and compliantly after the WTO panel ruling, which vetoes the denial of copyright protection to certain censored works. In 2010, China made a small revision of the 2001 Copyright Act. Having accepted the WTO ruling, the SCNPC removed the clause that denies copyright protection to prohibited works. Article 4 of the Copyright Act now reads:

"Copyright owners should not exercise their copyrights in a manner that violates the Constitution or relevant laws, or harms the public interest. The State will supervise publication and distribution of the works in accordance with law."[145]

Indeed, this provision looks like a Chinese version of Article 17 of the BC. Literally, copyright protection is now extended to all "works," regardless of the restrictions on publication and distribution imposed by the censorship authorities under other laws and regulations. The compliance could, however, only be understood as truncated and *ex parte*: censorship keeps on operating despite the WTO panel ruling because the amendments do not affect the underlying censorship system even literally. Ultimately, it will also be questionable how effective China's enforcement of copyright protection for a work can be. For instance, it is unclear whether the overseas copyright owners will be able to obtain damages if their works cannot be published or distributed in China. The calculation of damages is based on "actual losses," which the Chinese courts have been reluctant to acknowledge,[146] as long as the right holder fails to obtain permission to publish or distribute the work in China.

Nevertheless, the amendments are an indication that China's copyright law is moving in the direction of free expression, though the amendments cover up the underlying question about whether China's

---

[145] The Copyright Act of the PRC, Art. 4, adopted 7 September 1990, revised 27 October 2001 and 26 February 2010 (2010 Copyright Act).

[146] J. Tao, 'Problems and New Development in the Enforcement of Intellectual Property Rights in China', in P. Torremans, H. L. Shan, and J. Erauw (eds.), *Intellectual Property and TRIPS Compliance in China: Chinese and European Perspectives* (Cheltenham-Northampton: Edward Elgar, 2007), p. 107, at 112.

national copyright system should be more pro-A2R or pro-A2K. In a sense, Article 4(1) of the 2001 Copyright Act, which declares that certain works could not enjoy copyright protection, seems to be anti-A2R. It is, however, also anti-A2K in nature considering the enforcement of China's censorship regime. Theoretically, works whose copyrights are no longer protected by law would fall into the public domain and become available to everyone. China has, however, indicated explicitly that it "will always enforce copyrights against infringing edited versions, even when there is no edited version authorised by the author," though the WTO panel wonders how this would be possible under Chinese law.[147] In fact, under the existing system of combining censorship and administrative enforcement of copyright, any attempt to access works that fail content review in China, even in the form of piracy, will be totally banned to ensure "effective action," which, according to China, "is in a sense an alternative form of enforcement against infringement."[148]

At the initial stage of copyright development, the publication of one's ideas often depended on the patronage or financial support of the State or public facilities. The establishment of China's national copyright system was, however, a revolutionary event in facilitating A2R: it made an author's financial independence (and, thus, creative freedom) possible by putting the destiny of their works in the hands of the market, though A2R was rather limited in the beginning. Furthermore, the advent of the wireless telecommunication technologies necessitated the protection of related rights (such as broadcasters' rights or TV/radio station's rights), in which case modern media facilities and industries thrived. Thus, A2R became a cornerstone of ensuring media freedom by providing creative industries with a channel of securing financial viability, regardless of whether the State is reluctant to do so.

In fact, A2R may not easily militate against A2K in the Internet age. The universal dissemination of digital technologies has made free expression an irreversible trend for copyright law because digital copyright gave copyright owners not only the collateral of having their works protected by an electronic fence (for example, through TPM and RMI) but also the option of giving up part or all of their copyright (for instance, by endorsing certain CC). Despite China's digital copyright reforms, which consolidate copyright owners' A2R, global A2K movements might have impacts on Chinese users and, ultimately, enhance the resilience of free

---

[147] *China–IPR*, para. 7.136.   [148] Ibid., para. 7.180.

expression considerably. For one thing, with the advent of CC in China,[149] Chinese copyright owners have had the option of reserving only part of their rights rather than claiming "all rights reserved" or leaving their works in the public domain. In that way, copyright owners may facilitate A2K at reasonable costs as long as they wish. Besides, numerous anonymous users of Baidu Baike, who have no interest in claiming their A2R through copyright protection, have also been able to promote A2K in China on an unprecedented scale.

4.2.3.   Reconsidering Some Kernel Access Rules in Terms of Free Expression

Articles 9 and 10 of the BC endorse the "fair practice" under national laws. In China, such fair practice exists largely in the framework of access rules under the Copyright Act. Essentially, access rules in Chinese copyright law aim to strike the balance between copyright internationalisation (that is, the need to conform to the international copyright treaties) and the government's interest in maintaining the "public order" (largely through censorship). Under such conditions, copyright law deals with the potential conflict between A2R and affordable A2K. The following part reconsiders and evaluates the most representative access rules under the 2010 Copyright Act in the light of this approach.

4.2.3.1.   The status of censorship in copyright law

Article 1 of the Copyright Act lays down the legislative goals of copyright law as (1) "protecting the copyright of authors in their literary, artistic and scientific works and rights related to copyright"; (2) "encouraging the creation and dissemination of works which would contribute to the construction of socialist spiritual and material civilisation"; and (3) "promoting the development and flourishing of socialist culture and sciences."[150] This fundamental provision remains intact as it was in the 1990 Copyright Act. The three goals are interrelated to each other. Accordingly, copyright protection aims, first of all, to protect the private interest of copyright owners in A2R. This should not, however, collide with the goal nurturing the public interest in A2K at reasonable costs. Last but not least, both goals are subject to the overall objective of the

---

[149]   The CC started in China in 2003. See Creative Commons China Mainland [知识共享中国大陆], at http://creativecommons.net.cn/about/history/.

[150]   The 2010 Copyright Act, Art. 1.

socialist culture and science, that is, the government's interest in maintaining the public order and defining it in terms of "socialist" values.

As illustrated in the foregoing discussions, copyright protection in China has followed these goals in a unique way. When copyright standards are low and insufficient to protect the private interest in A2R, the incentive to create works (and free speech) would diminish, although the public interest in having affordable A2K seems to be endorsed. Virtually, the Chinese government adopted this approach to legitimise its power to regulate publication of individual works and impose censorship. By contrast, where copyright standards are raised (for example, by granting right holders high royalties), the government imposed a more powerful administration mechanism to enforce copyright protection, albeit with an aim to intensify the censorship. This diluted mechanism of copyright enforcement, though it obviates the need to solicit authorisation and permission from copyright owners to disseminate their works, could prejudice A2K (and the free flow of information). Therefore, although Chinese copyright law allegedly wields the balance between the private interest and the public interest, the government's interest in conducting censorship prevails and suppresses either A2R or A2K. In that sense, Article 1(3) is the key to understanding the rest of the provisions under the Copyright Act and other copyright regulations.

Further, Article 1 of the Information Network Rules issued recently by the SPC provides that "in adjudicating disputes relating to infringement of the right to communicate information on networks, the courts should exercise their discretionary power in accordance with law and take into account the interests of right holders, ISPs and the public."[151] These rules show that, in digital copyright protection, striking the balance between the private interest and the public interest is not only a legislative goal but also a judicial approach. Thus, the existing Chinese copyright law highlights the balancing approach in order to prioritise the State's interest. In redesigning the national copyright system, however, the State claims to focus merely on the balance between the private interest and the public interest. In principle, these legislative goals should be interpreted in accordance with Articles 7 and 8 of TRIPS, which set forth the pro-A2K functions of copyright law explicitly. Such an approach can be perceived as the radiating effect of Articles 7 and 8 of TRIPS.

---

[151] Information Network Rules, Art. 1.

4.2.3.2.   Censorship and administrative
copyright enforcement

It seems that Article 17 of the BC, together with Articles 7 and 8 of TRIPS, provide legitimate basis for maintaining the public order under Chinese copyright law. After the Copyright Act was amended in 2010, Article 4 has taken on a different outlook, while adhering to the principle of maintaining the public order. Obviously, the "public interest" still refers to the public order as defined by the government. Thus, despite a revision in 2013, the Information Network Regulation has retained the original censorship provision.[152] Whereas the legal effect of the Copyright Act literally trumps that of the regulation, this provision could still be triggered by Article 48 of the Copyright Act, which allows copyright administrative authorities to take administrative measures against copyright infringements if they find the public interest violated.

Since the very beginning, Chinese copyright law has allowed copyright owners to submit their claims of damages for copyright infringement directly to local administrative authorities. In that connection, copyright administrative authorities have been empowered to govern matters relating to the public order such as registration, confirmation of certain rights, and imposing administrative penalties. Where the private interest in A2R and the public interest in affordable A2K are infringed, local authorities are invariably more efficient and prompt than courts in locating such damages and find the most expedient way to curb further damages. In this way, ordinary Chinese citizens could understand and accept copyright law more easily, when they witness administrative authorities enforcing copyright law.

In fact, the dualistic system of copyright enforcement has turned into a fundamental institutional design in the PRC. Indeed, in most countries of the world only courts can grant remedies in the event of copyright infringement, which take the form of either civil or criminal liabilities. In fact, the SPC established a specific chamber for IP in October 1996, which is playing an important role in judicial practice related to copyright protection. What is unique about copyright enforcement in the PRC, however, is the system of administrative liabilities that can be imposed by copyright administrative authorities at various levels of the Chinese government. To a certain extent, this is because the Chinese national copyright system has followed the development of international

---

[152] Information Network Regulation, Art. 3.

copyright law in a passive way, and China has not yet found a completely satisfying pattern of enforcing copyright protection.

No doubt the dualistic system of copyright enforcement has contributed to the implementation of the copyright standards that China promised to maintain under the international copyright treaties. For instance, after the NCB issued the so-called "most stringent ban on copyright infringement in history" in 2015,[153] more than two million unauthorised music works were removed immediately from the Internet.[154] This means, however, that the Chinese government is in full control of the dissemination of most copyrighted works in China. In March 2013, the State Council merged the GAPP with the SARFT into the State Administration of Press, Publication, Radio, Film and Television of the PRC [国家新闻出版广播电影电视总局], still equivalent to the NCB. This might be seen as a new step to coordinate the control of free expression through copyrighted works. Further, the government often carries out a series of special campaigns to implement copyright protection. Admittedly, misuse of power may result from the vague definition of the public interest and the extensive power granted to the copyright administration.

Should China, then, give up such a dualistic system of copyright enforcement? As the court system is not fully independent, copyright administrative authorities will probably continue to play a major role in IP enforcement in dealing with rampant copyright infringement. More important, the dualistic framework of copyright protection is rooted in the political system of the PRC, where there has been no clear border between the functions of the executive branch and those of the judicial branch. Since the establishment of the PRC, a number of quasi-judicial functions have been conferred on executive branches. The judicial reforms since 2014 seek to increase independence of courts by disentangling the personnel appointments and financial arrangements of courts from local governments, but still place such power at the provincial level of the executive branch.[155] Unless the political reform in China takes place at a

---

[153] NCB, Notice on Ordering Online Music Service Providers to Stop the Dissemination of Unauthorised Music Works [《关于责令网络音乐服务商停止未经授权传播音乐作品的通知》], 8 July 2015.

[154] 'The Most Stringent Copyright Order in History Takes Effect: 2,2 Million Music Works Disappear Overnight' ['史上最严版权令生效 220多万首音乐作品一夜消失'], West China Metropolis Daily [《华西都市报》], 6 August 2015, at www.wccdaily.com.cn/shtml/hxdsb/20150806/297472.shtml.

[155] S. Tiezzi, 'Beijing's Blueprint for Judicial Reform', The Diplomat, 12 July 2014.

fundamental level, China would probably not load the court system with the entire task of weighing the balance between A2R and affordable A2K in copyright protection.

4.2.3.3.   Free use as the core free-expression-oriented access rule

In Chinese copyright law, "free use" refers to the most significant type of access rules. It allows the general public to gain access to works protected by copyright without permission from or paying remuneration to the right holder. Article 22 of the Chinese Copyright Act is such a statutory provision that defines "free use" under twelve circumstances. Further, Articles 6–7 of the Information Network Regulation prescribe the free use doctrines in the digital environment. Arguably, these doctrines may serve purposes relating to freedom of expression directly, or may do so indirectly by promoting education and culture.

4.2.3.3.1.   Freedom of expression

4.2.3.3.1.1. *Citation: freedom of speech*   Both the Copyright Act and the Information Network Regulation allow "appropriate quotation from another person's published work in one's own work for the purpose of introducing or commenting a certain work, or explaining a certain point" as a free use.[156] Indeed, citation as a free use enables the general public to collect and disseminate information and allows individuals to exercise their freedom of expressing critical or satirical opinions about certain published ideas in various forms. In fact, Article 10(1) of the BC permits "quotations from a work," which are "compatible with fair practice" such as quotations from "newspaper articles and periodicals in the form of press summaries." Thus, citation fits into the public interest in exercising the freedom to publish and freedom of speech.

In 2006, the famous Chinese director Kaige Chen [陈凯歌] sued Ge Hu [胡戈] for online copyright infringement on the ground that Hu made a parody of about 20 minutes based completely on the pictures of Chen's film but substituted the voice of the players with synchronised dialogues composed by Hu himself.[157] Although the new film became a completely different story and represented a different interpretation of the pictures, Hu uploaded the new film onto the Internet available for the

---

[156] The 2010 Copyright Act, Art. 22.1(2). Information Network Regulation, Art. 6(1).
[157] J. Li [李建中], 'An Open Letter to Kaige Chen' ['致陈凯歌大师的一封公开信'], *Shanghai Morning Post* [《上海晨报》], 14 February 2006.

public. According to Chen, Hu infringed his moral rights, whereas Hu held that this was a free use. In the end, Chen withdrew the action under great social pressure.

In fact, this case can be compared with the US case of *Campbell* v. *Acuff-Rose Music, Inc*, where the Court differentiated "biting criticism that merely suppresses demand" from "copyright infringement, which usurps it" in case of parody.[158] Under the US law, a "transformative" use of a work for the purpose of parody can be regarded as fair use,[159] as long as such use has no negative effect on the potential market of the original work.[160] Indeed, Hu's parody was purely recreational and aimed to criticise Chen's film and make comments on certain other social affairs. The author simply exercised his freedom of speech and employed new digital technologies to serve this goal. Even though the Chinese Copyright Act doesn't provide parody explicitly as a free use, it would go against the ultimate goal of copyright law in promoting advancement of knowledge if Hu had been found to infringe Chen's copyright simply because of the parody. In fact, the Copyright Act and the Information Network Regulation might have provided the legal basis for justifying Hu's act as a reasonable free use, if the Court had been given the chance to interpret such an act of making parody as citation.

4.2.3.3.1.2. *News report/comments on current topics/public speech: freedom of the media*   Not only individuals, but also journalists in the media can cite a work for the purpose of news report. Again, both the Copyright Act and the Information Network Regulation provide that "reuse or citation, for any unavoidable reason, of a published work in newspapers, periodicals, at radio stations, television stations or any other media for the purpose of reporting current events" is a free use.[161] Moreover, the Copyright Act goes on to permit publication and broadcasting in the media of "a speech delivered at a public gathering,"[162] whereas the Information Network Regulation permits "making available to the public a speech delivered at a public gathering."[163] Both provisions comply with Article 2*bis* (1) of the BC, which excludes

---

[158] *Campbell* v. *Acuff-Rose Music, Inc.*, 510 US 569 (1994) II D.   [159] Ibid.
[160] *Princeton University Press* v. *Michigan Document Services Inc.*, 99 F 3d 1381 (6th Cir. 1999).
[161] The 2010 Copyright Act, Art. 22.1(3). Information Network Regulation, Art. 6(2).
[162] The 2010 Copyright Act, Art. 22.1(5).
[163] Information Network Regulation, Art. 6(8).

"political speeches and speeches delivered in the course of legal proceedings" from copyright protection.

In addition, the Copyright Act allows "reprint or rebroadcasting by the
media ... of an article ... on current political, economic or religious
topics."[164] Similarly, the Information Network Regulation permits
"making available to the public articles on current political or economic
topics already published on the Internet."[165] These provisions conform to
Article 10*bis*(1) of the BC, which allows "reproduction by the press, the
broadcasting or the communication to the public by wire of articles
published in newspapers or periodicals on current economic, political
or religious topics. . . ."[166]

In the Internet age, the free use of published news/political speeches
can be a significant breakthrough for ordinary citizens to strive for
their freedom of expression. In China, official websites of public media
are under strict government control, where news or comments or
political speeches are reproduced or cited. It is, however, practically
impossible to prevent such content from being transmitted instantan-
eously to the public through private websites, personal blogs (such as
Sina Weibo), mobile text communication services (such as WeChat),
or by "climbing the firewall" [翻墙] with widespread technologies of
circumventing Internet censorship. These instruments have become
most influential in facilitating the free flow of information in China,
even though these media facilities are also under constant supervision
and censorship.

For these reasons, China is currently seeking to impose a more powerful network of Internet control via new laws. In 2013, the SPC and the
SPP issued a judicial interpretation that criminalises the act of disseminating online information that might constitute defamation and offense
against the State on the basis that such information has been clicked for
over 5,000 times or reproduced for over 500 times.[167] The 2015 Draft of
the Cyber Security Act of the PRC even juxtaposes copyright protection
and the substantial contents of censorship (such as those jeopardising
state security, endorsing terrorism or pornography) as legitimate

---

[164] The 2010 Copyright Act, Art. 22.1(4).
[165] Information Network Regulation, Art. 6(7).   [166] BC, Art. 10*bis* (1).
[167] Interpretation on Several Issues concerning the Specific Application of Law in the
Handling of Defamation through Information Networks and Other Criminal Cases
[《最高人民法院、最高人民检察院关于办理利用信息网络实施诽谤等刑事案件适
用法律若干问题的解释》], Art. 2, 6 September 2013.

legislative goals of the law.[168] Such efforts might render the role of administrative enforcement of copyright protection in China even more outstanding. It would be, however, a real challenge for the government to screen out all the undesirable online content in time.

4.2.3.3.2. Education For a country with the world's largest population, education is an extremely important pro-A2K public interest and a prerequisite for exercising freedom of expression. In China, the most significant activities of public education that are closely related to copyright-protected works include teaching, research, library, and translation into minority languages and Braille.

4.2.3.3.2.1. Teaching and research Because education is a fundamental policy of almost all the governments around the world, it is a common practice to allow free use for the sake of teaching and research. Article 10 (2) of the BC allows exceptions for educational purposes. Thus, the Copyright Act and the Information Network Regulation permit research and teaching staff to reproduce or translate a published work in a small quantity.[169] It must be noted, however, that free use under both provisions refers only to those *pro bono* educational activities rather than commercial educational activities. Besides, such use is strictly confined to unpublished translation and a small quantity of reproduction.

4.2.3.3.2.2. Library use A library is a professional institution for collecting and disseminating knowledge and information for the purpose of promoting education because it provides free access to copyright-protected knowledge goods for the public. As such, a library represents a significant copyright-related public policy of the State. In most countries of the world copyright law would allow free use of published works in the library.[170] In fact, Article 22.1(8) of the Copyright Act also permits "reproduction of a work in its collections by a library, archive, memorial hall, museum, art gallery, and so on for the purpose of display, or preservation of a copy, of the work."[171] This provision, however, does not necessarily justify free use in a pro-A2K way.

---

[168] The Draft of the Cyber Security Act of the PRC, Art. 9, The 12th SCNPC, the 15th Session, June 2015, at www.npc.gov.cn/npc/xinwen/lfgz/flca/2015-07/06/content_1940614.htm.

[169] The 2010 Copyright Act, Art. 22.1(6). Information Network Regulation, Art. 6(3).

[170] *Authors Guild Inc. et al.* v. *Google Inc.*, No. 13-4829-cv (2nd Cir. 2015).

[171] The 2010 Copyright Act, Art. 22.1(8).

In the 2002 *Chen* case,[172] the defendant collected the plaintiff's academic works and uploaded them into the digital library without permission or paying remuneration to the plaintiff. Users of the library may browse or download its works upon paying a small sum of subscription fees. The defendant tried to justify its act on the ground of the public interest in A2K at affordable costs, stating that this is a nonprofit project. The Beijing Haidian District People's Court, however, found that providing digital copies to users on the Internet constitutes copyright infringement of the plaintiff's exclusive right to make available to the public. It seems, at first, that the Court did not support the defendant's suggestion of granting an ad hoc exception to libraries on pro-A2K grounds.

In a similar vein, in the 2004 *Zheng* case,[173] the Court dismissed the defendant's public interest defence, holding that the digitisation of the plaintiff's work constitutes an infringement of the right to make available under the 2001 Copyright Act. Yet, the Court found that the defendant's digital library was not funded by public funding and, thus, not a public library. Therefore, the free use doctrines in Article 22 do not apply to this case. However, requiring a library to be a public funded project in China often means subjecting A2K to government control per se. In the 2005 *Jiang* case,[174] the defendants shared the digital library of CNKI in which 132 of the plaintiff's works amounting to more than one million words were collected without his permission. Although these works had been purchased and downloaded online, the Court held that the defendants' act was free use under Article 22(4) of the Copyright Act because the CNKI project had been authorised by the NCB and, thus, was a project in the public interest.

Ultimately, whether courts would adopt a pro-A2R or a pro-A2K approach may still depend on an interpretation of the public interest.

---

[172] *Chen* v. *Superstar Digital Technology Co. Ltd* [陈兴良诉超星数字技术有限公司], Beijing Haidian District People's Court, (2002) Hai Min Chu Zi [海民初字] No. 5702, 27 June 2002.

[173] *Zheng* v. *Shusheng Digital Technology Co. Ltd* [郑成思诉北京书生数字技术有限公司], Beijing Haidian District People's Court, (2004) Hai Min Chu Zi [海民初字] No. 12509, 20 December 2004; Beijing First Intermediate People's Court, (2005) Yi Zhong Min Zhong Zi [一中民终字] No. 3463, 10 June 2005.

[174] *Jiang* v. *CNKI et al.* [蒋星煜诉上海虹口书城、清华同方光盘股份有限公司、中国学术期刊(光盘版)电子杂志社、清华同方知网(北京)技术有限公司], Shanghai Second Intermediate People's Court, (2005) Hu Er Zhong Min Wu (Zhi) Chu Zi [沪二中民五(知)初字] No. 326, 15 December 2006.

The relevant laws and regulations, however, fail to provide an explicit definition of the public interest. When the State Council issued the Information Network Regulation in 2006, Article 7 of that regulation allows the digitisation of such works by libraries, museums, and other institutions for the same purpose as defined under Article 22.1(8) of the 2001 Copyright Act, extending free use for library purposes to the digital environment.[175] Such free use, however, can only be granted where "a copy in the collection is on the brink of damage or is damaged, lost or stolen, or of which the storage format is outmoded, and which is unavailable or only available at a price obviously higher than the marked one on the market."[176]

4.2.3.3.2.3. *Translation into a minority nationality language and Braille*
The PRC is a multinational state composed of 56 nationalities, where most minorities live in the less wealthy provinces in the western and the northern parts of China. The minorities usually don't have their own written language, and they share many other languages as well. These minorities are often regarded as backward in their economies and disadvantaged in their social status. Historically, they have learned from the Han nationality through the standard Chinese language in order to facilitate their economic and cultural development. For these reasons, both Article 22.1(11) of the Copyright Act and Article 6(5) of the Information Network Regulation allow translation of a published work in Chinese Han language into any minority nationality language as free use.

The following conditions, however, must be satisfied to qualify for such free use: first, the works are created by a Chinese citizen, legal entity, or any other organisation rather than by a foreigner or a person without nationality; second, the works must be written in the Han language rather than any other language; third, the works must have been published; and fourth, the translated works must be published only in China and not in any foreign country.[177] Indeed, these rules resemble those contained in Article II of the Berne Appendix, which provides a compulsory license for developing countries regarding the translation right. This free use doctrine, however, illustrates the policy goal of the Chinese government in facilitating the dominant ideology in the minority regions.

---

[175] Information Network Regulation, Art. 7(1).
[176] The 2010 Copyright Act, Art. 22.1(8). Ibid., Art. 7(2).
[177] The 2010 Copyright Act, Art. 22.1(11). Information Network Regulation, Art. 6(5).

Besides, blind people cannot read as ordinary people, but rely on touching the Braille to understand and study, which leaves these people at a disadvantageous position. To help these people better gain A2K and participate in cultural life, copyright laws around the world have provided exceptions for these people as free use. Article 22.1(12) of the Copyright Act permits "transliteration of a published work into Braille and publication of the work so transliterated."[178] The works referred to in this provision are not limited to those created by Chinese authors as under Article 22.1(11), so that any types of works by anyone can be transliterated into Braille. Article 6(6) of the Information Network Regulation continues to apply this doctrine in the digital environment, but limits the doctrine to the use for "non-commercial purposes."[179]

4.2.3.3. Culture   Cultural development is an important public interest that contributes to forming public opinions and promotes free expression. In the Copyright Act, however, free use of works for promoting cultural development often contributes to private purposes such as use of artistic works in the public, free performance, and entertainment.

4.2.3.3.1. Use of artistic works in the public   To guarantee the right to study, research and appreciate artistic works freely, Article 22.1(10) of the Copyright Act allows copying, drawing, photographing, or video recording of an artistic work located or on display in an outdoor public place as free use.[180] This doctrine does not apply in the digital environment. Accordingly, such artistic works must be located "in an outdoor public place," while the form of free use is confined only to the said acts, which militates against direct form of contact such as print. Because such works are displayed in the public for the purpose of allowing the public to study and appreciate them, it is difficult to prevent the public from committing the preceding said acts. In such cases, it would be unfeasible and unnecessary to acquire permission from the right holder of, say, a statute. Such free use is a common practice in many countries around the world. In fact, Articles 3(3) and 17 of the BC refer to the use of such works for the purpose of "exhibition."

---

[178] The 2010 Copyright Act, Art. 22.1(12).
[179] Information Network Regulation, Art. 6(6).
[180] The 2010 Copyright Act, Art. 22.1(10).

4.2.3.3.3.2. *Free performance*   Article 22.1(9) of the Copyright Act provides for free use in the form of "gratuitous live performance of a published work, where no fees are charged to the public, nor payments are made to the performers."[181] Just as the use of artistic works in the public, this doctrine does not apply in the digital environment, either. In addition, such performance is subject to stringent conditions. First, it must be free to the public, and performers may not receive any remuneration. Second, free use exists only when "published works" are performed for free, whereas unpublished works do not fit into this doctrine. Finally, such free performance cannot prejudice the entitlements of the right holder (for example, indicating identity of authorship). Such a free use doctrine may help enrich the cultural life of ordinary Chinese people because free performance assumes significant value in China as a long tradition (such as comic repartee or skit), which often allows performers to criticise the society or even politics openly. Nevertheless, this provision does not seem to be entirely consistent with Article 11(1)(i) of the BC, which allows authors of dramatic/musical works to "enjoy the exclusive right of authorising the public performance of their works, including such public performance by any means or process."

4.2.3.3.3.3. *Entertainment*   Article 22.1(1) of the Copyright Act allows free use of published works "for purposes of the user's own personal study, research or self-entertainment."[182] Thus, a private free use for the purpose of self-entertainment is subject to two conditions: first, it must be for one's own private use and may not be disseminated to others; second, it must be noncommercial. Some Chinese scholars, however, suggest that the word *self-entertainment* be deleted because use of published works for self-entertainment should not be a reasonable free use.[183] Indeed, copyright laws of major countries do not include self-entertainment as a private fair use.[184] In China, "self-entertainment," together with "study" and "research," is allowed for free in most cases only to provide a relaxed environment for ordinary Chinese citizens who

---

[181] Ibid., Art. 22.1(9).   [182] Ibid., Art. 22(1).

[183] K. Hu [胡开忠], 'Limitation and De-limitation of Copyright' ['著作权的限制与反限制'], in H. Liang [梁慧星] (ed.), *Civil and Commercial Law Review* [《民商法论丛》] (北京: 法律出版社, 1997), p. 577.

[184] See, e.g., Gesetz über Urheberrecht und verwandte Schutzrechte (German Act on Copyright and Related Rights), done on 9 September 1965, last revised on 14 December 2012, § 53(1).

may gain access to information and data for cultural development, which fits into the public interest in A2K at affordable costs.

4.3. Redesigning National Access Rules in the New Copyright Act of the PRC in the Light of Free-Expression-Oriented International Standards

As it became necessary to find a more adequate instrument to implement its national copyright policies, China started to launch a new revision of its Copyright Act in 2012.[185] This draft is of great importance for China to redesign its access rules as a tool of regulating free expression. So far the submitted draft has been identified as a "user-unfriendly" document.[186] In a sense, this reflects the fact that A2K, a core factor underlying free expression, remains a challenge in the course of promoting copyright protection in China.

4.3.1. The Process of Drafting a New National Copyright Act

After three decades of economic reforms and numerous international negotiations, China has established a modern national copyright system with the Copyright Act as the most fundamental source of copyright law. Besides, there are a number of legal sources of administrative regulations including the RICA, the RIICC, the RPSC, the Information Network Regulation, the Regulations of Copyright Collective Management (RCCM) [《著作权集体管理条例》],[187] and the Provisional Measures of Remuneration Payment Concerning the Phonograms of Broadcasting

---

[185] In 2012 the NCB published two drafts of revising the current Copyright Act and solicited public opinions for improving the drafts. For the fundamental principles and the history of making the draft see the NCB, Brief Illustration to the Revised Draft of the Copyright Act of the PRC (March 2012), 4–10, at www.ncac.gov.cn/cms/html/309/3502/201203/740608.html. The original draft of revision (31 March 2012) is available at www.ncac.gov.cn/cms/html/309/3502/201203/740608.html. The second draft of revision (6 July 2012) is available at www.ncac.gov.cn/cms/html/309/3502/201207/759779.html. The third draft of revision (October 2012) is available at http://wenku.baidu.com/view/5f6c312e58fb770bf78a5528.html. The final revision draft (6 June 2014), which has been submitted to the State Council (Final Revision Draft), is available at www.jetro.go.jp/ext_images/world/asia/cn/ip/law/pdf/origin/opinion20140606.pdf.
[186] H. Xue, 'A User-Unfriendly Draft: 3rd Revision of the Chinese Copyright Law' (2012) 7:4 J Int'l Commercial L Tech 350.
[187] Regulations of Copyright Collective Management of the PRC, 28 December 2004.

Stations and Television Stations [《广播电台电视台播放录音制品支付报酬暂行办法》].[188] Even criminal law in China defines copyright infringement as a crime under certain circumstances.[189] Alone the NCB had issued nine department regulations and forty-four specific rules by 2012.[190] The highest judicial authorities in the PRC (including the SPC and the SPP) have issued at least six judicial interpretations, as well as guiding rules with respect to specific application of laws in civil and criminal trials. In addition, the legislative authorities and governments in the provinces, autonomous regions, and municipal cities have promulgated numerous copyright rules.

However, the 2001 and 2010 amendments of the 1990 Copyright Act have not changed the basic tenor of copyright rules that derived from a planned economy. Although both amendments of the 1990 Copyright Act aimed to cater to the needs of acceding to the WTO and the ruling of the DSB of the Sino–US IP dispute, respectively, they no longer reflect the economic and social development of the PRC in an overall sense. With the deepening globalisation of knowledge economy and widespread use of information technology, the Chinese society is undergoing a full-scale transformation. As intellectual creation is playing an irreplaceable role in national development strategy, it becomes urgent for China to make a complete overhauling of the existing national copyright system in terms of free expression.

In July 2011, the State Council invited experts from all over the country to start the legislative project of amending the Copyright Act. The NCB set up a working team composed of representatives from the government, industries, and research institutions. Since July 2011 opinions have been solicited from all circles of the society, while prestigious copyright research institutions in China have been entrusted to draft an expert amendment. After three drafts were brought together in January 2012, the NCB convened a conference to discuss the drafts. Thereafter, the work was accomplished in February 2012, and a second conference was held in March 2012 to discuss the draft.

On the basis of the opinions gathered at the conference, the NCB made several amendments and published the first Revision Draft on 31 March

---

[188] The Provisional Measures of Remuneration Payment Concerning the Phonograms of Broadcasting Stations and Television Stations [《广播电台电视台播放录音制品支付报酬暂行办法》], 10 November 2009.
[189] Brief Illustration to the Revised Draft of the Copyright Act of the PRC, p. 3.
[190] See, e.g., the Criminal Act of the PRC, Art. 217.

2012, on its website to solicit opinions from the society. Various circles of people from China and abroad participated in the debate on the amendments of the Copyright Act. In May 2012, the third conference was held to allow experts from both legislative departments and judicial authorities to discuss those opinions thus gathered. In July 2012, the second draft amendments were published online for soliciting opinions from the whole society. In October 2012, the NCB convened another conference and produced a third draft of the amendments of the Copyright Act. The final updated draft, which was published online for public opinions in June 2014, was submitted to the State Council earlier in 2015 (Final Revision Draft) [送审稿].

4.3.2. *The Guiding Principles for Future Copyright Reforms*

4.3.2.1. The principle of copyright internationalisation

As the first principle of copyright reforms, copyright internationalisation was a most important driving force for the 1990 Copyright Act and the two amendments in 2001 and 2010. Indeed, the Chinese government cares a lot about polishing its image as a responsible economic power in international economic relations. Through numerous IP and trade negotiations in the past decades, China has learned to follow the need to check regularly the gap that exists between Chinese copyright law and relevant international copyright treaties. Where it appears necessary and appropriate, China would adapt its national copyright system to international copyright standards and turn international law into national law. A most important example is that the Final Revision Draft contains rules concerning rental rights and updates rules concerning the TPM and the RMI.

4.3.2.2. The principle of localisation

The legislators in China always bear in mind the local needs of economic and social development in order to find a solution to deal with domestic issues. Today, the right holder in China has been well informed of copyright protection and is fully aware of the private interest in A2R. Moreover, the publication industry in China has steadily boomed with widespread use of the digital technology, while the Chinese government will need to reconsider how to maintain the control of China's media industry. As the PRC is at a crucial crossroad of social transformation, it is highly important to establish a national copyright system that takes into account the realistic needs of economic, social, and cultural development. Thus, legislators often see it as undesirable to adapt China's national copyright laws by following the international copyright treaties "blindly." As such, the Final Revision Draft responds positively to the needs of copyright industries and encompasses rules concerning applied art works and the three-step test.

4.3.2.3.   The principle of interest balancing

Consequently, it is necessary to find equilibrium between copyright internationalisation and China's needs of localisation, in particular, the "public order" defined by the Chinese government. In other words, there is a conflict between free-expression-oriented copyright law and censorship-oriented copyright law. In revising the Copyright Act, China has made it a fundamental principle to maintain the balance between A2R and A2K at reasonable costs. By doing so, copyright law may either facilitate or hinder freedom of expression of individuals and freedom of information of the general public. It is, thus, crucial for legislators in China to reevaluate the existing national access rules regularly in terms of these considerations. This task remains to be accomplished, as China's IP and trade negotiations increasingly ratchet up the request for reshaping a free-expression-oriented framework.

4.3.3.   The Legal Framework of Access Rules under the New Final Revision Draft

4.3.3.1.   The pro-A2R rules: ensuring the financial independence of copyright owners from the State

As this study shows, pro-A2R rules are significant not only in securing economic benefits for copyright owners, but also in ensuring their financial independence from the State (which is the prerequisite of creative freedom). The development of copyright law renders three generations of such creators outstanding: traditional individual copyright owners, media industries/facilities, and right holders in the digital environment. The proposals in the Final Draft cover A2R by all of them.

4.3.3.1.1.   More complete A2R rules for traditional copyright owners
First, the Final Revision Draft proposes pro-A2R adjustments to several types of authorship. For instance, it addresses a specific

Chinese A2R-related issue, that is, the potential tension between individual authorship and the "ownership" by the "working units" to which such authors belong. Thus, an individual performer will enjoy authorship over her/his own performance, whereas the organising unit will enjoy the right to use the performance freely as long as its business license permits.[191] If, however, the organising unit enjoys authorship over collective performance, individual performers are entitled to reasonable remuneration.[192]

Second, Article 9 of the Final Revision Draft introduces the idea/expression dichotomy. Thus, the universal prerequisites of subject matter, which exist sporadically in various regulations, will be integrated and laid down uniformly in the new Copyright Act. What's more, Article 5 of the Final Revision Draft defines "literary, artistic and scientific works" explicitly as "intellectual creations that assume originality and can be fixed in a tangible form." Other readjustments ensure the principle of national treatment. For example, works of applied art have not been protected so far under the existing copyright law. However, Article 6 of the RIICC grants protection to foreign works of applied art whose term of protection, as under Article 7(4) of the BC, is 25 years after its completion. Such imbalance that goes beyond national treatment is a serious flaw. Article 5(2)(ix) of the Final Revision Draft will grant protection to works of applied art with a term of 25 years uniformly.

Finally, copyright collective management is an indispensable rule of ensuring A2R, while the current Copyright Act fails to include essential rules that are provided in the RCCM. In that connection, the Final Revision Draft allows copyright owners to materialise their A2R through sophisticated procedures.[193] Other commentators, however, criticise the copyright collective management organisation (CCMO) as an arbitrary institution[194] because the CCMO in China is an exclusive organ that is subordinate to the Chinese government. Free expression, which rests on A2R and A2K in this circumstance, will become more vulnerable if government institution intervenes in the CCMO.

---

[191] Final Revision Draft, Art. 36.   [192] Ibid.   [193] Ibid., Arts. 61–7.

[194] C. Xu [徐词], 'I Must Protect You: the Revision Draft of the Copyright Act Is Trapped in Controversy' ['我就要来保护你?—著作权法修改草案陷入争议漩涡'], *The Southern Weekly* [《南方周末》], 20 April 2012.

4.3.3.1.2. Expanding economic rights for the media industry The right of making available online under Article 10(12) of the 2001 amendments reflects a broadly defined and technology-neutral right over works transmitted through different media facilities. The Final Revision Draft further provides new rights that expand A2R for the media industry. For example, Article 13 of the Final Revision Draft incorporates the digitisation of works into the reproduction right, allows alternative forms of transferring the ownership under the distribution right, and grants rental rights over works fixed in phonograms. Article 11 of the Final Revision Draft also proposes important revisions of the neighbouring rights by defining the "right to broadcast" as "the right to transmit to the public" (non-peer-to-peer). These proposals could promote the financial independence of media facilities in China.

With the development of digital technology and network technology, the traditional commercial model of distributing tangible phonograms is close to dying out. Therefore, it becomes an urgent task for the music industry to design new rights for the sake of sustainable development. In recent years, the music industry (in particular the phonogram companies) in China has lobbied for granting the right of making available and performance rights to producers of phonograms. Thus, under Article 40 of the Final Revision Draft, performers and producers of phonograms are entitled to remuneration in two circumstances: first, transmission of the phonograms through wireless or cable means; second, disseminating or performing the phonograms through technological equipment. Besides, the existing rights of broadcasting and television stations, which cover primarily wireless and cabled transmission of programs, are extended to the Internet. Article 42 of the Final Revision Draft grants broadcasting and television stations the right to permit a third party to transmit, record, and reproduce their programs. This right, which differs from the right to make available to the public through the Internet, could broaden the scope of A2R for the media industry.

4.3.3.1.3. Digital copyright: linking copyright to free expression Article 47(6) and (7) of the 2001 Copyright Act provide for new enforcement measures authorising criminal sanctions and civil remedies against the use of a device for the circumvention of TPM and the intentional removal or tampering with electronic RMI. Nevertheless, these access rules, which aim at ensuring A2R, are flawed and untenable: there is no explicit provision about TPM and RMI except for these two remedy provisions that are placed under the title of "liabilities," though Article 4 of the 2006 Information Network Regulation provides for the TPM in the digital environment.[195] In contrast, the Final Revision Draft sets forth a separate chapter for the TPM and the RMI,[196] changes the existing definition of "technological measures" and "rights management electronic information," respectively,[197] and applies them in both the traditional and the digital environment.[198] The Final Revision Draft, however, also allows circumvention of the TPM and RMI for the purpose of classroom teaching and research, noncommercial use by blind persons, carrying out executive and judicial functions, or testing the security of computer systems or networks.[199]

Importantly, Article 73 of the Final Revision Draft establishes the "safe harbour" doctrines for ISPs in the light of the US model. The provision exculpates an ISP from the liability for providing connection, searching or hosting services to allegedly infringing contents by alleviating them of the obligation to examine the rights information of the contents. To be indemnified against liabilities for copyright infringement, ISPs may have a duty to detect, identify, and filter infringing materials or activities on their system or networks. Further, a copyright owner may notify the relevant ISP in written form of the details concerning potentially infringing contents and request the ISP to remove them. Upon receipt of such notice, the ISP shall immediately take measures to deal with such content, in which case ISPs will not be liable for damages. In contrast, if the ISP knows, or ought to know, that the materials in question are infringing without taking any necessary steps, it will bear joint liability.

However, these provisions of enhancing A2R in the digital environment might also produce chilling effects on A2K and the free flow of information, as it is typically with safe harbour law.[200] Obviously, ISPs are obliged to monitor the Internet and impose a filtering system. In China, there is reason to believe that ISPs will have more pressure and even an incentive to carry out censorship in the name of fulfilling the obligation of checking copyrightable contents. Therefore, a free-

---

[195] Information Network Regulation, Art. 4. [196] Final Revision Draft, Arts. 68–71.
[197] Ibid., Art. 68. [198] Ibid., Art. 69–70. [199] Ibid., Art. 71.
[200] See, e.g., CJEU, Case 314/12. See also *Twentieth Century Fox* v. *Newzbin Ltd* [2010] EWHC 608 (Ch) (29 March 2010); *Twentieth Century Fox et al.* v. *British Telecommunications Plc* [2011] EWHC 1981 (Ch).

expression-oriented interest-balancing approach and a test of proportionality would be indispensable to prevent copyright owners and ISPs from misusing their rights.

4.3.3.2.   Pro-A2K rules: securing information flow in terms of international standards

In addition, the Final Revision Draft has drawn on different models that represent international standards and creates mechanism that may, at least, facilitate the free flow of information in the copyright scenario. It is, however, difficult to predict the effects of the proposals.

4.3.3.2.1.   Uncertain free use doctrines   As the Final Revision Draft aims to introduce some universal principles, the new system of free use is being reshaped primarily in the US model. The overall effect of such a free use doctrine on promoting A2K, however, seems to be shrinking. Under the current Copyright Act, free use of knowledge goods may be allowed for the purpose of "a person's own private study, research or self-entertainment."[201] Article 43(1) of the Final Revision Draft contains an important revision. It deletes "self-entertainment" as a free use and makes it clear that only reproduction of the excerpts of published works will be permitted for the said purpose. It seems that the Final Revision Draft aims to enhance the protection of the private interest in A2R without taking much regard for the public needs for self-entertainment at lower costs.

Another proposal can be perceived as a step toward adopting the "substantiality" test under the US fair use doctrine.[202] The Copyright Act allows "appropriate quotation from a published work in one's own work for the purposes of introduction of, or comment on, a work, or demonstration of a point."[203] Article 43(2) of the Final Revision Draft, however, requires that the quoted part of any works should not constitute the "main or substantial" part of the works being used. The Final Revision Draft also aims to apply the free use doctrine in the digital environment. Thus, the existing free use doctrine, which is granted for the purpose of news report, comments on the issues of politics, economy, religion, and public speech, extends from the traditional media to the "information networks."[204]

---

[201] The 2010 Copyright Act, Art. 22(1).
[202] *Sony Corporation of America et al.* v. *Universal City Studios Inc.*, at 50.   [203] Ibid.
[204] Final Revision Draft, Art. 43(3)–(5).

Notably, just as the US fair use doctrine has been characterised as an "open-ended" provision,[205] a new clause in the form of an open-ended provision is inserted into the Final Revision Draft, which allows for "other uses" of works "without the permission from, and without payment of remuneration to, the copyright owner, provided that the name of the author and the title of the work are mentioned and the other rights enjoyed by the copyright owner by virtue of this Act are not infringed upon."[206] It will only be possible to evaluate the effect of such an open-ended fair use doctrine in China after the provision is put into practice.

Finally, Article 43 of the Final Revision Draft provides that all the said fair uses "shall not influence the normal exploitation of the work, or unreasonably prejudice the legitimate interests of the right holder." This is almost a verbatim duplication of Article 13 of TRIPS and reflects the aim of legislators to achieve the consistency between the new Copyright Act and TRIPS. Given the flexibilities in interpreting Article 13, Chinese courts would be able to decide whether to impose an expansive or a shrinking approach of interpreting the limitation and exception rules.

4.3.3.2.2. More feasible rules of compulsory license   The Final Revision Draft also retools the compulsory license to facilitate A2K at reasonable costs under certain special circumstances. In the past two decades of legal practice, almost no users of compulsory license paid remuneration to right holders. Nor was anyone held liable for their failure to do so. Because A2R cannot be guaranteed, there were proposals that the compulsory license should be abolished. Nonetheless, the fundamental values and functions of compulsory license, which lie primarily in promoting A2K and information flow, would still fit into China's domestic economic and social development. The regime failed to work well simply because there was no effective system of paying remuneration and remedies. Therefore, the Final Revision Draft made some adjustments to the current access rule of compulsory license.

Accordingly, compulsory license will be confined to three circumstances. First, in compiling textbooks for "the nine-year compulsory education or state education planning," one can make free use of

---

[205] S. Ricketson, WIPO Study on Limitations and Exceptions of Copyright and Related Rights in the Digital Environment, p. 69, Standing Committee on Copyright and Related Rights, 9 Session, Geneva, June 23 to 27, 2003, WIPO Doc.SCCR/9/7 (E), dated 5 April 2003.

[206] Final Revision Draft, Art. 43(13).

different types of works including "excerpts of already published works or short literary works or music works, or single fine artworks, photographic works or graphs."[207] Second, literary works published in newspapers and periodicals can be reprinted as reference materials in any other newspaper and periodicals without permission from the authors, unless the first publishers enjoy exclusive rights to reprint as authorised by authors and have explicitly forbidden others to reprint.[208] Third, broadcasting and TV stations may, without the permission from copyright owners, broadcast their published works (except for audiovisual products).[209] These types of access rules continue to serve the public interest of ordinary Chinese citizens in gaining A2K at reasonable costs.

Under such a system of compulsory license, however, public users will have to follow certain procedural conditions. First, users of the said two types of compulsory license must apply for registration at the relevant CCMO prior to its first use. Second, they shall indicate the names of authors and the titles and sources of the works being used. Third, within one month of its use of the work, users must make payment according to the national standards either to the right holder (direct payment) or through the CCMO to the right holder (indirect payment).[210] Because the standards of remuneration for compulsory license are clearly related to the public interest, the government takes these matters into account as part of its public policy and will provide for such standards specifically. In case a party dissents with the remuneration standards, the State Council may organise a committee to award arbitrary rulings.[211] Such adjustments will both meet the needs of the public in gaining timely A2K at affordable costs and ensure the legitimate rights and interest of rights holders in having A2R.

4.3.3.3.   More refined enforcement rules relating to the public interest

While China relies heavily on administrative enforcement of copyright protection, there is no clear definition about the "prejudice against the public interest" in Article 48 of the Copyright Act under which circumstances administrative branches may take measures. This would impair the legitimacy of access rules relating to the public interest. Therefore, the second Revision Draft substitutes the wording "prejudice against the public interest" with "prejudice against the order of

---

[207] Final Revision Draft, Art. 47.   [208] Ibid., Art. 48.   [209] Ibid., Art. 49.
[210] Ibid., Art. 50.   [211] Ibid., Art. 62.

socialist market economy."[212] The Final Revision Draft, however, no longer refers to the vague "public interest." This does not mean that China will abolish the prevalent administrative enforcement mechanism in copyright law. Rather, the Final Revision Draft has made technical improvements by specifying what kind of administrative measures (such as warning, confiscating illegal gains or instruments, and imposing fines) the copyright administrative organs can take under specific circumstances.[213]

4.4. Conclusion

After its accession to the WTO, the PRC has had a wide range of choices in international negotiation platforms concerning copyright protection. China has taken an active part in various multilateral IP negotiations at WIPO. Moreover, China has learned to avail itself of the DSM to negotiate with its trade partners on difficult issues that cannot be solved easily through bilateral negotiations. The Sino–US Copyright Dispute is of particular importance for sounding alarm of the lack of a free-expression-oriented copyright system in China. In addition, China has continued to position itself in bilateral IP and trade negotiations with significant partners, including the United States and the EU, to address copyright-related issues such as new problems posed by the information technology. The ACTA and the TPP, however, remain a challenge for China and the world because both agreements contain inherent demands for a free-expression-oriented copyright system, and they would be incomplete treaty law without China playing a role in the system.

Through international IP and trade negotiations, the Chinese national economy is increasingly being integrated into the global knowledge economy. Being fully aware of the significance of global economic rules, China is experiencing an economic slowdown and facing the challenge of carrying out profound structural reforms. Although the current administration seems to offer a bleak prospect on loosening the control of free expression, the domestic and international pressure for furthering China's economic and social development renders a free-expression-oriented copyright system irreversible. Indeed, China has taken pains to work out its own national IP strategy

---

[212] Second Revision Draft, Art. 73.   [213] Final Revision Draft, Art. 77.

in 2008, which encompasses important measures to improve A2R and A2K in its national copyright system. In fact, both international copyright treaties and international copyright-related negotiations provide important impetus for redesigning China's national copyright system. Since the ruling of the WTO panel on *China–IPR*, censorship is, literally, no longer a prerequisite for copyright protection in Chinese copyright law, although censorship will continue to be an underlying factor that affects the outcome of copyright protection.

Throughout the process of international negotiations China has accumulated sufficient experiences and legal resources for redesigning its national copyright system. Essentially, China's contemporary copyright system is censorship-oriented: it is still a product based largely on China's planned economy prior to the 1990s. The birth of China's national copyright system and the two revisions done to the Copyright Act (and the other relevant regulations) are also largely the result of external pressure. It is time to reconsider the legal framework of access rules that may lead to a free-expression-oriented copyright system. The current framework consists of certain conflicting elements, including the provisions on censorship (albeit more clandestinely), the administrative enforcement, and the free use doctrines on free expression and other A2K-related cases. It remains a challenge to render these rules more coherent.

At this moment, China is engaged in a new revision of the Copyright Act, which aims to redesign the overall national copyright system in terms of the need for copyright internationalisation and domestic economic and social development. The final Revision Draft shows that the results of China's three decades of hard international IP and trade negotiations are fruitful. Certainly, after the minds of most Chinese have been soaked in a censorship-driven society for thousands of years, one might doubt whether the fruits of copyright-related international negotiations – China's interest balancing approach *inter alia* – would really ensure the financial independence of copyright owners in both traditional and digital context. However, there is reason to believe that the facilities of modern copyright law, together with the new technologies, could facilitate the impetus of intellectuals to exercise their free speech and the irreversible process of free information flow among the public. In the nineteenth century, no one could foresee that copyright, an unexpected by-product of censorship left unnoticed by the emperors, together with international negotiations, which used to be a humiliating symbol of the decline of the central empire, would turn out to be a gift for Chinese intellectuals at the beginning of the twentieth century. A century later, one may have more reasons to believe that, in an age of networked information, copyright and international negotiations, as a robust engine of free expression, remain a blessing for China, regardless of the intransigent mind-set and sophisticated tentacles of the Leviathan.

BIBLIOGRAPHY

Books

Alford, W. P., *To Steal a Book Is an Elegant Offence: Intellectual Property Law in Chinese Civilization* (Stanford, CA: Stanford University Press, 1995).

Allen, Y. J. [林乐知] et al. (eds.), *International Communique* [《万国公报》], 60 vols. (上海: 上海书店, 2014), vol. 36, Book 183.

Bao, T. [包天笑], *The Reminiscence of the Chuanying Mansion* [《钏影楼回忆录》] (台北: 文海出版社, 1980).

Benkler, Y., *The Wealth of Networks: How Social Production Transforms Markets and Freedom* (New Haven, CT and London: Yale University Press, 2006).

Bently, L. and Sherman, B., *Intellectual Property Law*, 3rd edn (Oxford: Oxford University Press, 2009).

Bodde, D., *China's First Unifier: A Study of the Ch'in Dynasty as Seen in the life of Li Ssu* (Hong Kong: Hong Kong University Press, 1967).

Bodde, D. and Morris, C., *Law in Imperial China: Exemplified by 190 Qing Dynasty Cases* (Cambridge, MA: Harvard University Press, 1971).

Carter, T. F., *The Invention of Printing in China and Its Spread Westward* (New York: Columbia University Press, 1925).

Coase, R. and Wang, N., *How China Became Capitalist* (Basingstoke: Palgrave Macmillan, 2012).

Cohen, J. E. et al., *Copyright in a Global Information Economy* (New York: Aspen Publishers, 2006).

Correa, C. M., *Trade Related Aspects of Intellectual Property Rights: A Commentary on TRIPS* (Oxford: Oxford University Press, 2007).

Cui, J. [崔建农], *The Red Past Events: Chinese Films in 1966–1976* [《红色往事 1966–1976 年的中国电影》] (北京: 台海出版社, 2001).

Dimitrov, M., *Piracy and the State: The Politics of Intellectual Property Rights in China* (Cambridge: Cambridge University Press, 2012).

Dinwoodie, G. B. and Dreyfuss, R. C., *A Neofederalist Vision of TRIPS: The Resilience of the International Intellectual Property Regime* (Oxford: Oxford University Press, 2012).

Drahos, P., *A Philosophy of Intellectual Property* (Aldershot: Dartmouth Publishing Co., 1996).

Editing Committee of the Journals of the Chinese Modern History of Economy [中国近代经济史资料丛刊编辑委员会], *The Commercial Negotiations after the Boxer Protocol* [《辛丑合约订立以后的商约谈判》] (北京: 中华书局, 1994).

Efroni, Z., *Access-Right: The Future of Digital Copyright Law* (Oxford: Oxford University Press, 2011).

Fairbank, J. K. and Goldman, M., *China: A New History*, 2nd enlarged edn (Cambridge, MA: Belknap Press of Harvard University Press, 2006).

Feng, P., *Intellectual Property in China* (Hong Kong: Sweet & Maxwell Asia, 1997).

Feng, Y. [冯友兰], 'The Written Speech at the Second Conference of the Sixth Session of the National CPPCC' ['全国政协六届二次会议的书面发言'], in Feng, Y., *The Collected Works of Sansong Tang* [《三松堂全集》], 15 vols. (郑州: 河南人民出版社,1994), vol. XIII.

Gervais, D., *TRIPS: Drafting History and Analysis*, 3rd edn (London: Sweet & Maxwell, 2008).

He, Q.[何勤华](ed.), *The Essential Essays of Jurisprudence of the Republic of China: Civil and Commercial Law* [《民国法学论文精粹·民商法律篇》], 6 vols. (北京: 法律出版社, 2004), vol. 3.

Holdsworth, W., *A History of English Law*, 2nd edn, 12 vols. (London: Methuen Publishing Ltd, 1939, reprinted 1966), vol. VI.

Huang, L. [黄林], *Study on the Publication Industry under the New Politics during the Period of the Late Qing Dynasty* [《晚清新政时期图书出版业研究》] (长沙: 湖南师范大学出版社, 2007).

Huang, Q. [黄勤南](ed.), *The New Textbook of Intellectual Property Law* [《新编知识产权法教程》] (北京: 中国政法大学出版社, 1995).

Jiang, P. and Shen, R. [江平、沈仁干], *Lectures on the Copyright Law of the PRC* [《中华人民共和国著作权法讲析》] (北京: 中国国际广播出版社, 1991).

Jiang, Z. [江泽民], *On Science and Technology* [《论科学技术》] (北京: 中央文献出版社, 2001).

Joyce, C. et al., *Copyright Law*, 5th edn (New York: Lexis Publishing, 2000).

Kong, Q., *China and the World Trade Organization: A Legal Perspective* (Singapore: World Scientific Publishing, 2002).

Kuang, Y. [匡亚明], *Comments on Confucius* [《孔子评传》] (山东: 齐鲁书社, 1985).

Lai, X. [来新夏], *The History of Chinese Publication Industry* [《中国图书事业史》] (上海: 上海人民出版社, 2000).

Levenson, J., *Modern China and Its Confucian Past: The Problems of Intellectual Continuity* (Garden City, New York: Anchor Books, 1964).

Li, M. [李明山], *The Chinese Modern Copyright History* [《中国近代版权史》] (开封: 河南大学出版社, 2003).

Li, M. et al. [李明山 等], *The Contemporary Chinese History of Copyright* [《中国当代版权史》] (北京: 知识产权出版社, 2007).

Li, Y. [李育民], *The Treaty System in Modern China* [《近代中国的条约制度》] (长沙: 湖南师范大学出版社, 1995).

Liu, A. P. L., *Communication and National Integration in Communist China* (Berkeley: University of California Press, 1971).

Liu, C. [刘春田], *Twenty Years of China's Copyright 1978–1998* [《中国知识产权二十年 (1978–1998)》] (北京: 专利文献出版社, 1998).

Locke, J., *Two Treatises of Government*, 2nd edn (Cambridge: Cambridge University Press, 1690, *reprinted* 1967).

Long, D. E. and D'Amato, A., *A Coursebook in International Intellectual Property* (St. Paul, MN: West Group, 2000).

Lü, H. [吕海寰], *Memorials Submitted by Haihuan Lü* [《吕海寰奏稿》] (台北: 文海出版社, 1997), vol. I.

MacFarquhar, R., *The Origins of the Cultural Revolution: Contradictions among the People, 1956–1957* (New York: Columbia University Press, 1974), vol. 1.

Marx, K., *Grundrisse: Foundations of the Critique of Political Economy (Rough Draft) 1857–1858* (Harmondsworth: Penguin, 1973).

Masouyé, C., *Guide to the Berne Convention for the Protection of Literary and Artistic Works* (Geneva: WIPO, 1978).

Miu, Y. [缪咏禾], *The History of Printing in the Ming Dynasty* [《明代出版史稿》] (南京: 江苏人民出版社, 2000).

Netanel, N. W., *The Copyright's Paradox* (New York: Oxford University Press, 2008).

Pi, H. [皮后峰], *The Biography of Yan Fu* [《严复大传》] (福州: 福建人民出版社, 2003).

Ploman, E. W. and Hamilton, L. C., *Copyright: Intellectual Property in the Information Age* (London and Boston: Routledge & Kegan Paul, 1980).

Rehbinder, M., *Urheberrecht: Ein Studienbuch*, 15th edn (München: C. H. Beck, 2008).

Renouard, A. C., *Traité des Droits d'Auteurs dans la Littérature, les Sciences et les Beaux-arts* 2 vols. (Paris: J. Renouard et cie, 1838), vol. I.

Ricketson, S. and Ginsburg, J. C., *International Copyright and Neighbouring Rights: The Berne Convention and Beyond*, 2nd edn (Oxford: Oxford University Press, 2006).

Senftleben, M., *Copyright, Limitations and the Three-Step Test: An Analysis of the Three-Step Test in International and EC Copyright Law* (The Hague: Kluwer Law International, 2004).

Shanghai Library (ed.), *Letters of the Teachers and Friends of Wang Kangnian* [《汪康年师友书札》], 4 vols. (上海: 上海古籍出版社, 1986), vol. II.

Shao, Z. [邵之棠], *Collection of Political Essays of the Empire* (Vol. 6, Culture and Education)[《皇朝经世文统编》] (台北: 文海出版社, 1980), vol. 6.

Song, Y. [宋原放](ed.), *The History of Publication in China: The Pre-Modern Part*, [《中国出版史料·近代部分》], 3 vols. (武汉: 湖北教育出版社, 2004).

Sterling, J. A. L., *World Copyright Law*, 3rd edn (London: Sweet & Maxwell, 2008).

Štrba, S. I., *International Copyright Law and Access to Education in Developing Countries* (Leiden: Martinus Nijhoff, 2012).

Tang, G., *Copyright and the Public Interest in China* (Cheltenham/Northampton: Edward Elgar, 2011).

Taubman, A., *A Practical Guide to Working with TRIPS* (Oxford: Oxford University Press, 2011).

von Jhering, R., *Der Zweck im Recht*, 3rd edn, 2 vols. (Leipzig: Breitkopf & Härtel, 1893), vol. I.

von Savigny, F. C., *System des heutigen römischen Rechts*, 3 vols. (Leipzig: Veit, 1840), vol. I.

Wang, C. and Zhang, X. (eds.), *Introduction to Chinese Law* (Hong Kong: Sweet & Maxwell Asia, 1997).

Wang, S. [王绳祖] (ed.), *The History of International Relations: From the Middle of the Seventeenth Century to 1945* [《国际关系史(十七世纪中叶-一九四五》] (北京: 法律出版社, 1986).

Wang, S. [王栻], *The Collections of the Works by Fu Yan* [《严复集》], 5 vols. (北京: 中华书局, 1986), vol. III.

Xiong, Y. and Zhou, W. [熊月之、周武], *Shanghai: The Chronicle of a Modern Metropolis* [《上海-一座现代化都市的编年史》] (上海: 上海书店, 2007).

Xue, S. [薛松奎], *The Memory of the Empire: A Memorandum of the Late Qing Dynasty by the NYT* [《帝国的回忆: <纽约时报>晚清观察纪》] (北京: 三联书店, 2002).

Yao, F. [姚福生], *The Editing History in China* [《中国编辑史》] (上海: 复旦大学出版社, 1990).

Ye, D. [叶德辉], *Light Comments among the Bookstacks* [《书林清话》] (北京: 中华书局, 1957).

Ye, S. and Yu, Z. [叶树声, 余政辉], *A Brief History of Book Printing by Jiangnan Heren in the Ming and Qing Dynasties* [《明清江南和人刻书史略》] (合肥: 安徽大学出版社, 2000).

Zhang, Z. [张之洞], *The Entire Collections of Zhang Wenxianggong* [《张文襄公全集》], 4 vols. (北京: 中国书店, 1990), vol. IV.

Zheng, C., *Chinese Intellectual Property and Technology Transfer Law* (London: Sweet & Maxwell, 1987).

Zheng, C., *Copyright Law* [《版权法》] (北京: 中国人民大学出版社, 1997).

Zheng, C., *On Intellectual Property* [《知识产权法学》] (北京: 法律出版社, 2003).

Zheng, C. and Pendleton, M., *Copyright Law in China* (NSW, CCH Australia Ltd for CCH International, 1991).

Zhou, L. and Li, M. [周林, 李明山], *Study Literature on the Chinese History of Copyright*, [《中国版权史研究文献》] (北京: 中国方正出版社, 1999).

Articles in Books

Ba, J. [巴金], 'On Copyright' ['谈版权'], in Ba, J., *The Book of Telling the Truth* [《说真话的书》] (成都: 四川人民出版社, 1995), p. 823.

Balkin, J. M., 'The Constitution in the National Surveillance State', in Balkin, J. M. and Siegel, R. B. (eds.), *The Constitution in 2020* (Oxford: Oxford University Press, 2009), p. 197.

Broude, T. and Shany, Y., 'The International Law and Policy of Multi-Sourced Equivalent Norms', in Broude, T. and Shany, Y. (eds.), *Multi-Sourced Equivalent Norms in International Law* (Oxford: Hart Publishing, 2011), p. 1.

Chen, J., 'Modernisation, Westernisation, and Globalisation: Legal Transplant in China', in Oliveira, J. C. and Cardinal, P. (eds.), *One Country, Two Systems, Three Legal Orders – Perspectives of Evolution* (Berlin/Heidelberg: Springer, 2009), p. 91.

Elms, D. K. and Lim, C. L., 'An Overview and Snapshot of the TPP Negotiations', in Lim, C. L., Elms, D. K., and Low, P. (eds.), *The Trans-Pacific Partnership: A Quest for A Twenty-First-Century Trade Agreement* (Cambridge, Cambridge University Press, 2012), p. 21.

Füller, J. T., '*Art. 9.2*', in Stoll, P.-T., Busche, J., and Arend, K. (eds.), *WTO-Trade-Related Aspects of Intellectual Property Rights* (Leiden: Martinus Nijhoff, 2009), p. 250.

Hu, K., [胡开忠], 'Limitation and De-limitation of Copyright' ['著作权的限制与反限制'], in Liang, H. [梁慧星] (ed.), *Civil and Commercial Law Review* [《民商法论丛》] (北京: 法律出版社, 1997), p. 577.

Hugenholtz, P. B., 'Adapting Copyright to the Information Superhighway', in Hugenholtz, P. B. (ed.), *The Future of Copyright in a Digital Environment* (The Hague: Kluwer Law International, 1996), p. 81.

Kuriyama, C., 'APEC and the TPP: Are They Mutually Reinforcing?', in Lim, C. L., Elms, D. K., and Low, P. (eds.), *The Trans-Pacific Partnership: A Quest for a Twenty-First-Century Trade Agreement* (Cambridge: Cambridge University Press, 2012), p. 242.

Mao, Z. [毛泽东], 'The Talk at the Meeting on Literature and Arts in Yan'an' ['在延安文艺座谈会的讲话'], in Mao, Z., *Selected Works of MAO Zedong* [《毛泽东选集》], 5 vols. (北京: 人民出版社, 1991), vol. III, p. 847.

Mao, Z., 'Taking in a Number of Intellectuals' ['大量吸收知识分子'], in Mao, Z., *Selected Works of MAO Zedong*, vol. II, p. 618.

Mao, Z., 'The Analysis of the Classes in the Chinese Society' ['中国社会各阶级的分析'], in Mao, Z., *Selected Works of MAO Zedong*, vol. I, p. 3.

Okediji, R. L., 'Sustainable Access to Copyrighted Digital Information Works in Developing Countries', in Maskus, K. E. and Reichman, J. H. (eds.), *International Public Goods and Transfer of Technology under a Globalized Intellectual Property Regime* (2005), p. 142.

Pendleton, M. D., 'Intellectual Property Regimes of Selected Asia-Pacific Jurisdictions', in Wild, K. C. D. M. and Islam, M. R. (eds.), *International Transactions: Trade and Investment, Law and Finance* (Sydney: The Law Book Co. Ltd, 1993), p. 361.

Shen, R., 'The Making of the Copyright Law and Its Legislative Spirit' ['著作权法的制定和立法精神'], in the SPC (eds.), *Lectures on the PRC's Copyright Law* [《著作权法讲座》] (1991), p. 109.

Song, M. [宋木文], 'Speech (in Hangzhou) at the Seminar of the Leadership of Copyright Administration around the Country' [在杭州全国版权局局长研讨班上的讲话], in Song, M. [宋木文] (ed.), *Collections of Essays on Publication by Song Muwen* [《宋木文出版文集》] (北京: 中国书籍出版社, 1996), p. 681.

Strömholm, S., 'Copyright – Comparison of Laws', in Ulmer, E. and Schricker, G. (eds.), *Copyright: International Encyclopedia of Comparative Law* (Tübingen: Mohr Siebeck, 2007), vol. 14.

Tao, J., 'Problems and New Developments in the Enforcement of Intellectual Property Rights in China', in Torremans, P., Shan, H. L., and Erauw, J. (eds.), *Intellectual Property and TRIPS Compliance in China: Chinese and European Perspectives* (Cheltenham-Northampton: Edward Elgar, 2007), p. 107.

Van Staden, A. and Vollaard, H., 'The Erosion of State Sovereignty: Towards a Post-Territorial World?', in Kreijen, G. et al. (ed.), *State, Sovereignty, and International Governance* (New York: New York University Press, 2002), p. 165.

Wechsler, A., 'Spotlight on China: Piracy, Enforcement, and the Balance Dilemma in Intellectual Property Law', in A. Kur (ed.), *Intellectual Property Rights in a Fair World Trade System: Proposals for Reform of TRIPS* (Cheltenham: Edward Elgar, 2011), p. 61.

Xiao, X. [肖峋], 'Solving Controversial Problems in Copyright Legislation from the Perspective of the Practice in China' ['从我国的实际出发解决版权(著作权)立法中有争议的问题'], in China Copyright Study Association (ed.), *Selected Essays on Copyright Studies* [《版权研究文选》] (上海: 商务印书馆, 1995), p. 25.

Yang, W. and Fu, Q. [杨文玉、傅强国], 'On the US 301 Section' ['试论美国三零一条款'], in Zheng, C. [郑成思] (ed.), *Study on Intellectual Property* [《知识产权研究》] (北京: 方正出版社, 1996), vol. I, p. 56.

Yu, P. K., 'Intellectual Property, Economic Development, and the China Puzzle', in Gervais, D. J. (ed.), *Intellectual Property, Trade and Development: Strategies to Optimize Economic Development in a TRIPS-plus Era* (Oxford: Oxford University Press, 2007), p. 173.

Yu, P. K., 'The US-China Dispute over TRIPS Enforcement', in Antons, C. (ed.), *The Enforcement of Intellectual Property Rights: Comparative Perspectives from the Asia-Pacific Region* (Alphen: Kluwer Law International, 2011), p. 239.

Zheng, C. [郑成思], 'Information Industry Property and Copyright Law' ['信息产权与版权法'], in *Selected Essays on Copyright Studies*, p. 89.

Zhou, L. [周林], 'Several Clues to the Study of Chinese Copyright History' ['中国版权史研究的几条线索'], in Zhou, L. and Li, M. [周林、李明山] (eds.), *Literature of Study on Chinese Copyright History* [《中国版权史研究文献》] (北京: 中国方正出版社, 1999), p. 10.

Journal Articles

André, K, 'Reflections on the Future Development of Copyright' (1983) *Copyright* 373.

Boytha, G. and Benard, A., 'Socialist Copyright Law – A Theoretical Approach' (1976) 109 *RIDA* 63.

Butterton, G. R., 'Pirates, Dragons and U.S. Intellectual Property Rights in China: Problems and Prospects of Chinese Enforcement' (1996) 38 *Ariz L Rev* 1081.

Callandrillo, S. P., 'An Economic Analysis of Intellectual Property Rights: Justifications and Problems of Exclusive Rights, Incentives to Generate Information, and the Alternative of a Government-Run Reward System' (1998) 9 *Fordham Intell Prop Media Ent L J* 301.

Chen, G., 'Piercing the Veil of State Sovereignty: How China's Censorship Regime into Fragmented International Law Can Lead to a Butterfly Effect' (2014) 3:1 *Global Constitutionalism* 31.

Chon, M., 'Intellectual Property and the Development Divide' (2006) 27(6) *Cardozo L Rev* 2813.

Davies, G., 'The Public Interest in Collective Administration of Rights' (1989) *Copyright* 81.

Gale, B., 'The Concept of Intellectual Property in the People's Republic of China: Inventors and Inventions' (1978) 74(2) *China Quarterly* 350.

Ginsburg, J. C., 'Berne Without Borders: Geographic Indiscretion and Digital Communications' (2002) 2 *Intell Prop Q* 114.

Ginsburg, J. C., 'From Having Copies to Experiencing Works: The Development of an Access Right in US Copyright Law' (2003) 50 *J Cop Soc USA* 113.

Ginsburg, J. C., 'News from the US' (1999) 180 *RIDA* 127.

Ginsburg, J. C., 'Toward Supranational Copyright Law? The WTO Panel Decision and the "Three Step Test" for Copyright Exemptions' (2001) 187 *RIDA* 3.

Grossman, G. M. and Lai, E. L. C., 'International Protection of Intellectual Property' (2004) 94 *Am Econ Rev* 1635.

He, Q. [何清涟], 'The Status Quo and Prospects of China under Authoritarian Rule' ['威权统治下的中国现状与前景'] (2004) 2 *Modern China Studies* [《当代中国研究》] 5.

Howser, R., 'From Politics to Technocracy – and Back Again: The Fate of the Multilateral Trading Regime' (2002) 96 *AJIL* 94.

Hsia, T. and Haun, Y., 'Law of the PRC on Industrial and Intellectual Property' (1983) 38 *L Contemp Probs* 479.

Hu, K. [胡开忠], 'On the Philosophical Ground of Theory Concerning the Limitations to Copyright' ['著作权限制与反限制的法哲学基础研究'] (1996) 1 *Journal of Law and Business* [《法商研究》] 21.

Husted, B. W., 'The Impact of National Culture on Software Piracy' (2000) 26 *JBE* 197.

Joyce, C. and Patterson, L. R., 'Copyright (and Its Master) in Historical Perspective' (2003) 10 *J Intell Prop L* 239.

Kapzynski, A., 'The Access to Knowledge Mobilization and the New Politics of Intellectual Property' (2008) 117 *Yale L J* 804.

Kitch, E. W., 'Elementary and Persistent Errors in the Economic Analysis of Intellectual Property' (2000) 53 *Vand L Rev* 1727.

Landes, W. M. and Posner, R. A., 'An Economic Analysis of Copyright Law' (1989) 18 *J Legal Stud* 325.

Leval, P. N., 'Toward a Fair Use Standard' (1990) 103 (5) *Harv L Rev* 1105.

Li, C., 'Resumption of China's GATT Membership' (1987) 21 *JWT* 4.

Li, Z. [李宗辉], 'Legal Transplantation and Traditional Creation in the Hiatus: Comments on the 1910 Copyright Code' ['夹缝中的法律移植与传统创造:《大清著作权律》述评'] (2010) 5 *Journal of the Southwestern University of Politics and Law* [《西南政法大学学报》] 14.

Litman, J., 'Readers' Copyright' (2011) 58 *J Cop Soc USA* 325.

Liu, G. [刘杲], 'Crossing the History: The Stories before and after China's Accession to the International Copyright Treaties' ['历史的跨越—我国加入版权公约的前前后后'下] Part II (1999) 4 *China Publishing Journal* 52.

Liu, G. [柳谷书], 'Several Questions of Worldwide Interest in the Chinese Copyright Law' ['举世关心的著作权法中的几个问题'] (1991) 4 *China Patent & Trademark* [《中国专利与商标》] 19.

Long, D. E., 'Copyright and the Uruguay Round Agreements: A New Era of Protection or an Illusory Promise?' (1994) 22 *AIPLA Q J* 531.

Massey, J. A., 'The Emperor Is Far Away: China's Enforcement of Intellectual Property Rights Protection 1986–2006' (2006) 7 *Chi J Int'l L* 231.

Miller, S. E., 'The Posse Is Coming to Town . . . Maybe: The Role of United States Non-Governmental Organisations in Software Anti-Piracy Initiatives as China Seeks WTO Accession' (2000) 7 *ILSA J Int'l Comp L* 111.

Netanel, N. W., 'Copyright and a Democratic Civil Society' (1996) 106 *Yale L J* 283.

Nimmer, M. B., 'Does Copyright Abridge the First Amendment Guarantees of Free Speech and Press?' (1970) 17 *UCLA L Rev* 1180.

Olian, I. A., 'International Copyright and the Needs of Developing Countries: The Awakening at Stockholm and Paris' (1974) 7 *Cornell Int'l L J* 81.

Qin, J. Y., 'WTO-Plus Obligations and Their Implications for the World Trade Organization Legal System: An Appraisal of the China Accession Protocol' (2003) 37(3) *JWT* 483.

Raustiala, K., 'Density and Conflict in International Intellectual Property Law' (2007) 40 *U C Davis L Rev* 1021.

Reichman, J. H., 'From Free Riders to Fair Flowers: Global Competition under the TRIPS Agreement' (1997) 29 *NYU J Int'l L Pol* 11.

Reichman, J. H., 'Intellectual Property in International Trade: Opportunities and Risks of a GATT Connection' (1989) 22 *Vand J Transnat'l L* 747.

Ruse-Khan, H. Grosse, 'The Role of TRIPS in a Fragmented IP World' (2012) 43 (8) *IIC* 881.

Shaver, L. B., 'Defining and Measuring A2K: A Blueprint for an Index of Access to Knowledge', *I/S: A Journal of Law and Policy for the Information Society* (2008) Vol 4 Issue 2, 3, at http://ssrn.com/abstract=1021065.

Sidel, M., 'Copyright, Trademarks and Patent Laws in the People's Republic of China' (1986) 21(2) *Texas Int'l L J* 270.

Sidel, M., 'The Legal Protection of Copyright and the Rights of Authors in the PRC, 1949–1984: Prelude to the Chinese Copyright Law' (1986) 9 *Columbia J Art L* 479.

Song, M. [宋木文], 'On the Revisions of Chinese Copyright Law' ['关于我国著作权法的修改'] (2001) 6 *Copyright* [《著作权》] 30.

Sun, H., 'Overcoming the Achilles Heel of Copyright Law' (2007) 5 *Northwestern J Tech IP* 265.

Torremans, P. L. C., 'Is Copyright a Human Right?' (2007) *Mich St L Rev* 271.

Trachtman, J. P., 'The Constitutions of the WTO' (2006) 17 *Eur J Int'l L* 623.

von Lewinski, S., 'EC proposal for a Council Directive harmonizing the term of protection of copyright and certain related rights' (1992) 23 *IIC* 785.

Wang, Q. [王清], 'The Commercial Press and the Chinese Modern Copyright Protection' ['商务印书馆与中国近代版权保护'] II (1993) *Studies on Publication* [《出版发行研究》] 55.

Wang, T. [王铁崖], 'China and International Law: History and Today' ['中国与国际法—历史与当代'] (1992) *Chinese Yearbook of International Law* [《中国国际法年刊》] 22.

Wu, K., 'Ming Printers and Printing' (1942–43) 7(3) *Harvard J Asiat Stud* 230.

Xiu, Z. [修志君], 'The Dissemination and Influence of Modern International Law in China' ['近代国际法在中国的传播及影响'] (2006) 23:3 *Journal of the Normal College of Qingdao University* [《青岛大学师范学院学报》] 81.

Xue, H., 'A User-Unfriendly Draft: 3rd Revision of the Chinese Copyright Law' (2012) 7:4 *J Int'l Commercial L Tech* 350.

Yang, R. H. [杨瑞华], 'The First Case on Harming the Public Interest' ['损害"公共利益"第一辩案'] 2004 (3) *Modern Towns* [《现代乡镇》] 24.

Yu, P. K., 'From Pirates to Partners: Protecting Intellectual Property in China in the Twenty-First Century' (2000) 50 *Am U L Rev* 131.

Yuan, Y. [袁逸], 'The History of Plagiarism in China' ['中国古代剽窃史'] (1992) 1 *Copyright*[《著作权》]48.

Zhao, J. [赵建文], 'The Status of International Treaties in the Chinese Legal System' ['国际条约在中国法律体系中的地位'] (2010) 6 *Chinese Journal of Law* [《法学研究》] 190.

Zhao, S. [赵胜], 'The Bar of Printing in the Song Dynasty' ['宋代的印刷禁令'](1987) 4 *Journal of the Hebei Normal University* [《河北师范大学学报》] 39.

Zhu, B. [朱兵], 'Copyright Legislation Is an Important Content of the Socialist Legal System' ['建立和完善中国特色社会主义文化法律制度'] (2012) 20 *People's Congress of China* [《中国人大》] 8.

Conference/Working Papers/Reports/Speeches

Committee to Protect Journalists, Falling Short: As the 2008 Olympics Approach, China Falters on Press Freedom, A Special Report of the Committee to Protect Journalists (August 2007).

Floridi, L., 'ACTA – The Ethical Analysis of a Failure, and Its Lessons', ECIPE Occasional Paper, No. 4/2012.

Harpaz, M. D., 'China and the WTO: New Kid on the Developing Bloc?', 5 and 17 (Hebrew University of Jerusalem, Faculty of Law, Research Paper No 2-07, 2007), at www.ssrn.com/abstractid=961768.

Hugenholtz, P. B., and Okediji, R. L., 'Conceiving an International Instrument on Limitations and Exceptions to Copyright' (2008), at www.ivir.nl/publicaties/hugenholtz/finalreport2008.pdf.

Human Rights Watch, *Freedom of Expression and the Internet in China: A Human Rights Watch Backgrounder* (2001), at www.hrw.org.

Ilias, S. and Fergusson, I. F., Congressional Research Service Report for Congress, Intellectual Property Rights and International Trade, 20 December 2007, *Congressional Research Service*, Washington, DC.

Long, Y., Vice Minister, Head of the Chinese Delegation, 'Address at the Sixteenth Session of the Working Party on China', 4 July 2001, at www.china-un.ch/eng/qtzz/wtothsm/t85632.htm.

Nzelibe, J., 'The Case against Reforming the WTO's Enforcement Mechanism', 32 (Northwestern School of Law, Pub Law & Legal Theory, Series No. 07–12 2007), at http://ssrn.com/abstracts=9801002.

Rogers, T. and Szamosszegi, A., *Fair Use in the US Economy: Economic Contribution of Industries Relying on Fair Use* (CCIA: September 2007) at www.ccianet.org/wp-content/uploads/library/FairUseStudy-Sep12.pdf.

Newspaper Articles and Press Release

'Alibaba's Maturity Mismatch', *The Economist*, 24 July 2014, at www .economist.com/blogs/freeexchange/2014/07/chinese-finance.

'Anti-Pornographic and Anti-Illegal Publications, Purifying the Internet 2014' ['扫黄打非净网2014'], at www.xinhuanet.com/legal/shdf/.

'China Claims Success in Copyright Crackdown', *Reuter Bus Rep*, 3 August 1994.

'China Internet Association Advocates the Sharing of a Common Black List to Combat Online Pornographic Information' ['中国互联网协会倡议建立黑名单共享机制 抵制网络淫秽色情信息'], *Xinhua Net*, 23 April 2014, at http://news.xinhuanet.com/legal/2014-04/23/c_1110375964.htm.

Chen, J. [陈家俊], 'Journalists from Hong Kong Accused of the Crime of Illegal Business Operation' ['港传媒人在深圳被控非法经营罪'], *Deutsche Welle*, 06 November 2015, at www.dw.com/zh/港传媒人在深圳被控非法经营罪/a-18832754.

Chu, B. [储百亮], 'XI Jinping Admonishes the CCP to Remember the Lessons of the Former Soviet Union' ['习近平警告中共记取前苏联教训'], *The NYT*, 15 February 2013, at http://cn.nytimes.com/world/20130215/c15xi/.

Committee to Protect Journalists, '2001 Prison Census: 118 Journalists Jailed', 26 March 2002, at https://cpj.org/imprisoned/attacks-on-the-press-in-2001-journalists-in-prison.php.

European Commission, EU–China Economic and Trade Joint Committee Debriefing, Brussels, 4 November 2005, at http://trade.ec.europa.eu/doclib/docs/2005/november/tradoc_125721.pdf.

Faison, S., 'US and China Sign Accord to End Piracy of Software Music Recordings and Film', *NYT*, 27 February 1995, A1.

Feng, J. [冯建华], 'From Beijing to Berne: China's Process of Copyright Protection' ['从北京到伯尔尼——中国版权保护历程'], *Beijing Weekly Review*, 3 August 2007, at www.china.com.cn/book/zhuanti/qkjc/txt/2007-08/03/content_8624228.htm.

GAPP, 'LIU Binjie: the Work of "Anti-pornography and Anti-illegal Publications" Must Follow Five Key Points Strictly' ['柳斌杰:"扫黄打非"工作要严把"五个关口"'], 11 January 2012, at www.gov.cn/gzdt/2012-01/11/content_2042269.htm.

Guan, Y. [管育鹰], 'Development of the Chinese Intellectual Property System in Globalisation' ['全球化背景下中国知识产权法律制度的发展'], at www .iolaw.org.cn/showArticle.asp?id=2774.

'Intellectual Property Protection - Presence and Prospect' ['知识产权保护'], *Law & Order Daily* [《法制日报》], 30 June 1994, 2.

'In the Campaign of Purifying the Internet 1222 Pornographic Websites Have Been Dealt with' ['净网行动处理淫秽色情网站1222家'], *People's Daily* [《人民日报》], 21 June 2014.

Li, J. [李建中], 'An Open Letter to Kaige Chen' ['致陈凯歌大师的一封公开信'], *Shanghai Morning Post* [《上海晨报》], 14 February 2006.

'LI Keqiang: China Remains Open towards the US' Promotion of the TPP' ['李克强:中国对美国推动TPP持开放态度'], *China Economy Weekly* [《中国经济周刊》], 19 October 2015, at http://finance.sina.com.cn/china/20151019/231423516298.shtml.

'LI Keqiang, RCEP and TPP Can Go Hand in Hand and Benefit Mutually' ['李克强:RCEP和TPP可并行不悖、相互促进'], *China News Service*, 10 April 2010, at www.chinanews.com/gn/2014/04–10/6048467.shtml.

Lim, B. K., 'China Court Favours Disney in Key Copyright Suit', *Reuter Asia-Pac Bus Rep*, 4 August 1994.

'LIU Qibao: Building a Cleaner Cultural Domain in Online and Offline Environment' ['刘奇葆:营造更加清朗的网上网下文化空间'], *Xinhua Net*, 19 January 2015, at http://news.xinhuanet.com/legal/2015-01/19/c_1114051457.htm.

Liu, Z. [刘政], 'Jiyun Tian in the Great Reforms' ['改革风云中的田纪云'], *Southern Weekly* [《南方周末》], 07 January 2009.

Lu, W. [陆文军], 'The EU Ambassador to China: Conflict Is by No Means Mainstream of EU–China Trade Relations' ['摩擦绝非中欧贸易主流'], *Xinhua News Net*, 7 March 2007, at http://news.xinhuanet.com/fortune/2007-03/07/content_5814346.htm.

'Mandelson Urges China to Tackle Piracy, Hints at WTO Action', *EU Business*, 26 November 2007.

Nystedt, D., 'Baidu May Be Worst Wikipedia Copyright Violator', *IDG News Service*, 6 August 2007, at https://web.archive.org/web/20070930182947/www.pcworld.com/article/id,135550-c,copyright/article.html.

Peng, Z. [彭志平], 'YU Qiuyu Tops the Ranking of the Richest Writers from the Mainland' ['大陆富豪作家排行 余秋雨占鳌头'], *China Times* [《中国时报》], 17 December 2006.

Program on Information Justice and Intellectual Property, 'Over 75 Law Profs Call for Halt of ACTA', 28 October 2010, at www.wcl.american.edu/pijip/go/blog-post/academic-sign-on-letter-to-obama-on-acta.

Sanger, D. E., 'Japan's Ghost in China Pact: US Tries to Avoid Old Trade Mistakes', *NYT*, 27 February 1995, Dl.

'Seven Instantaneous Telecommunication Companies Launched Rectifying Measures to Echo the Specific Campaign of Regulating the Internet' ['全国七大移动即时通信商启动整顿措施响应移动互联网治理专项行动'], *Xinhua Net*, 30 May 2014, at http://news.xinhuanet.com/legal/2014-05/30/c_1110927841.htm.

Shakespeare, S., 'Chinese Ban "Rude" Songs at Prince William's Gala Dinner', *Daily Mail*, 4 March 2015, at www.dailymail.co.uk/news/article-2978504/SEBASTIAN-SHAKESPEARE-Chinese-ban-rude-songs-Prince-William-s-gala-dinner.html.

State Intellectual Property Office of the PRC, 'The Volume of Registration of Copyrighted Software in Our Country Multiplied in the First Half of 2009' ['2009年上半年我国软件著作权登记量同比成倍增长'], at www.sipo.gov.cn/yw/2009/200907/t20090708_467794.html.

Stevenson, R. W., 'US Cites China for Failing to Curb Piracy in Trade', *NYT*, 1 May 1996, D4.

'The Anti-Pornographic and Anti-Illegal Publications Working Office Releases Ten Significant Statistics of Anti-Pornographic and Anti-Illegal Publications in 2014' ['全国扫黄打非办公布2014扫黄打非十大数据'], *Xinhua Net*, 25 December 2015, at http://news.xinhuanet.com/legal/2014-12/25/c_1113778449.htm.

'The Great Firewall: The Art of Concealment', Special Report: China and the Internet, *The Economist*, 6 April 2013, at www.economist.com/news/special-report/21574631-chinese-screening-online-material-abroad-becoming-ever-more-sophisticated.

'The Most Stringent Copyright Order in History Takes Effect: 2,2 Million Music Works Disappear Overnight' ['史上最严版权令生效 220多万首音乐作品一夜消失'], *West China Metropolis Daily* [《华西都市报》], 6 August 2015, at www.wccdaily.com.cn/shtml/hxdsb/20150806/297472.shtml.

Tiezzi, S., 'Beijing's Blueprint for Judicial Reform', *The Diplomat*, 12 July 2014.

'Trade War Averted: Chinese Officials, Individuals Welcome Sino–US Copyright Accord', BBC Summary of World Broadcasts, 28 February 1995, part 3.

'US, China Edging Back to Table', *Chicago Tribune*, 7 February 1995, 3.

Weisman, S. R., 'China Talks Don't Resolve Major Issues', NYT (24 May 2007) C1.

Whittaker, Z., '"Last Rites" for ACTA? Europe Rejects Antipiracy Treaty', 4 July 2012, CNet, at www.cnet.com/news/last-rites-for-acta-europe-rejects-antipiracy-treaty.

Wiseman, P., 'Top Story in 2015: China's Sharp Economic Slowdown', The TandD.com, 26 December 2015, at http://thetandd.com/business/top-story-in-china-s-sharp-economic-slowdown/article_16a59d2f-69f6-5d54-a29e-8326b175a320.htm.

Wong, E., 'China Blocks Web Access to "Under the Dome" Documentary on Pollution', *NYT*, 8 March 2015, at http://cn.nytimes.com/china/20150308/c08dome/dual/.

Wong, G. and Chu, K., 'US Trade Group Seeks Relisting of Alibaba's Taobao as "Notorious"', *The Wall Str J*, 06 October 2015, at www.wsj.com/articles/u-s-trade-group-says-alibabas-taobao-should-be-relisted-as-notorious-for-fakes-1444096618.

Wood, S., 'Baidu's Perfect Paradox: Free Speech and the Right to Censor', *The Conversation*, 9 April 2014, at http://phys.org/news/2014-04-baidu-paradox-free-speech-censor.html.

Wu, J. [吴敬琏], 'We Can Safeguard the Extreme Leftism Only by Curbing Crony Capitalism' ['遏制权贵资本主义才能防极左'] *Beijing Daily* [《北京日报》], 05 May 2009.

Wu, Y. [吴雨], 'XI Jinping: We Can't Say No. to Our History of the First 30 Years' ['习近平:不能否定前30年历史'], *Deutsche Welle*, 05 January 2013, at www.dw.com/zh/习近平不能否定前30年历史/a-16500930.

XinhuaNet.com, 'XI Jinping: Literature and Art Should Not Get Lost in the Tide of Market Economy' ['习近平:文艺不能在市场经济大潮中迷失方向'], 15 October 2014, at http://news.xinhuanet.com/politics/2014-10/15/c_1112840544.htm.

Xu, C. [徐词], 'I must Protect You: The Revision Draft of the Copyright Act Is Trapped in Controversy' ['我就要来保护你?—著作权法修改草案陷入争议漩涡'], *The Southern Weekly* [《南方周末》], 20 April 2012.

Yan, S., '3 Things about Alibaba's Move into Big Media', *CNN Money*, 13 December 2015, at http://money.cnn.com/2015/12/13/media/alibaba-scmp.

Zhong, D. [钟鼎文], 'The Publication Industry in China: A Decade towards the Market' ['中国出版业:走向市场化的10年'], *China Reading News* [《中华读书报》], 13 August 2004.

Other Online Resources

Business Software Alliance, 'Fifth Annual BSA and IDC Global Software Piracy Study' (2007), at http://globalstudy.bsa.org/2007.

Centre for World-Class Universities of Shanghai Jiao Tong University, the Academic Ranking of World Universities (ARWU), at www.shanghairanking.com.

China Anti-pornography and Anti-illegal Publications Net [全国扫黄打非网], at www.shdf.gov.cn/.

Creative Commons, Creative Commons Licenses, at http://creativecommons.org/licenses.

Foundation for a Free Information Infrastructure e.V., 'The World Faces Major Challenges Introduction', at http://action.ffii.org/acta/Analysis.

Han, S. [韩少功], 'The Depravation of Chinese Intellectuals in the 1990s' ['90年代中国知识分子的堕落'], *Tencent Da Jia* [腾讯大家], 26 April 2015, at http://dajia.qq.com/blog/478612012821892.html.

IIPA, Chart of Countries' Special 301 Placement (1989 to 2014) and IIPA 2015 Special 301 Recommendations, at www.iipa.com/pdf/2015SPEC301HISTORICALCHART.pdf.

Kuhn, R. L., 'American Scholar Reveals Zemin Jiang's Seldom Anger and Criticism of Hong Kong Journalists' ['美学者披露江泽民少见发火并批评香港记者始末'], news.ifeng.com [凤凰网历史], 24 December 2013, at http://news.ifeng.com/history/zhongguoxiandaishi/detail_2013_12/24/32417303_0.shtml.

Liu, S. [刘绍棠], *Unbearable to Recall the Past* [《往事不堪回首》], at www.oklink.net/99/1208/sywc/102.htm.

Max Planck Gesellschaft, Open Access, at http://openaccess.mpg.de.

Office of the USTR, www.ustr.gov.

Open Source Initiative: The Open Source Definition, at http://opensource.org/osd.

Public Knowledge, 'Key Issues: The Anti-Counterfeiting Trade Agreement (ACTA)', at www.publicknowledge.org/issues/acta.

Testa, J., The Thomson Reuters Journal Selection Process, at http://wokinfo.com/essays/journal-selection-process.

The News Office of the State Council, 'The New Progress of Intellectual Property Protection in China' [《中国知识产权保护的新进展》], 21 April 1994, at http://politics.people.com.cn/GB/1026/3338425.html.

WTO, *Handbook on Accession to the WTO*, 'Chapter 4: The Accession Process — the Procedures and How They Have Been Applied', at www.wto.org/english/thewto_e/acc_e/cbt_course_e/c4s1p1_e.htm.

Wu, H. [吴海民], *Towards the Berne Convention: The Memorandum of Chinese Copyright* [《走向伯尔尼—中国版权备忘录》], at www.oklink.net/a/0008/0822/zouxiang/index.html.

Yu, P. K., 'Causes of Piracy and Counterfeiting in China' (2007) *Guanxi: The China Letter*, at www.peteryu.com/guanxi.pdf.

INDEX

CAMBRIDGE INTELLECTUAL PROPERTY AND INFORMATION LAW

Titles in the series (formerly known as Cambridge Studies
in Intellectual Property Rights)

Normann Witzleb, David Lindsay, Moira Paterson and Sharon Rodrick *Emerging Challenges in Privacy Law: Comparative Perspectives*

Paul Bernal *Internet Privacy Rights: Rights to Protect Autonomy*

Peter Drahos *Intellectual Property, Indigenous People and their Knowledge*

Susy Frankel and Daniel Gervais *The Evolution and Equilibrium of Copyright in the Digital Age*

Edited by Kathy Bowrey and Michael Handler *Law and Creativity in the Age of the Entertainment Franchise*

Sean Bottomley *The British Patent System and the Industrial Revolution 1700–1852: From Privileges to Property*

Susy Frankel *Test Tubes for Global Intellectual Property Issues: Small Market Economies*

Jan Oster *Media Freedom as a Fundamental Right*

Sara Bannerman *International Copyright and Access to Knowledge*

Andrew T. Kenyon *Comparative Defamation and Privacy Law*

Pascal Kamina *Film Copyright in the European Union, Second Edition*

Tim W. Dornis *Trademark and Unfair Competition Conflicts*

Ge Chen *Copyright and International Negotiations: An Engine of Free Expression in China?*

David Tan *The Commercial Appropriation of Fame: A Cultural Critique of the Right of Publicity and Passing Off*

Jay Sanderson *Plants, People and Practices: The Nature and History of the UPOV Convention*

Daniel Benoliel *Patent Intensity and Economic Growth*

CPSIA information can be obtained
at www.ICGtesting.com
Printed in the USA
LVOW07*1737191217
560258LV00005B/47/P